Ethnic Minorities, their Families and the Law

Edited by
JOHN MURPHY

·HART·
PUBLISHING

OXFORD – PORTLAND OREGON
2000

Hart Publishing
Oxford and Portland, Oregon

Published in North America (US and Canada) by
Hart Publishing c/o
International Specialized Book Services
5804 NE Hassalo Street
Portland, Oregon
97213-3644
USA

Distributed in the Netherlands, Belgium and Luxembourg by
Intersentia, Churchillaan 108
B2900 Schoten
Antwerpen
Belgium

Hart Publishing Ltd is a specialist legal publisher based in Oxford, England.
To order further copies of this book or to request a list of other
publications please write to:

Hart Publishing Ltd, Salter's Boatyard, Oxford OX1 4LB
Telephone: +44 (0)1865 245533 or Fax: +44 (0)1865 794882
e-mail: mail@hartpub.co.uk
www.hartpub.co.uk

British Library Cataloguing in Publication Data
Data Available
ISBN 1 901362–59–0 (cloth)

Typeset by Hope Services (Abingdon) Ltd.
Printed in Great Britain on acid-free paper
by Biddles Ltd, Guildford and King's Lynn.

For my mother,
CATHERINE MURPHY
and for
ANNE JACOBSEN

Preface

Between them, the Children Act 1989 and the Family Law Act 1996 mark the dawn of a new era in family law. Gone are the days of fault-based divorces, retrograde domestic violence laws (providing remedies only to those who were married or in long-term, stable, cohabitational relationships) and local authority abuses of wardship. They have been superseded, as we begin the new Millennium, by an era in which children's rights have emerged in statutory form and greater recognition has been afforded to relationships outside marriage, whether heterosexual or homosexual. And yet, despite this new enlightenment, the specific concerns of ethnic minority families have been largely disregarded. In the whole of the Children Act, for example, only two provisions make specific reference to racial and ethnic considerations. Moreover, they only apply to children either who are being looked after by a local authority or who are "in need" within the local authority's boundaries.

This collection of essays is primarily intended to highlight some of the main areas of English domestic law and English conflicts law in which a good deal more thought needs to be given to the way in which ethnic minority families are *in practice* affected by our ostensibly colour-blind legislation. One essay—John Dewar's—provides a helpful comparative study of the way in which Australian law has got to grips with implementing greater self-determination for the indigenous peoples while retaining a genuine commitment to multiculturalism. It contains many useful lessons.

The book is arranged into three parts. The first deals with the law relating to children. The second—"private lives and public duties"—concerns the duties owed to ethnic minority families (and their individual members) by local authorities, the courts and the police. The final section contains essays with an international dimension. Some of the essays might have been placed in either two sections of the book. To an extent, the kind of overlaps that make this so are inevitable: family law has no fixed boundaries and is anything but a discrete body of law. The essays have, therefore, been placed according to *my* conception of a "best-fit".

In compiling this collection, I have incurred many debts. First, I should like to thank all the contributors—I would never have found the time to write all of the material myself, and even if I had, I would not have done it nearly so well. Secondly, I am grateful to those people who kindly read and commented on drafts of my contributions: Emilios Avgouleas, Hugh Bevan and David Booton. Finally—and this cannot be understated—I am hugely grateful to Richard Hart whose encouragement never wavered, and whose patience was exemplary during the very long time between the idea for this collection being raised and the final manuscript being delivered.

John Murphy
Manchester
1 November 1999

Contents

Contributors   xiii
Table of Cases   xv
Table of Legislation   xix

Part I Children

1   Images of Child Welfare in Child Abduction Appeals
    Michael Freeman   1

    Introduction   1
    Assessing a Risk   5
    An Objecting Child   7
    Non-Convention Cases   9
    Looking at Other Systems—A Value Framework   11
    Conclusion   14

2   Local Authority Support for Ethnic Minority Children
    Martin L. Parry   15

    Introduction   15
    Provision of Services   18
    Children Looked After by Local Authorities   24
        Placement   26
        Leaving Local Authority Accommodation   28
    Conclusion   30

3   Child Welfare in Transracial Adoptions:
    Colour-blind Children and Colour-blind Law
    John Murphy   33

    Introduction   33
        Two Urban Myths   35
        Transracial Adoptions are Harmful?   35
    Transracial Adoptions Damage Minority Community Interests   38
    Legal Improprieties of Race-matching   40
        Race-matching as Racial Discrimination   40
        The Centrality of Child Welfare   42
    Reform Measures   44
        Practical Measures   44
        Legal Steps   46
    Conclusions   48

Part II   International Issues

4   Recognition of Foreign Divorces: Unwarrantable
Ethnocentrism
Abla Mayss   51

Introduction   51
Historical Overview   52
The Scheme of the Current Law   54
  Divorces Obtained within the British Isles   54
  Overseas Divorces   55
Conclusions   68

5   The Discretionary Refusal of Recognition
of Foreign Marriages
John Murphy   71

Introduction   71
Public Policy and Cultural Imperialism   74
Cultural Values: Reasons and Non-reasons   77
Cultural Values in the Non-recognition of Child Marriages   80
Conclusion   85

6   Indigenous Children in Australian Law
John Dewar   87

Introduction   87
Self-determination and Multiculturalism Defined   89
Child Protection and Child Placement: Towards "Self-determination"?   92
  The "Stolen Generation"   92
  The Aboriginal Child Placement Principle (ACPP)   92
Towards Greater Self-determination?   96
Family Law: Towards "Multiculturalism"?   98
  Family Structures and Family Values   99
  Re CP: The Tiwi Island Case   102
  Recuperating the "Best Interests" Principle?   105
Conclusion   108

7   Rhetoric and Reality in Inter-country Adoptions:
Divergent Principles and Stratified Status
John Murphy   111

Introduction   111
The Welfare of the Child in Inter-country Adoptions   113
  Convention Adoptions   113
  Other Adoptions   115

Safeguards (?) Against Wrongful Adoption   118
The Recognition of Inter-county Adoptions   121
Conclusion   124

Part III   Miscellaneous Issues

8   Double Jeopardy: Race and Domestic Violence
     Ada Kewley   129

Introduction   129
Women Trapped in Violent Relationships   130
Domestic Violence and Contact Orders   131
Race and the Legal System   133
    Institutions and Procedures   135
    Race, Gender and Criminal Law   137
Problems in Policing Domestic Violence   139
    Introduction   139
    Particular Problems of Policing and Race   140
Domestic Violence and Immigration   141
Conclusion   142

9   State Support for Housing Ethnic Minority Households:
     Spatial Segregation and Ghettoisation?   143
     David Cowan

Introduction   143
Spatial Segregation and Ghettoisation   145
    The 1991 Census: General   145
    The 1991 Census: Ghettoisation   147
    The 1991 Census: Spatial Segregation   147
State Support: The Effects of Colour Blindness   149
    Home Ownership   150
    Council Housing   152
    Housing Associations   153
    Private Renting   154
The Politics of Segregation   155
Conclusion   159

10   Healthcare Law for a Multi-faith Society
     Jonathan Montgomery   161

Introduction   161
Three Principles   162
    Autonomy   162
    Best Interests   163
    Sanctity of Life   166

Religious Dimensions to Assessing Competence   168
Categorical Imperatives in the Structure of Welfare
Decision Making   172
Conclusions   177

Index   181

Contributors

David Cowan, Lecturer in Law, University of Bristol

John Dewar, Professor of Law and Dean, Griffith University, Brisbane

Michael Freeman, Professor of Law, University College London

Ada Kewley, Lecturer in Law, University of Hull

Abla Mayss, Lecturer in Law, University of Liverpool

Jonathan Montgomery, Reader in Health Care Law, University of Southampton

John Murphy, Senior Lecturer in Law, University of Manchester

Martin Parry, Reader in Law, University of Hull

Table of Cases

A v N (Committal: Refusal of Contact) [1997] 1 FLR 533..............................132
A, Re [1992] Fam 182...3
Abidin Daver, The [1984] AC 398 10
Adams v Adams [1970] 3 All ER 572; [1971] P 188..................................56, 73
Adoption Application (Adoption of Non-Patrial), Re [1992] 1 WLR 596 121
Adoption Application (Non-Patrial: Breach of Procedures), Re [1993]
   2 WLR 110–11, 116–17
Airedale NHS Trust v Bland [1993] 1 All ER 821, 1 FLR 1026; [1994]
   1 FCR 485..162–4, 166–7
Alhaji Mohamed v Knott [1969] 1 QB 1 ....71, 74, 81–2
Apt v Apt [1947] P 127 74
Armitage v Att-Gen [1906] P 135 53–4
B and R and the Separate Representative (1995) Fam LR 594...99, 103–4, 106–7
B v B: Family Law Reform Act (1995) 21 Fam LR 676 88
B v K [1993] 1 FCR 382..8
B, Re [1987] 2 All ER 206 ....165, 173
Banik v Banik [1973] 3 All ER 45 131
Barret v Enfield London Borough Council [1999] 3 All ER 193......................43
Berkovits v Grinberg [1995] 1 FLR 477..57, 62–3, 70
Berthiaume v Dastous [1930] AC 79 71
B's Settlement, Re [1940] Ch 54 9–10
C (Adoption: Legality), Re [1999] 1 FLR 370 ....111, 114–18, 120–1, 124
C (MA), Re [1966] 1 All ER 838 6
C, Re [1989] 1 FLR 403 5–6
C, Re [1996] 2 FLR 43 165
C, Re [1998] 1 FCR 1 ....173–44, 176–7
C, Re [1999] 1 FLR 1145 7
Chaudhary v Chaudhary [1985] FLR 476 ....60, 68
Cheni v Cheni [1965] P 65/85 ....72, 74
CP, Re (1997) 21 Fam LR 486 ....91, 102–3, 105–6, 108
D (A Minor) (Contact: Mother's Hostility), Re [1993] 2 FLR 1 133
D (An Infant) (Adoption: Parent's Consent), Re [1977] AC 602 113
D v D [1994] 1 FLR 137...9, 56, 65
D, Re [1998] 1 FCR 498...168
E, Re [1993] 1 FLR 386 174–76
El-Ryami v El-Ryami [1958] CLY 497 52
F, Re [1989] 2 FLR 376..162–64
F, Re [1995] 2 FLR 31..5–6

Frenchay NHS Trust v S [1994] 2 All ER 403 164
G, Re [1995] 1 FLR 64..5
Gibbs v Capewell (1995) 128 ALR 577...96
Gillick v West Norfolk and Wisbech AHA [1985] 3 All ER 402;
    [1986] AC 112 ....8, 82, 168
Goudge (1984) FLC 91 106
H (A Minor) (Adoption: Non-Patrial), Re [1997] 1 WLR 791 113
H, Re [1998] 3 FCR 174..168
Har-Shefi v Har-Shefi (No 2) [1953] P 20 ....52, 54
Harvey v Farnie (1882) 8 AC 43..52
Hornett v Hornett [1971] P 255 66
Indyka v Indyka [1969] 1 AC 33 53
Ingra v Ingra [1951] P 404 66
J (A Minor) (Contact), Re [1994] 1 FLR 729 132
J (A Minor) (Wardship: Adoption: Custodianship), Re [1987] 1 FLR 455 27
J, Re [1990] 3 All ER 930..173, 179
J, Re [1992] 4 All ER 614..164
JA, Re [1998] 1 FLR 231 ....9, 11
JK (Adoption:Trans-Racial Placement), Re [1991] 2 FLR 340 27
K (A Minor) (Wardship: Adoption) [1991] 1 FLR 57....................................44
K, Re [1995] 1 FLR 977 ....4, 8
Kendall v Kendall [1977] 3 All ER 471 67
Kruger v Commonwealth of Australia (1997) 146 ALR 126...........................92
L v L (Child Abuse: Access) [1989] 2 FLR 16..132
L, Re [1993] 2 FLR 401 6
L, Re [1998] 2 FLR 810 ....17–72, 177
Lee v Lau [1967] P 14 52
M, Re (1990) 25 July (unreported)...7
M, Re [1995] 1 FLR 1021 5
M, Re [1995] 2 FLR 224 11
M, Re [1996] 1 FLR 315..6
Mabo v Queensland (No 2) (1992) 175 CLR 1 87
Manchester City Council v F [1993] 1 FLR 419 25
MB, Re [1997] 2 FLR 426 (CA)...163, 169
McCabe v McCabe [1994] 1 FLR 410 74
McKee v McKee [1951] AC 352...9
Minister of State for Immigration and Ethnic Affairs v Ah Hin Teoh 183
    CLR 273 88
Mississippi Choctaw Band of Indians v Holyfield 109 SCt 1597 (1989) 91, 96
N (A Minor) (Adoption), Re [1990] 1 FLR 58 ....18, 27, 36, 38, 44, 47
N v N [1995] 1 FLR 107...3–4, 8
N, Re [1991] 1 FLR 413...5
N, Re [1993] 2 FLR 124...4
O (Contact: Imposition of Conditions), Re [1995] 2 FLR 124 132

O, Re [1993] 2 FLR 149 176
Ogden v Ogden [1908] P 46 71
P (A Minor) (Adoption), Re [1990] 1 FLR 96...27, 44
P v P [1992] 1 FLR 155 ....5, 9
P v S [1992] 2 FLR 492 8
Pilling v Abergele UDC [1950] 1 KB 636 78
Quazi v Quazi [1980] AC 744 ....52, 57, 59–60, 68
Qureshi v Qureshi [1971] 1 All ER 325 57
Qureshi v Qureshi [1972] Fam 173 54
R, Re [1993] 2 FLR 757 176
R (No 1) (Inter-Country Adoption), Re [1999] 1 FLR 1014 ....117–18, 120
R (Inter-Country Adoptions: Practice), Re [1999] 1 FLR 1042 120
R v Adams [1957] Crim LR 365 166
R v Arthur (1981) 12 BMLR 1 166
R v Birmingham Licensing Planning Committee, ex p Kennedy [1972]
    2 QB 140 78
R v Camplin [1978] AC 705 138
R v Cox (1992) 12 BMLR 38 166
R v Immigration Appeal Tribunal and Seada Bi, ex p Secretary of State for the
    Home Department [1984] FLR 147 60
R v Lancashire County Council ex p M [1992] 1 FLR 109 27
R v Newham LBC, ex p Gorenkin (1998) 26 HLR 278.................................157
R v Registrar General of Births, Deaths and Marriages, ex p Minhas [1977]
    QB 1 57
R v Secretary of State for Social Security, ex p Joint Council for the
    Welfare of Immigrants [1996] 4 All ER 385 145
R v Secretary of State for the Home Department, ex p Fatima [1986]
    2 All ER 32, [1986] AC 527 61–3
R v Secretary of State for Health, ex p Luff [1992] 1 FLR 59.......................116
R v Thornton [1992] 1 All ER 306 138
R, Re [1981] 2 FLR 416 10
R, Re [1993] 2 FLR 757 176
R, Re [1995] 1 FLR 716 8
R, Re [1996] 3 FCR 473 168
Radwan v Radwan (No 2) [1972] 3 All ER 1026...73
Ratanachai v Ratanachai (1960)/[1960] CLY 480.....................................52, 60
Russ v Russ [1963] P 87; [1964] P 315...53, 57, 72
S v S [1992] 2 FLR 492 7–8
S, Re [1991] 2 FLR 388 11
S, Re [1993] 1 FLR 26 169
S, Re [1994] 1 FLR 297 9
S, Re [1994] 1 FLR 819 8
S, Re [1994] 2 FLR 1065 ....170, 171, 175
S, Re [1995] 2 WLR 38, [1995] 3 All ER 290 164

S, Re [1999] 1 FLR 843...6
Sabbagh v Sabbagh [1985] FLR 29..66
Schloendorff v Society of New York Hospital (1914) 105 NE 92..................162
Sharif v Sharif [1980] Fam Law 216..57, 59–60, 67
Sidaway v Bethlem RHG [1985] 1 All ER 643 ....162, 164, 169
Simonin v Mallac (1860) 2 Sw & Tr 67...71
St George's Healthcare NHS Trust v S [1998] 2 FCR 685 ....163, 169
T, Re [1992] 2 FLR 458...168–70, 177
Tahir v Tahir 1993 SLT 194...68
Travers v Holley [1953] P 246..53
Varanand v Varanand (1964) 108 SJ 693..60
Vervaeke v Smith [1983] 1 AC 145...72
W v Essex County Council [1998] 2 FCR 269...17
W, Re [1992] 2 FCR 785 168
W, Re [1995] 1 FLR 878..4,
Wik Peoples v Queensland (1996) 134 ALR 637 87
Wood v Wood [1957] P 254..66
X (Minors) v Bedfordshire County Council [1995] 2 AC 633.........................17
Z v Z [1992] 2 FLR 291 57
Z, Re [1999] 1 FLR 1270 9
Zaal v Zaal [1982]/[1983] 4 FLR 284...57, 59, 68

Table of Legislation

EUROPEAN

Brussels II Convention on Jurisdiction and the Recognition and Enforcement
    of Judgements in Matrimonial Matters 1988
    Art. 13 69
    Art. 14 69
Convention on Consent to Marriage 78
    Art. 1(1) 78
European Convention on Human Rights and Fundamental Freedoms............7
    Art. 2 168
    Art. 8 46
    Art. 12 78
Hague Convention 1993 ....3, 8–9, 13–14, 112, 114–15, 121–4
    Art. 1(a) 112–13
    Art. 2(1) 122
    Art. 4(b) 112–15
    Art. 4(c)(i) 122
    Art. 4(c)(iii) 122
    Art. 4(d)(iv) 122
    Art. 12 14
    Art. 13 ....4, 5, 8, 14
    Art. 13(b) 4, 7
    Art. 14..118
    Art. 16..118
    Art. 23(1) 122
    Art. 24..122
    Art. 26..122
    Art. 26(1) 123
    Art. 26(2) 122–3
    Art. 27..123
    Art. 27(1) 123
Hague Convention on the Adoption of Children 1965................................112
Hague Convention on Recognition of Divorces and Legal Separations 1968 ...53

INTERNATIONAL

Australian Constitution 1967 92

Draft Declaration on the Rights of Indigenous Peoples
  Art. 6 97
International Covenant on Civil and Political Rights
  Art. 1 97
  Art. 6 168
  Art. 27 97
United Nations Convention on the Rights of the Child 7, 11, 14, 85, 88, 112–13
(UNCROC) 91
  Art. 2 ....17, 172
  Art. 3 14
  Art. 8 17
  Art. 11 14
  Art. 14 172
  Art. 18 19
  Art. 19 ....7, 85
  Art. 20 ....17, 112
  Art. 21 112
  Art. 21(b) 114
  Art. 30 ....17, 91, 97, 103, 107
  Art. 35 14
United Nations Declaration on Social and Legal Principles Relating to the
  Protection and Welfare of Children 112

NATIONAL

Australia

Australian Family Law Reform Act 1995 ....16, 88
Child Protection Bill 1998 (*Qld*)
  cl 6 95
Children and Young Persons Act 1989 (*Vic*)
  s 119 95
Children (Care and Protection) Act 1987 (*NSW*)
  s 87 94
Children Protection Act (*SA*) ....no year fn 29 pge 95
  s 5 95
Family Law Act 1975 (*Cth*) 87, 99, 100, 107
  s 60B 88, 100
  s 60B(2) 107
  s 60B(2)(a) 100
  s 60B(2)(b) 101
  s 60B(2)(c) 100
  s 60B(2)(d) 100
  s 60D(1) 99

s 60D(3) 99
s 60H 99
s 61B 100
s 61C 99, 100
s 61D(1) 100
s 65C (c) 100
s 68F 99, 100, 105, 108
s 68F(b) 100
s 68F(c)(ii) 100
s 68F(e) 100
s 68F(f) 100
s 68F(i) 99
s 68F(j) 99
s 68F(2) 99
s 68F(2)(f) 103, 107
s 68J 99
s 68L 103
Family Law Reform Act 1995..99
Marriage Act 1961 73

Pakistan
Pakistan Muslim Family Laws Ordinance 1961 ....51, 57, 59, 61, 63
s 1(2) 57

United Kingdom
Abortion Act...1967
s 1(1)(a) 166
Adoption Act 1676...46, 114
s 6..27, 34, 40, 42, 47, 113, 117–19
s 11 ....117, 119, 121, 125
s 11(1) 117
s 11(3) 117–18
s 23(1) 119
s 24 ....119, 121
s 24(2) 117
s 32 119
s 33 119
s 33(1) 119
s 34 119
s 57 ....117, 119, 121
s 57(2) 121
s 57(3) 121
s 74(3) 117, 119
Adoption (Intercountry Aspects) Act 1999................................112–13

Asylum and Immigration Act 1996
  s 95(1) 156
Child Abduction and Custody Act 1985 3
Children Act 1989 ....4, 15–19, 21–3, 26–30, 46, 85, 119
  s 1 ....34, 46
  s 1(1) 3, 16, 27
  s 1(3) 16, 24
  s 1(3)(g) 16
  s 1(4) 16
  s 1(4)(b) 24
  s 3 16
  s 8 ....16, 27
  s 17(1) 19, 20
  s 17(5) 23
  s 17(10)(a) 19
  s 17 (10)(b) 19
  s 17 (10)(c) 19
  s 17(11) 19
  s 20 ....24, 144, 156
  s 22 16
  s 22(1)(2) 24
  s 22(3) 24–6, 29
  s 22(5) 24, 42, 47
  s 22(5)(c) 16, 20, 24, 26, 28, 41
  s 26(1)(2) 29
  s 30(1) 19
  s 31 24
  s 31(2)(a) 119
  s 34 28
  s 46(1)(a) 119
  s 61(1)(c) 29
  s 61(3)(c) 24
  s 64(1)(c) 29
  s 64 (3)(c) 24
  s 83(6) 20
  Sched. 2 para. 1A 22
  Sched. 2 para. 1(1) 20
  Sched. 2 para. 1(2) 23
  Sched. 2 para. 10(a) 18
  Sched. 2 para. 11 ....16, 23
  Sched. 2 para. 15 28
  Sched. 2 para. 16 28
  Sched. 2 para. 17(1) 26, 28
  Sched. 15 119

Children and Young Persons Act 1933
  s 1 85
Children (Scotland) Act 1995
  s 17(4)(c) 24
Crime and Disorder Act 1998 158
Domicile and Matrimonial Proceedings Act 1973...............................53
  s 16(1) 61
Draft Adoption Bill 1996..46
Family Law Act 1986 ....54–55, 59–60, 63–4, 66–7
  s 44 ....54, 63–4
  s 44(1) 61–2
  s 44(2) 54
  s 45 54
  s 46 64
  s 46(1) 55–7, 60, 62–5
  s 46(2) 56, 64, 66
  s 46(2)(c)..56, 64
  s 51 ....55, 57, 64
  s 51(1) 64
  s 51(2) 65
  s 51(3) 65
  s 51(3)(a)(i) 56, 65
  s 51(3)(b)...66
  s 51(3)(c) 67
  s 51(4) 66
  s 52 (1)(a) 54
  s 52(5)(b)...64
  s 52 (3) 54
  s 52 (4) 54
  s 52 (5)(a) 54
  s 54 (1) 57
Family Law Act 1996 ....133, 136, 139, 144
  s 47(2) 139
Housing Act (**Year?**)..142
Housing Act 1996 ....152, 158–9
  ss 161 156
  ss 185–8..156
Housing Act 1988 153–4
  s 58 149
Housing Grants, Construction and Regeneration Act 1996...............151
Homicide Act 1957
  s 3 137
Human Rights Act 1998
  s 3...7

ss 6–8 7
Marriage Act 1949 62
  s 2 81
Matrimonial and Family Proceedings Act 1984 ....58, 68
  s 12(1) 58
Mental Health Act 1983 178
National Assistance Act 1948
  s 21 156
Offences Against the Person Act 1861 133
Race Relations Act 1976 ....19, 33, 149
  s 1(a) 40
  s 20 15
  s 20(1) 40
  s 20(1)(b) 40
  s 20(2)(g) 40
  s 23(2) 40
  s 37 (1)(a) 45
  s 37 (1)(b) 45
  s 71 ....15, 149
Recognition of Divorces and Legal Separations Act 1971 ....54, 59, 63–4, 67
  s 46(2) 58
  s 1 53
  ss 2 53
  ss 6 53
  s 2 ....53, 59, 61
  s 3 53
  s 6 53
  s 6(3) 64
  s 8 ....57, 60

United States of America
Indian Child Welfare Act 1978 ....35, 93, 97

REGULATIONS

Adoption Agency Regulations 1983 118
  Reg. 9 47
Arrangements for Placement of Children (General) Regulations 1991,
    SI 1991/890
  Regs. 3–4 25
  Sched. 1–4 25
British Agencies for Adoption Practice Notes 47
Practice Guidance and Regulations on Part III of the Children Act 17
Review of Children's Cases Regulations SI 1991/895 29

PART I
Children

1

Images of Child Welfare in Child Abduction Appeals

MICHAEL FREEMAN*

I INTRODUCTION

THE ABDUCTION OF a child—a phenomenon often involving members of ethnic minority groups—is the hangover from the concept of the child as
"property".[1] Two international Conventions, one from the Council of Europe,
the other the Hague Convention, have attempted to tackle the problem of international child abduction. The United Kingdom is a signatory to both
Conventions, and both are incorporated in the Child Abduction and Custody
Act 1985. The two Conventions have similar aims—to return abducted children
promptly to home countries, so that any dispute as to their care can be determined there. The Conventions set their faces against the abductors gaining any
tactical advantage from their wrongful behaviour. They can also be seen as
intended to deter abductions. There is, accordingly, a presumption in favour of
returning the child, and a reluctance to investigate the merits of disputes over
residence and upbringing. In Children Act proceedings (at least in those which
relate to a child's upbringing),[2] the child's welfare is paramount.[3] But in the context of the Conventions, the courts have interpreted welfare as congruent with
the restoration of the child to her home environment.

A striking illustration of this is the case *N v. N*[4] where the mother had
abducted the three children from Australia. In the words of the judge:

> The mother is seeking to obliterate the father from her life and the lives of the children,
> almost as though he were dead. If she succeeds in distancing him by ten thousand or
> more miles, directly or indirectly discouraging contact, what will be the long-term
> effect on the children of losing a devoted father in such way?[5]

---

* University College. London.

[1] See, e.g., M.A. Mason, *From Father's Property to Children's Rights* (New York: Columbia
University Press, 1994).
[2] See *Re A* [1992] Fam 182.
[3] Children Act 1989, s. 1(1).
[4] [1995] 1 FLR 107.
[5] *Ibid.*, at 112.

There was some evidence, though the court thought that this should be evaluated in Australia, that this "devoted" father had sexually abused one of the children (the eight year-old-daughter). The court held that it had to weigh the psychological harm of returning the children against the psychological consequences of refusing such a return. Given that both risks were substantial, the court held that it had to speculate as to which was the more substantial and, further, in "exercising the discretion in such circumstances, due weight [had to] be given to the important primary purpose of the Convention to ensure the swift return of abducted children".[6] In the event, the welfare of the children was said to be important, but not a paramount consideration.[7]

The only reference in the Conventions—and thus in the Act—to children's welfare is in one of the Article 13 defences (which was an issue in *N* v. *N*).[8] To read welfare as important, rather than as paramount, is therefore a judicial construction rather than a literal reading of the legislative Act. Nonetheless it is necessary if the underlying objectives of the Conventions are to be carried through. What ought to be noted, however, is that not only is the emphasis on the child's welfare different in abduction cases, it is also located within a different objective. In Children Act cases, where paramountcy *is* the guiding principle, the courts are concerned with the best interests of the child whose upbringing is in question. But in international child abduction cases, the courts are concerned not just with the interests of the abducted child in the case in issue, but also with the interests of abducted children more generally. As Balcombe LJ explained in *Re N*:[9]

> The fact that the assistance of the court is invoked . . . does not make this ordinary adversarial litigation between the father and the mother as the judge seems to have thought. Not merely is there a statutory duty to apply the Convention if the necessary facts are present, but in applying the Convention the court is concerned with the interests of the child in question and of abducted children generally.[10]

The most contentious part of the Convention—and the one which has caused most interpretational problems both in England and elsewhere—is the package of "defences" to international child abduction contained in Article 13. The "message" of the Convention is clear, and the English courts comply with it. So they "set their face against the removal of the child".[11] This should have led to Article 13 being construed strictly, but regrettably the courts have not been consistent.

---

[6] [1995] 1 FLR 107, at 113.
[7] *Ibid.*, at 144. See also *Re K* [1995] 1 FLR 977.
[8] Art. 13(b) of the Hague Convention. This provision is discussed at some length, *infra*, in part II of this chapter.
[9] [1993] 2 FLR 124.
[10] *Ibid.*, at 131.
[11] *Re W* [1995] 1 FLR 878, 889 *per* Wall J.

II ASSESSING A RISK

Probably the most contentious provision empowers a court to refuse to return a child if there is "a grave risk that his or her return would expose the child to physical or psychological harm or otherwise place the child in an intolerable situation".[12] There are few English cases where this defence has succeeded.[13] This is the only provision in the Convention where the issue of the child's welfare can be legitimately raised, but the courts, aware as they are of the objectives of the Convention, have done their best to frustrate the endeavours of those who would invoke it. Thus, in *Re N*[14] Bracewell J said:

> it is plain that it is not a trivial risk and it is not a trivial psychological harm which is envisaged and which has to be justified and, furthermore, I am satisfied that the intolerable situation envisaged has to be something extreme and compelling.[15]

In *P v. P*,[16] the mother claimed that if the court ordered the return of the children to the USA she would become deeply unhappy, and this, in turn, would make the children unhappy as well. The argument was said to be "beside the point". But this was not because the courts were inhumane. "On the contrary" it was said, "there is a humane purpose underlying it in ensuring that children are not subjected to disruption through arbitrary movement by one parent".[17] On the other hand, the courts have accepted that psychological harm can include that suffered by the abducting parent. In *Re G*,[18] for instance, the court was convinced that to return a child to Texas would lead to the mother's mental condition worsening and a prognosis that the mother might become psychotic. Accepting the evidence provided by a consultant psychiatrist to the effect that the mother's psychotic state would import the likelihood that the mother "would be unable to look after the child",[19] Ewbank J concluded:

> I am satisfied that this is a case where Art 13 does apply and that I am not bound to send these children back to the USA, and taking into account all the circumstances of the case, I do not propose to make an order that these children should go back to the USA. In my view, the effect of an order returning the children to the USA would be that there would be a serious deterioration in the mother's condition and the children would be affected.[20]

It has also been judicially accepted that harm in this context can include financial detriments.[21] But the courts refuse to listen to the idea that a child would be

---

[12] Art. 13(b).
[13] The first was *Re F* [1995] 2 FLR 31.
[14] [1991] 1 FLR 413.
[15] *Ibid.*, at 419. See also *Re C* [1989] 1 FLR 403.
[16] [1992] 1 FLR 155.
[17] *Ibid.*, at 161.
[18] [1995] 1 FLR 64.
[19] *Ibid.*, at 68.
[20] *Ibid.*, at 70.
[21] *Re M* [1995] 1 FLR 1021.

in danger if she returned unaccompanied. In *Re C*,[22] the mother said she would refuse to accompany the child if he were to be returned to Australia. She asserted that the child would therefore suffer severe psychological harm. The Court of Appeal rejected this contention effectively on the basis that the mother ought to be estopped from relying on a psychological danger that she herself had created. Moreover, in *Re L*,[23] a baby of eighteen months was returned to Texas in the face of evidence that the mother might not get a visa to accompany him, and despite affidavits provided by two psychologists that stated that separation of a mother and a child of this age would be likely to cause grave psychological harm. Hollis J was of the view that, even if the mother failed to obtain a visa, the child would not be exposed to psychological harm of the necessary degree, reasoning that "[h]e knows, of course, his father although he has not seen him since last September" and "[h]e knows his paternal grandmother although less well than his father".[24] The evidence for these claims is not clear. On the face of it, this is an extraordinary decision, redolent of much-criticised cases in other contexts,[25] and one which it is thought, could never be reached today outside the context of an international abduction.

One of the few cases in which the defence has succeeded is *Re F*.[26] In that case, there was evidence both of domestic violence towards the mother and of physical abuse of the child.[27] The combined effect was of nightmares and bed-wetting. Additionally, the child suffered from asthma. It was said that returning the child to the surroundings in which he had previously been not simply a witness to marital discord, but also a victim of it, would on the facts create a grave risk that his return would expose him to psychological harm and would place him in an intolerable situation. Even so, Butler-Sloss LJ admitted that she reached this conclusion with "considerable hesitation" noting in passing that, to her knowledge "there is no case which has been heard in an English appellate court in which that standard has been reached".[28]

The contrast with two very recent cases is striking. In *Re S*,[29] the return of a nine-year-old girl to Sweden was ordered, though there was genuine concern on the part of social services both in Camden and in Sweden that the cohabitant of the mother (the child had been brought to England on a vacation visit and not returned by the father) had sexually abused the girl. "Comity of nations"[30] seemed to weigh more with Sir Stephen Brown P than the girl's "understandable reluctance"[31] to go back to Sweden. Once in Sweden the uncomfortable process

[22] [1989] 1 FLR 403.
[23] [1993] 2 FLR 401.
[24] *Ibid.*, at 405.
[25] For example, *Re C (MA)* [1966] 1 All ER 838, the so-called "blood-tie adoption" case that caused considerable controversy.
[26] [1995] 2 FLR 31.
[27] See also, *Re M* [1996] 1 FLR 315.
[28] *Supra*, n. 26, at 38.
[29] [1999] 1 FLR 843.
[30] *Ibid.*, at 848.
[31] *Ibid.*, at 849.

of disclosure would be repeated, this time, it seems, by the police.[32] So, together, the child and her mother would be placed in an "investigation home" where at least she would be relatively safe. It would then be up to the Swedish social authorities to find a way of protecting her.

Similarly, in *Re C*,[33] the Court of Appeal, overruling the first instance judge, ordered the return to California of children aged nine and eight despite the fact that this would mean, *inter alia*, contact with a father who beat them with a belt buckle. The judge was reassured that contact would be safe because it would be supervised. But he also quoted from the welfare report to the effect that "the children's thoughts and feelings about the father are dominated by their painful memories of what they consider to be his cruel and harsh mistreatment of them".[34] This, it will be observed, was readily discounted. So keen are we to uphold our international obligations to secure the return of abducted children that we forget that we also have an international obligation towards the children themselves (under the United Nations Convention on the Rights of the Child) to protect them from abuse.[35] The response—that this latter obligation ranks lower in the scale since it is not a directly enforceable right under English law—is further ammunition for those who would like to see the United Nations Convention "brought home" in a manner similar to that in which the European Convention on Human Rights and Fundamental Freedoms has been.[36]

III AN OBJECTING CHILD

The Conventions also allow the courts to refuse to return a child in the face of that child's objections. But as a rider to this, the child has to have reached "an age and degree of maturity at which it is appropriate to take account of its views".[37] The Court of Appeal has ruled that the child's objection is an entirely separate matter from paragraph (b) of Article 13, and that there is no need to establish that the child will be at risk of physical or psychological harm before the discretion comes into play.[38]

---

[32] *Ibid.*, at 845.

[33] [1999] 1 FLR 1145.

[34] *Ibid.*, at 1147.

[35] Art. 19.

[36] Contrary to what is often said, the Human Rights Act 1998 does not incorporate the European Convention on Human Rights and Fundamental Freedoms into English law. Rather, the Act provides, first, that wherever possible primary and subordinate legislation must be interpreted in a way which is compatible with Convention rights (s. 3), and secondly, that it is unlawful for any public authority to act in a way that is incompatible with a Convention right (ss. 6–8).

[37] Art. 13.

[38] In *S* v. *S* [1992] 2 FLR 492 Balcombe LJ was emphatic (at 499) that "the part of Art. 13 which relates to the child's objections to being returned is completely separate from para (b)". See also *Re M* (1990) 25 July (unreported) *per* Sir Stephen Brown P.

The Convention does not specify an age.[39] Nor does it embody a *Gillick*-type competency test.[40] In *Re R*,[41] Balcombe LJ was prepared to listen to the objections of a child of seven-and-a-half, though Millett LJ was not. Seven would appear to be the earliest age at which the English courts seem to have taken note of a child's objection.[42] What is required is not just "instinct", but "the discernment which a mature child brings to the question's implication for his or her best interests in the long and the short term".[43] Often the child's objection will be to a separation from the abducting parent, rather than to being returned to the home environment.[44] Frequently, too, the child's views will have been influenced by the abducting parent, and when the courts have deemed this to be so they have given little or no weight to those views. Balcombe LJ's remark in *S v. S*[45] is typical: "if the court should come to the conclusion that the child's views have been influenced by some other person, for example the abducting parent. then it is probable that little or no weight will be given to those views".[46]

Even if the child has reached the requisite level of maturity, her return may still be ordered, the child's views being merely one, not necessarily prevailing, consideration.[47] (The seven-year-old girl in the case in which this was said appeared afraid to return to a home in which she recollected severe physical chastisement).[48] Where a child of sufficient maturity has expressed a wish to remain, the court must decide just how much weight to attribute to the child's views, bearing in mind the purposes of the Convention. Thus, in *S v. S*,[49] the court was alert to the danger that Article 13 could be interpreted in a manner which would undermine the notion that it is normally in the best interests of children that they should promptly be returned to the country from which they have wrongfully been removed. Balcombe LJ remarked that to give effect to a child's views where these have been influenced by some other person would be "to drive a coach and horses through the primary scheme of the Hague Convention".[50] In fact, in *S v. S*, the court took the view that the nine-year-old's reason for not wishing to be returned to France—she found being educated in English far easier—both independent and valid, and it upheld it.

[39] There is no chronological threshold in Balcombe LJ's judgment in *Re R*: see [1995] 1 FLR 716, 730.
[40] See Lord Scarman's speech in *Gillick* v. *West Norfolk and Wisbech AHA* [1986] AC 112.
[41] [1995] 1 FLR 716.
[42] *B* v. *K* [1993] 1 FCR 382; *P* v. *S* [1992] 2 FLR 492.
[43] *Re S* [1994] 1 FLR 819, 827 *per* Waite LJ.
[44] See *S* v. *S* [1992] 2 FLR 492.
[45] [1992] 2 FLR 492.
[46] *Ibid.*, at 501. See also Thorpe J's approval of this approach in *N* v. *N* [1995] 1 FLR 107, 112.
[47] See *Re K* [1995] 1 FLR 977. But this statement was made *obiter* because it was held that the child in this case had *not* reached the age and maturity required.
[48] *Ibid.*, at 996.
[49] [1992] 2 FLR 492.
[50] *Ibid.*, at 491.

IV NON-CONVENTION CASES

When the Convention was drawn up and when the United Kingdom passed its legislation, there were comparatively few Convention countries. And in terms of understandings of child welfare the differences were not pronounced. In relation to child welfare, therefore, the Convention/non-Convention dichotomy may not always be as significant as interpretations of child welfare within Convention countries (Burkina Faso and many ex-Soviet Republics including Asiatic ones are Hague signatories). Where debates have arisen, however, is in relation to the application of Hague-type principles to non-Convention countries.

In non-Convention cases the welfare of children is the paramount consideration.[51] Accordingly, "the principles of the Convention are applicable only to the extent that they indicate what is normally in the interests of children".[52] But there is a concern that the courts are too willing to apply Hague principles to non-Convention cases. The courts have said that they will do so only where the non-Convention country applies principles not significantly different from those of the English courts.[53] But in *Re S*,[54] the case in which this statement was made, the children concerned were returned to Pakistan where, according to expert evidence, they could be deprived of the care of their mother if she re-married, formed a liaison with a man other than a close relation or was deemed unsuitable (for example, by living an un-Islamic way of life). The underlying assumption of the Convention is that:

> the courts of all its signatories are equally concerned to ensure, and equally capable of ensuring, that both parties receive a fair hearing, and that all issues of child welfare receive a skilled, thorough and humane evaluation.[55]

But the children in *Re S* were returned to a system whose principles are not compatible with the welfare standard applied by the English courts. This does not always happen, however. In *Re JA*,[56] both Singer J and the Court of Appeal refused to return a two-year-old girl to her father in Sharjah. But the two courts gave different reasons for their decisions. Singer J relied on acquiescence and presumably therefore would have returned the child had the father not indicated an earlier willingness for her to remain. Ward LJ, however, situating his reasoning firmly within pre-Convention principles,[57] held that it would be an "abnegation of the duty of this court to the ward under its protection to surrender the determination of the ward's future to a foreign court whose regime may be inimical

---

[51] *D v. D* [1994] 1 FLR 137; *Re Z* [1999] 1 FLR 1270.
[52] *D v. D* [1994] 1 FLR 137, 144 *per* Balcombe LJ.
[53] *Re S* [1994] 1 FLR 297.
[54] *Ibid.*
[55] *P v. P* [1992] 1 FLR 155, 161 *per* Waite J.
[56] [1998] 1 FLR 231.
[57] *Re B's Settlement* [1940] Ch. 54; *McKee v. McKee* [1951] AC 352.

10   *Michael Freeman*

to the child's welfare".[58] He referred to the limited powers of the Emirates' courts and to the fact that there was no indication that welfare was the applicable test there. So, he said:

> if the mother returns to Sharjah with the child, there is no power in the court to permit her to return to this country if the father objects to that move, whatever the best interests of the child dictate. Once the mother and the child return to the Emirates, they are effectively locked in there.[59]

But there was also a welfare consideration (or transferred welfare consideration) in the opinion of Ward LJ. He was convinced by the argument that the mother's health—not merely her happiness—was at risk if she was forced to return to the Emirates. This was perceived as a risk of consequential harm to the child. If this swung the balance in favour of the mother and non-return to the child's habitual residence, one has to conclude that the mother (and the child) were fortunate to be able to point to psychiatric evidence (it can be found in the judgment)[60] which I suspect would fit any abducting mother ("adjustment disorder", "lowness of mood", "considerable anxiety accompanied by worry, disturbance in sleep and appetite and occasional bouts of crying").

The resurrection of pre-Convention sources is welcome, as is Ward LJ's reading of them. In particular, this is true of his emphasis on words in a judgment of Ormrod LJ in *Re R*[61] to the effect that "damage to a child's interest" from not making a summary order ought to be balanced against risks which include "the child being subjected to a regime of law under which the protection of their interests may be open to question".[62] Of course, there are dangers of chauvinism here in an arena in which comity is supposed to prevail.[63] Even worse, there is the suspicion that ethnocentrism (sometimes referred to as "anglo-centrism")[64] or just plain racism may intrude into decision making. These are dangers against which we must guard ourselves.

We are all further aware of the indeterminacy of the notion of welfare and best interests even within a purely domestic context.[65] Where the choice is between two jurisdictions, the problem is quite obviously accentuated. Even so, there are aspects of systems within rules, procedures and processes which militate against upholding a child's interests. There are inflexible rules related to age

[58] *Supra*, n. 57, at 243.
[59] *Ibid.*, at 244.
[60] *Ibid.*
[61] [1981] 2 FLR 416, 426.
[62] *Supra*, n. 57, at 243.
[63] And note Lord Diplock's language in a very different context—in *The Abidin Daver* [1984] AC 398, 411.
[64] Identified again in a very different context: see N. MacCormick, "Children's Rights: A Test Case for Theories of Right" in N. MacCormick, *Legal Right and Social Democracy: Essays in Legal and Political Philosophy* (Oxford: Clarendon Press, 1982) pp. 154–7.
[65] See R. Mnookin, "Child-Custody Adjudication: Judicial Functions in the Face of Indeterminacy" (1975) 39 *Law and Contemporary Problems* 226 and J. Montgomery, "Rhetoric and Welfare" (1989) 9 *Oxford Journal of Legal Studies* 395.

and gender.[66] There are systems which discriminate, often in effect penalising women and hence mothers. That we have done this ourselves in the past or come close to doing so (it is not so long ago that we abandoned custody presumptions, for example)[67] should not deflect us from trying to seek justice now, particularly when the future of vulnerable children is in issue. And we should remember that in all, or practically all, of the contested abduction cases the child is closely connected with this country, even if habitually resident elsewhere.

The courts have refused to be deflected by *forum conveniens* considerations,[68] but the truth of the matter is that often England is the most appropriate forum for the litigation of the dispute. In Convention cases, this is not a consideration that can properly be brought into the decision making process. On the other hand, it is not the least bit clear why this should not be a highly relevant factor.

V   LOOKING AT OTHER SYSTEMS—A VALUE FRAMEWORK

The question remains as to how we should look at a child's best interests in international abduction cases. It is possible to take three distinct approaches. The first emphasises monism or universalism.[69] This directs us to believe that there is an overriding value (or set of values). International documents—the United Nations Convention on the Rights of the Child is the most obvious paradigm—are committed (or largely so) to just such an approach. On this account, what amounts to the best interests of the child should vary very little from one country to another.

The second approach, long popular, emphasises cultural relativism. Relativism emerged, early in the last century, in reaction to cultural evolutionism, which was European and often distinctly racist.[70] Cultural relativism is a theory about the way evaluations or judgements are made. To the relativist, "evaluations are relative to the cultural background out of which they arise".[71] And, according to Benedict, tolerance is a key element of cultural relativism,[72]

---

[66] An example is discussed by Ward LJ in *Re JA* [1998] 1 FLR 231 at 243.

[67] And see *Re S* [1991] 2 FLR 388, 390 *per* Butler-Sloss LJ.

[68] See *Re M* [1995] 2 FLR 224.

[69] There are different models of monism: these range from the Platonic—the "Idea of the Good": see Plato, *The Republic* (Harmondsworth, Penguin, 2nd ed, 1974) (revised) pp. 504–9—to different versions of utilitarianism, using its simplest model of a felicific calculus (as in Jeremy Bentham's *Introduction to the Principles of Morals and Legislation* (Oxford: Oxford University Press, 1996)).

[70] See, e.g., G.W. Stocking Jnr, *Race, Culture and Evolution* (New York: Free Press, 1968).

[71] M. Herskovits, *Cultural Relativism: Perspectives on Cultural Pluralism* (New York: Random House, 1972) p. 14.

[72] *Patterns of Culture* (New York: Houghton Mifflin, 1934) p. 37. See also E. Hatch, *Culture and Morality: the Relativity of Values in Anthropology* (New York: Columbia University Press, 1983) pp. 99–100.

while for Herskovits it is necessary to recognise "the dignity inherent in every body of custom".[73]

The contemporary philosopher, Charles Taylor, talks of the presumption of the equal worth of cultures.[74] The attraction of relativism is difficult to ignore. It is rooted in egalitarianism, liberalism and modernism. It belongs—at least, on Charles Larmore's account[75]—to a disenchanted vision of the world. It is anti-assimilationist, it is anti-imperialist, it is hostile to ethnocentrism.[76] It is sympathetic to, and would wish to protect, the traditions and rights of indigenous peoples.[77] It has the value also, in a sort of Millian way,[78] of enhancing the prospects of achieving moral knowledge, though this presupposes the possibility of real communication across cultures which, of course, is not always possible.

Relativists regard all values as the products of the customs, practices and beliefs which have, as a matter of fact, developed within a particular tradition. They deny that any value has any authority, epistemological or moral, outside of this cultural context. They deny, also, that conflict between values belonging to different traditions can be settled in any reasonable way because, so they argue, what is reasonable is itself a product of particular cultures. And so they demand of us that we ask not whether social practices like child marriage or female circumcision are justified by the moral considerations that we find convincing, but rather whether they are sanctioned by the relevant social understandings of the cultures within which they are practised.

The fundamental problem with this approach is that the culture can only be judged by endogenous value judgements, so that moral principles which derive from outside that culture have no validity. In effect, morality becomes a slave to custom.[79] But the argument in favour of any practice must be more than simply that the practice exists. A culture which permits child marriage, for example, must be able to justify legitimising this practice by a stronger argument (or series of arguments) than that there is—if, indeed this is the case—social consensus. An examination of the social understandings within a culture may reveal that there is no social understanding at all, or that there are conflicting understandings, misunderstandings or inconsistencies. Female circumcision, to take one example, is often justified by Muslims by reference to the Koran—but it is not

[73] *Man and his Works* (New York: Alfred A. Knopf, 1947) p. 76.
[74] *Multiculturalism and "The Politics of Recognition"* (Princeton, NJ: Princeton University Press, 1992) p. 72.
[75] "Pluralism and Reasonable Disagreement" (1994) 11(1) *Social Philosophy and Policy* 61, at 71.
[76] See A.A. An-Na'im, "Religious Minorities under Islamic Law and the Limits of Cultural Relativism" (1987) 9 *Human Rights Quarterly* 1.
[77] See W. Kymlicka, *Liberalism, Community and Culture* (New York: Oxford University Press, 1989) and A. Gewirth, "Is Cultural Pluralism Relevant to Moral Knowledge" [1994] *Social Philosophy and Policy* 22, at 35.
[78] See J.S. Mill, *On Liberty* (first published in 1859).
[79] Mill referred to the "despotism of custom" in *On Liberty*. See also A. Gutmann, "The Challenge of Multiculturalism in Political Ethics" (1993) *Philosophy and Public Affairs* 171.

there![80] Often, an examination will reveal that the so-called dominant under-standing is in reality the understanding of the dominant.[81] Many cultural prac-tices when critically examined turn upon the interpretation of a male élite (an oligarchy, clergy or judiciary): if there is now consensus, this was engineered, an ideology constructed to cloak the interests of only one section of society.[82]

Pluralism, which is the third and preferred approach, must be distinguished from relativism. For the cultural pluralist there are values independent of the context of the culture in question to which we can appeal in settling conflicts. Perhaps the biggest difference between relativism and pluralism is that the lat-ter identifies primary values and therefore standards independent of a particu-lar culture by which it can be judged. There are certain needs which do not vary either temporally—they are historically constant—or culturally—they are the requirement of people everywhere. There are physiological needs (food, cloth-ing, shelter); psychological needs (comfort, affection, companionship, stimula-tion); social needs (dignity, respect, privacy). There are, in other words, certain minimum requirements of human welfare. They must be met whatever the con-ception of what constitutes a good life, and regardless of what other values are upheld in any particular culture.[83]

The monistic approach is unhelpful to any child abduction debate, though in a sense the presumption of return embodied in the Hague Convention is such a standard. Relativism is also not helpful. We cannot pretend that there is noth-ing to choose between the approach to child welfare in different systems. It is simply not true that "anything goes". Pluralism may offer an answer. Standards independent of culture can be identified. It is for this reason that we should not contemplate returning a child to a country where she would not be properly fed or where she cannot be educated or where she would be violated by being forced into a marriage or compelled to undergo genital mutilation or where her needs would not be uppermost in any custody determination.

There is, I believe, in pluralism a framework which would assist the courts in making the difficult decisions that confront them when having to justify not returning a child to the country of her habitual residence. It may be argued in response that the framework offered by pluralism would plunge the judiciary into the non-justiciable. The argument would be that the judges are well quali-fied to evaluate systems of justice (procedures, processes, rules and principles of legal systems) but that their competence ends where issues of policy arise. But the boundary between principle and policy is unreal and unsustainable. A care-ful reading of reasoning processes of the judiciary in the difficult cases they have

---

[80] The practice does not exist in the teachings of any formal religion.

[81] A point made forcefully by Gutmann: see A. Gutmann, *op cit*. n. 79, p. 176.

[82] Also argued by Stephen A. James in relation to female circumcision in African societies: see S.A. James, "Reconciling International Human Rights and Cultural Relativism: The Case of Female Circumcision" (1994) 8 *Bioethics* 1.

[83] And see J. Kekes, "Pluralism and the Value of Life" (1994) 11(1) *Social Philosophy and Policy* 44, at 49.

to decide in this area will demonstrate how difficult it is to maintain this boundary.

But if this is a process to commend in the context of non-Convention cases, should it stop there? The decision to admit countries to the Convention is currently taken on unduly narrow criteria—in fact little different from those employed by our judges. A framework could be created to assist the vetting process. And pluralism could offer this guidance as it could to judges even when the Convention applies. Nor should it be thought that explorations of this nature would take the judiciary beyond the remit of the Convention. Rather, it could be incorporated into the language of Article 13. Those who drew up this provision neither put flesh on a concept such as "intolerable situation" nor put that concept into any theoretical framework. The approach I have identified would fill both those lacunae.

VI CONCLUSION

We have been too ready to accept, and accept uncritically, that "welfare" bears a different meaning in the context of child abduction from that which it possesses elsewhere in legislation and litigation concerning children. Welfare is not necessarily congruent with a restoration of the *status quo ante*. Many, if not most, abductions are wrongful. Some, however, could more aptly be described as rescues. What is imperative is that we find better ways of protecting victims of abductions (and rescues) than those currently employed.

A final thought: what would the Convention have looked like had it been considered after the passing of the United Nations Convention on the Rights of the Child in 1989, rather than some years before it? The United Nations Convention, it is true, specifically repudiates abduction[84] and requires States to take all measures to combat it.[85] But it also states that "in all actions concerning children . . . the best interests of the child shall be a primary consideration".[86] And it requires children to be given participatory rights in legal proceedings that go way beyond those accorded in Hague Convention litigation.[87] Hague Convention practice falls far short of these child-centred norms. It is time to rethink it.

---

[84] Art. 35 states that "States Parties shall take all appropriate national, bilateral and multilateral measures to prevent the abduction, the sale of or the traffic of children for any purpose or in any form".

[85] See Art. 11.

[86] Art. 3.

[87] See Art. 12.

2

Local Authority Support for Ethnic Minority Children

MARTIN L. PARRY*

I INTRODUCTION

BEFORE THE CHILDREN Act 1989[1] it was far from clear whether or not ethnic minority children in need of local authority support had any right[2] to have their ethnic identity recognised. Certainly no such right had been written into primary child care legislation. In addition, local authority social services departments frequently failed to respond adequately to the needs of ethnic minorities in their provision of services to children in need.[3] There was a disproportionately high representation of children from some ethnic minorities[4] in local authority care.[5] Ethnic minority children were often considered to be "hard to place" and, along with other such perceived groups, often unsuitable for

---

* University of Hull. I am grateful to Kate Riley for her research assistance.

[1] For an assessment of the response of the previous legislation to the needs of ethnic minorities see Ince, *Making it Alone: a Study of the Care Experiences of Young Black People* (London: British Agencies for Adoption and Fostering, 1998) ch. 1. The Race Relations Act 1976 duty upon local authorities is a general one to eliminate unlawful racial discrimination and promote equality of opportunity and good relations between persons of different racial groups: s. 71 and also s. 20, see, e.g., *Conwell v Newham London Borough Council* [2000] 1 All ER 696. See further, Commission for Racial Equality; Association of Directors of Social Services, *Multiracial Britain: the Social Services Response* (London: CRE; ADSS, 1978); Commission for Racial Equality, *Race Equality in Social Services Departments: a Survey of Opportunity Policies* (CRE, 1989). The 1976 Act has not been used to promote service provision for ethnic minority families: see MacDonald, *All Equal Under The Act?* (London: Race Equality Unit, 1991) p. VIII.

[2] This essay does not address the nature and scope of children's "rights". For a comprehensive and scholarly analysis of the theoretical perspectives see Fortin, *Children's Rights and the Developing Law* (London: Butterworths, 1998) ch. 1.

[3] See Ahmad, *Services to Black People* (London: Race Equality Unit, 1988); MacDonald, *op cit.* n. 1, p. 12.

[4] Particularly mixed race—see Bebbington and Miles, "The Background of Children who enter Local Authority Care" (1989) 19 *British Journal of Social Work* 349—and African-Caribbean and African. In contrast Asian children have been under-represented, see Ince, *op cit.* n. 1, p. 1; Rowe, Hundleby and Garnett, *Child Care Now: a Survey of Placement Patterns* (London: British Agencies for Adoption and Fostering, 1989) ch. 12.

[5] See Rowe and Lambert, *Children Who Wait* (London: Association of British Adoption Agencies, 1973) pp. 95–7; id, "Black Children in Local Authority Care: Admission Patterns" (1990) 16 *New Community* 229; Garnett, *Leaving Care and After* (London: National Children's Bureau, 1992).

fostering, the preferred form of care.[6] If such children were fostered they were often not placed with carers from the same ethnic group.[7]

The Children Act 1989 itself has only partially remedied the situation. The pre-Act disregard of the needs of ethnic minority children suggested the need for a more proactive response given MacDonald's observation at the time that "black children and their families receive fewer welfare services and experience greater social control than their white counterparts".[8] Yet the "Introductory" Part I of the Act makes no specific reference to ethnicity when reaffirming the paramountcy of the child's welfare as the basis for judicial determination of any question relating to a child's upbringing.[9] In cases where the court is required to have regard to the so called "checklist",[10] the child's background is referred to only in general terms.[11] "Parental responsibility"[12] for children is a cryptic and "colour blind" concept. Even in Part III of the Act, which prescribes the responsibilities of local authorities to provide support for children and families, there is no statement of general principle regarding the consideration to be given to the child's ethnic background. Only in two specific contexts does it address the issue. First, and most importantly, in respect of the duties of local authorities in relation to children looked after by them,[13] the Act requires that the local authority, in making any decision with respect to such a child, "shall give due consideration to the child's religious persuasion, racial origin and cultural and linguistic background".[14] Secondly, more obscurely and solely in the context of provision of support services, the duty upon every local authority "to consider racial groups to which children in need belong"[15] is confined to instances in which it is making arrangements "for the provision of day care within their area; or . . . designed to encourage persons to act as local authority foster parents".[16]

The narrow focus of these provisions means that the Children Act 1989 does not adequately address, as a matter of fundamental principle, the needs of children of ethnic minorities and the duty upon all decision makers to give due consideration to those needs. It is regrettable that it was left to "Guidance and

---

[6] Ince, *op cit.* n. 1, p. 11.

[7] See Rowe, Caine, Hundleby and Keane, *Long-Term Foster Care* (London: Batsford, 1984).

[8] MacDonald, *op cit.* n. 1, p. 72.

[9] Children Act 1989, s. 1(1). Compare the Australian Family Law Reform Act 1995, Part VIII where the criteria by which the court determines what is in the child's best interests include certain cultural considerations (discussed at some length by Dewar in his essay in this collection).

[10] *Ibid.*, s. 1(3). The circumstances in which the court is required to consider the checklist are set out in s. 1(4): *viz*, contested s. 8 private law orders and all Part IV public law orders.

[11] *Ibid.*, s. 1(3)(g). The Law Commission in their Working Paper on custody suggested including "where relevant, the ethnic, cultural or religious background of the child and each of the parties": Working Paper No. 96, *Family Law Review of Child Law: Custody* (London: HMSO, 1986) para. 6.38.

[12] See Children Act 1989, s. 3.

[13] Whether the child is in their care as a result of a care order under Part IV of the Act or provided with accommodation under Part III: Children Act 1989, s. 22.

[14] Children Act 1989, s. 22(5)(c).

[15] Sched. 2 para. 11.

[16] *Ibid.*

Regulations" to state that "children should have the right to be cared for as part of a community which values the religious, cultural and linguistic identity of the child".[17] Such a right is more likely to be a reality than an aspiration if recognised in primary legislation and the introduction of statutory recognition would accord with the United Nations Convention on the Rights of the Child,[18] Articles 2, 8, 20 and 30 of which acknowledge that a child belonging to ethnic, religious or linguistic minorities has the right to enjoy his or her own culture and that due regard be paid to the child's ethnic, religious, cultural and linguistic background when he or she is deprived of his or her family environment. On the other hand, while child care practice would be better informed if child care legislation was to include such rights, simply enacting statutory recognition would not, *per se*, provide a panacea.[19] It is what happens in practice that matters. As Michael Freeman, citing Edelman,[20] correctly asserts "[t]he importance of legislation as a symbol . . . cannot be underestimated, but the true recognition of children's rights requires implementation in practice".[21] The *Practice Guidance and Regulations* on Part III of the Children Act 1989[22] go some way to addressing the lacuna in the primary legislation but the point, as Barn and others have indicated, is that although references to issues of race and ethnicity are incorporated in the *Guidance and Regulations* "it is important to emphasise the fragmented and minimalist way in which this is done".[23]

Consideration will be given in this essay to the nature, scope and effectiveness of the law and guidance applicable under Part III of the Act and to the research findings into the provision in practice of local authority support for children from ethnic backgrounds. It is important that the emphasis should be on ethnicity rather than colour[24] in view of the significant proportion of children from ethnic minorities in need of local support who are of mixed parentage. As the

---

[17] See Department of Health, *The Children Act 1989 Guidance and Regulations Volume 2: Family Support, Day Care and Educational Provision for Young Children* (London: HMSO, 1991) para. 6.28. Such *Guidance and Regulations* has statutory force: see *X (minors)* v. *Bedfordshire County Council* [1995] 2 AC 633 at 746 *per* Lord Browne-Wilkinson; *W* v. *Essex County Council* [1998] 2 FCR 269 at 274 *per* Stuart-Smith LJ.

[18] Cm. 1976 (London: HMSO, 1992)—ratified by the United Kingdom on 16 December 1991 and brought into force on 15 January 1992.

[19] For a sophisticated, autopoietic account of this view rooted in the belief that law, problematically, is a "closed social system" see King, *A Better World for Children: Explorations in Morality and Authority* (London: Routledge, 1997).

[20] *Political Language: Words That Succeed and Policies That Fail* (New York: Academic Press, 1977).

[21] Freeman, "Taking Children's Rights More Seriously" (1992) 6 *International Journal of Law and the Family* 52 at 60. See also, Grace, *Social Workers, Children and the Law* (Oxford, OUP, 1994).

[22] See Department of Health, *The Children Act 1989 Guidance and Regulations Volume 2, op cit.* n. 17, *Volume 3: Family Placements*, and *Volume 4: Residential Care* (London: HMSO, 1991).

[23] Barn, Sinclair and Ferdinand, *Acting on Principle: an Examination of Race and Ethnicity in Social Services Provision for Children and Families* (London: British Agencies for Adoption and Fostering, 1997) p. 11.

[24] See Smith and Berridge, *Ethnicity and Childcare Placements* (London: National Children's Bureau, 1993); Berridge, *Foster Care: a Research Review* (London: The Stationery Office, 1997).

Department of Health has insisted, "[c]are is needed to ensure that the terms "black" and "black family" are not used in isolation or in such a way as to obscure characteristics and needs".[25] The courts, too, have recognised that "emphasis on colour rather than cultural upbringing can be mischievous and highly dangerous when you are dealing in practical terms with the welfare of children".[26] It is the primary aim of this essay to focus in general rather than specific terms upon the importance of ethnicity in the context of Part III of the Children Act 1989. In so doing it is accepted that ethnicity is an important variable and that ethnic communities are not a single group but have their own diverse cultures, and that they may be in need of local authority support for a variety of different reasons.[27] Similarly, ethnic minority children in local authority accommodation have needs—for example, dietary, religious and personal and medical care—that are specific to their particular cultural background.[28]

II PROVISION OF SERVICES

Part III of the Children Act 1989 serves to exemplify the preventive, supportive and rehabilitative functions of local authorities which that Act seeks to promote. One of the underlying principles of the Act is that children are best brought up by their families[29] and that state intervention by means of compulsory court based powers, most usually a care order,[30] should be a last resort. That does not mean that local authority support should necessarily precede the use of compulsory powers, but for all but the most serious cases the Act acknowledges that children in need of protection may be in need of services and support, the provision of which will be sufficient to safeguard the child's welfare. There is an inextricable link between the provision of support services and minimal intervention which shapes the functions of local authorities. Research has revealed that this link is "frequently under-emphasised by professionals".[31]

[25] Department of Health, op cit. n. 17, para. 2.9. See also Department of Health (et al), Working Together to Safeguard Children (London: TSO, 1999) Paras 7.24–6.

[26] Re N (A Minor)(Adoption) [1990] 1 FLR 58 at 63 per Bush J.

[27] Community Relations Commission, A Home from Home? Some Policy Considerations on Black Children in Residential Care (London: CRC, 1977); McCulloch, Smith and Batta, "Colour as a Variable in the Children's Section of a Local Authority Social Services Department" (1979) 7 New Community 78; Johnson, "Citizenship, Social Work and Ethnic Minorities" in Etherington (ed.), Social Work and Citizenship (London: British Association of Social Workers, 1986); Barn, Black Children in the Public Care System (London: Batsford and British Agencies for Adoption and Fostering, 1993); Barn, Sinclair and Ferdinand, op cit. n. 23.

[28] See, e.g., Pearl, "Legal Issues arising out of Medical Provision for Ethnic Groups" in Grubb and Mehlman (eds.), Justice and Health Care: Comparative Perspectives (Chichester: John Wiley & Sons, 1995).

[29] See Department of Health, An Introduction to the Children Act 1989 (London: HMSO, 1989) para. 1.3. See also to this effect Children Act 1989, Sched. 2 para. 10(a).

[30] Under Part IV of the Children Act 1989 which provides also for supervision orders. See also Part V for other child protection orders and powers.

[31] See Department of Health, Child Protection Messages from Research (London: HMSO, 1995) p. 23.

Preventive work with ethnic minority families prior to the Children Act 1989 was shown to be particularly underdeveloped.[32] The work of Barn and others in their empirical examination of race and ethnicity in social services provision under the Children Act 1989 for children and families,[33] demonstrates that preventive work remains a low priority in the allocation of case work. Lack of time, energy and resources means that priority is given first, to child protection work; secondly, to "looked after"[34] children; and finally to preventive work.[35] Preventive work is perceived as a luxury. The rapid referral into local authority accommodation of children from ethnic minorities has been identified by the authors as a matter of concern[36] and raises important questions about the adequacy of the provision of social services support to ethnic minority children, and whether enough is being done to obviate the need to intervene in their families.

The extensive nature of the duties and powers invested in local authorities by the Children Act 1989 Part III[37] is such that their scope has to be limited in terms of those children to whom they are specifically targeted. For this reason, they are to be exercised only in relation to children "in need".[38] There is a general duty placed upon every local authority, and its various departments which are expected to work together, to safeguard and promote the welfare of children in need and so far as is consistent with that duty to promote the upbringing of such children by their families[39] by providing a range and level of services appropriate to those children's needs.[40] As official guidance states, the definition of need:

> is deliberately wide to reinforce the emphasis on preventive support and services to families . . . The child's needs will include physical, emotional and educational needs according to his age, sex, religion, culture and language and the capacity of the current carer to meet those needs.[41]

[32] See Barn, *op cit*. n. 27.

[33] See Barn, Sinclair and Ferdinand, *op cit*. n. 23, which examined the nature and pattern of local authority service provision to children from different ethnic groups and local authorities' practice and procedure in respect of the Children Act 1989 and the Race Relations Act 1976. Although the study was limited to three local authorities—one metropolitan borough, one shire county and one London Borough—they were very different and the findings should be of wider applicability, see Rejtman, "Meeting the Needs of Ethnic Minority Children and Young People in Care" (1997) 137 *Childright* 4.

[34] For the meaning of "looked after" see *infra*.

[35] See Barn, Sinclair and Ferdinand, *op cit*. n. 23, pp. 44–5.

[36] *Ibid.*, 57. See also Hunt Macleod and Thomas, *The Last Resort* (London: TSO, 1999) pp. 42 and 55–6.

[37] Which do not affect any other duties imposed on them by, or under, other legislation: Children Act 1989, s. 30(1).

[38] Children Act 1989, s. 17(10) provides that ". . . a child shall be taken to be in need if—(a) he is unlikely to achieve or maintain, or to have the opportunity of achieving or maintaining, a reasonable standard of health or development without the provision for him of services by a local authority under this Part; (b) his health or development is likely to be significantly impaired, or further impaired, without the provision for him of such services; or (c) he is disabled". In turn, "development" is defined as meaning "physical, intellectual, emotional, social or behavioural development" and "health" as "physical or mental health": *ibid.*, s. 17(11).

[39] *Ibid.*, s. 17(1).

[40] In line with *The United Nations Convention on the Rights of the Child*, Cm 1976 (London: HMSO, 1991) Art. 18.

[41] Department of Health, *op cit*. n. 17, para. 2.4.

The general duty seeks to encourage a proactive approach in preference to a reactive approach, by promoting upbringing within the family[42] rather than just preventing state intervention. In line with that approach, the specific duties of every local authority include taking "reasonable steps to identify the extent to which there are children in need within their area".[43] This specific duty upon local authorities is, however, one of identification of the extent of need within their area and thereafter to use their resources to provide a range of services to meet that need. Local authorities have the power to assess an individual child's needs but there is no duty to do so. In so far as local authorities do not assess children's individual need they must at least have "in need" criteria based on ethnicity. As MacDonald has observed "[t]here are inherent dangers for those who live in areas where the authority are reactive in their methods of measuring the extent of need" and where they "target a very restricted band of children and decide on narrow and inflexible criteria, either for political or for financial reasons, or both".[44] The first report to Parliament on the Children Act[45] showed that ten out of sixty local authorities who had been the subject of a research project on children in need undertaken on behalf of the Department of Health ranked black/ethnic minority families under the first limb of the "in-need" definition.[46]

A child in need includes one who is unlikely to achieve a reasonable standard of health or development without the provision of local authority support. The assessment of what constitutes a reasonable standard of health or development is to be made by the local authority but should be made in the context of the child's ethnic background.[47] The needs likely to be associated with a child's ethnic links include communicational and linguistic, dietary, cultural, religious, educational, emotional and physical needs. These needs are sometimes grouped under the four heads of racial, cultural, religious and linguistic needs.[48] To this end it is necessary for information to be recorded properly about all aspects of a child's ethnic background. Research has shown that although some information about the child's ethnic origin is usually available, other data, particularly about religious background, is not.[49]

Where a child is also disabled it "is crucial that at the centre of all policy and practice initiatives the needs of black and minority ethnic children with disabilities are considered in terms of both race and disability",[50] to prevent them from

[42] See, e.g., Children Act 1989, s. 17(1).

[43] *Ibid.*, Sched. 2 para. 1(1).

[44] See Macdonald, *op cit*. n. 1, p. 37.

[45] See Department of Health, *Children Act Report 1992* (London: HMSO, 1993) as required by s. 83(6) of the Children Act.

[46] *Ibid.*, at 34.

[47] See Macdonald, *op cit*. n. 1, pp. 72–8.

[48] See, e.g., Children Act 1989, s. 22(5)(c).

[49] See Colton, Drury and Williams, *Children in Need: Family Support under the Children Act 1989* (Aldershot: Avebury, 1995) ch. 8; Barn, Sinclair and Ferdinand, *op cit*. n. 23, p. 41 and *infra* n. 80.

[50] Begum, "Setting the Context: Disability and the Children Act 1989" in MacDonald, *op cit*. n. 1, p. XI.

being doubly disadvantaged.[51] So, for example, registers of children in need should ensure that ethnic monitoring, gender and disability are appropriately collated and cross-referenced. In 1993, a Social Services Inspectorate inspection[52] of four local authorities to determine progress being made in implementing the Children Act 1989 duties in relation to disabled children showed that:

> [f]urther work was needed in all four authorities to ensure that there is a more sympathetic and integrated approach to the provision of racially and culturally sensitive services. Authorities should evaluate the effectiveness of existing services given their low up-take by minority ethnic communities.[53]

Research also shows that ethnic monitoring has been used by some local authorities in order to assess the needs of different ethnic communities,[54] but, as Barn and others have pointed out,[55] such monitoring is not without its ethical dilemmas and its critics.[56] Some authorities may believe they are thereby carrying out their duty and "may see collection of data as a substitute for the improvement of the actual service provision". Ethnic monitoring of itself is, of course, no guarantee of proper service provision for ethnic minority children. Properly and sensitively used, however, it can provide an effective means of review of service provision and facilitate the appropriate targeting of limited resources in the light of different needs of the diverse ethnic communities. Such monitoring should encompass not only children and families in need or receipt of services, but also the extent to which ethnic minority children and families are able to receive a service from social workers from different ethnic backgrounds. In this context there seems to be much to commend balancing two principles: "a belief that *all* workers, regardless of their ethnicity, should be capable of providing a service to any client and that they should provide the best available service to meet the particular needs of each user".[57]

A child who qualifies as a child in need is eligible for a wider range of local authority services (and not just social services) than if he or she did not so qualify. Yet actual receipt of those services is subject once again to the local authority's discretion as to how to exercise its duties and powers in the light of its limited resources. Determining priorities of service provision for children in need is left to individual local authorities. A general concern identified by

---

[51] See Utting, *People Like Us: the Report of the Review of the Safeguards for Children Living away from Home* (London: The Stationery Office, 1997) para. 10.23.

[52] See Department of Health, *National Inspection of Services to Disabled Children and their Families* (London: HMSO, 1994).

[53] See Department of Health, *Children Act Report 1993* (London: HMSO, 1994) para. 2.31; see also para. 2.29. See also *infra* n. 80.

[54] See Butt, Gorbach and Ahmad, *Equally Fair* (London: Race Equality Unit; National Institute of Social Work, 1994).

[55] See Barn, Sinclair and Ferdinand, *op cit.* n. 23, pp. 12–13.

[56] See Ely and Denney, *Social Work in a Multi-Racial Society* (Aldershot: Gower, 1987); Ohri, "Politics of Racism—Statistics and Equal Opportunity" in Bhatt, Carr-Hill and Ohri (eds.), *Britain's Black Population: A New Perspective* (Aldershot: Gower, 1988, 2nd ed).

[57] See Barn, Sinclair and Ferdinand, *op cit.* n. 23, p. 30.

research is that local authority resources have been too narrowly directed to child protection at the expense of family support.[58] Resources should not be focused exclusively on assessing whether or not a child is at risk and if found not to be, for no support services to be offered.[59] Instead attention should be given to matching a wide range of individual children's needs, including ethnic needs, and services. As Ahmad states:

> [n]ot to take account of racial, cultural, religious and linguistic needs of a black child within his or her individual needs tantamounts to extracting the child out of his/her social reality. No social problems can be tackled or resolved outside the social reality. It is imperative that the black child's individual needs are met in the context of the child's racial and cultural needs.[60]

And as Morgan and Taylor assert, the success or failure of the Children Act 1989 in meeting the needs of ethnic minority children and their families depends upon the willingness of local authorities to use resources in and for the ethnic minority community.[61] The provision of services should be designed to match the individual child's needs rather than the child's individual needs being gauged solely according to the metric of the services which are actually provided. In making an assessment of the particular child, the local authority should monitor and take into account the child's needs relating to religious persuasion, racial origin, cultural and linguistic background and the extent to which these needs are being met by the current provision, if any, of services.[62] In practice, however, local authority support has tended to be service-specific rather than needs-led.[63]

Each local authority should, however, match the wide range of needs of ethnic minority children with appropriate services as part of its plan for the provision of children's services which all local authorities are required to prepare, publish and keep under review.[64] Local authorities must be aware that "[i]n some areas the local community may include too great a variety of ethnic groups to be reflected fully in [the] composition of staff". In such areas, as in others where local authorities may only rarely be called upon to provide a service for a child or family from a minority ethnic group, "local authorities will need to identify sources of advice and help . . ."[65] such as appropriate interpreters,

---

[58] Department of Health, *Child Protection: Messages from Research* (London : HMSO, 1995) p. 35; MacDonald *op cit.* n. 1, p. 59.

[59] See Association of Directors of Social Services and NCH Action for Children, *Children Still in Need: Refocusing Child Protection in the Context of Children in Need* (London: ADSS and NCH, 1996).

[60] Ahmad, "Setting the Context: Race and the Children Act 1989" in MacDonald, *op cit.* n. 1, p. IX.

[61] Morgan and Taylor, "A Study of Black Young People Leaving Care" (1987) 5/6 *Social Services Research* 10.

[62] Department of Health, *op cit.* n. 17, para. 2.7.

[63] See Association of Directors of Social Services and NCH Action for Children, *op cit.* n. 59, *p.* 4.

[64] See Children Act 1989, Sched. 2 para. 1A (as inserted). For examples of policy or equality statements relating to services for children from different ethnic groups see Barn, Sinclair and Ferdinand, *op cit.* n. 23, p. 27.

[65] Department of Health, *op cit.* n. 17, para. 2.9.

translators and the use of specialists to assist their social work staff to address ethnic issues when assessing and intervening in ethnic minority families. Local authorities are not expected to work in isolation and should facilitate service provision by other agencies by promoting partnerships to advance the welfare of children.[66] As part of that process, local authorities have a duty to publish information about the services that they and others provide to families with children in need.[67] That publicity should be sensitive to the needs of ethnic minority families.[68] Thereafter they should monitor and evaluate their service provision. Throughout, "the local authority will have to ensure that they are properly informed about the different racial groups to which children within their area who are in need belong". This is because "[l]ocal authorities should provide a range of services which should reflect (in scale as well as type) the needs of children and families from ethnic minority groups".[69]

One of the few duties in Part III of the Children Act 1989 specifically to address ethnic issues is the requirement in Schedule 2 paragraph 11 that "[e]very local authority *shall*,[70] in making any arrangements for the provision of day care within their area . . . have regard to the different racial groups to which children within their area who are in need belong". Among other things, the *Practice Guidance* also enshrines as a general principle (operative only in the context of informing good practice in day care, education and related services for young children and their families) that "the values deriving from different backgrounds—racial, cultural, religious and linguistic—should be recognised and respected".[71] It is regrettable that this "general principle" is of such limited scope when clearly it is of much wider relevance to the provision of services under Part III. Similarly, the need for professionals and others working with children to value and respect ethnic differences "so that each child is valued as an individual without racial or gender stereotyping"[72] is made in the context of standards in day care services for under eights and educational provision for under fives. Such respect should be central to all service provision because "minority ethnic families are amongst those living in the most difficult conditions in the country and have least access to support services."[73]

---

[66] Children Act 1989, s. 17(5). See Brandon, Thoburn, Lewis and Way, *Safeguarding Children with the Children Act 1989* (London: TSO, 1999) pp. 111–15.

[67] *Ibid.*, Sched. 2 para. 1(2).

[68] See Department of Health, *op cit.* n. 17, para. 2.36.

[69] *Ibid.*, para. 2.12.

[70] Emphasis added to highlight the fact that there is no discretion in this regard. For an anti-racist response including comprehensive ethnic monitoring, see MacDonald, *op cit.* n. 1, p. 75.

[71] See Department of Health, *op cit.* n. 17, para. 6.2

[72] *Ibid.*, para. 6.10. See also para. 6.11 for the expectations upon local authorities regarding their evaluation of the extent to which this provision of services is operating in a non-discriminatory way and that local authorities ensure that their review duty operates so as to enable all racial groups to contribute.

[73] See MacDonald, *op cit.* n. 1, p. 44; West (from the work of Dagg *et al*), *What Future for Our Children? Daily Experiences of Ethnic Minority Families* (London: Save the Children, 1996); *All the Same? Day Care and Ethnic Minority Children and Families* (London: Save the Children, 1996).

III CHILDREN LOOKED AFTER BY LOCAL AUTHORITIES

A child is "looked after" by a local authority if he is either in their care under a care order or is provided with accommodation by the authority for a continuous period of more than twenty-four hours.[74] Although the legal relationship between the local authority and, on the one hand, children in care, and on the other, children being provided with accommodation is clearly distinguishable (because of the voluntary nature only of the latter arrangement), the duties owed by local authorities to both groups of children are largely the same.[75] They include a duty when making any decision with respect to a looked after child to "give due consideration—to the child's religious persuasion, racial origin and cultural and linguistic background".[76] The vagueness of this provision has been criticised as "a watering down of anti-racism".[77] The requirement upon local authorities to give "due consideration" rather than "paramount consideration" to the child's ethnicity is consistent with the general duty in section 22(3) of authorities in relation to a child looked after by them "to safeguard and promote", rather than give paramount consideration to, the child's welfare. In neither regard does the legislation prioritise the weight to be given to the child's welfare. Ahmad considers that "the welfare of black children can neither be promoted, nor be protected fully without giving paramount consideration to their racial and cultural background",[78] but to do so would have required a reformulation of the general duty in section 22(3) regarding any child looked after by the authority. Ahmad's legitimate concern could have been met, however, by requiring local authorities to have regard "in particular" to the factors in section 22(5) in the same way as a court is required to have particular regard to certain factors in the so called "checklist" in section 1(3) when considering whether to make, vary or discharge a care or supervision order.[79]

In light of the duty in section 22(5)(c), it is surprising that no national statistics are kept regarding the ethnic composition of children looked after by local authorities. It is to be hoped that central government adopts the recommenda-

[74] Children Act 1989, s. 22(1)(2). For figures on looked after children, see Barn, Sinclair and Ferdinand, *op cit.* n. 23, p. 55. According to their study, 45% were provided with accommodation under s. 20 by voluntary arrangement, approximately 25% were subject to a final care order under s. 31 while the remainder were either in the early stages of the care process (that is, subject to an interim care order, emergency protection order or in police protection) or looked after for some other reason: *id*, p. 55.

[75] Local authorities have additional obligations to, and control over, those children who are in care, arising from the authority having parental responsibility.

[76] Children Act 1989, s. 22(5)(c). For a corresponding duty upon voluntary organisations and registered children's homes to children accommodated by them, see Children Act 1989, s. 61(3)(c) and s. 64(3)(c). For a similar duty in Scotland, see Children (Scotland) Act 1995, s. 17(4)(c).

[77] Stubbs, "The Children Act: An Anti-Racist Perspective" (1991) 5 *Practice* 226–9.

[78] Ahmad, *op cit.* n. 60, in MacDonald, *op cit.* n. 1, p. IX.

[79] Children Act 1989, s. 1(4)(b). However, for criticism demonstrating the potential ineffectuality of attempting to ensure a child's welfare by reference to open-ended criteria such as "regard in particular" see Montgomery, "Rhetoric and Welfare" (1989) *Oxford Journal of Legal Studies* 395.

tion of Barn and others that the Department of Health should take a lead in ethnic monitoring in respect of children looked after by local authorities.[80] That study found that the reasons for a child being looked after varied between different ethnic groups.[81] Of particular note and concern is that a majority of the children became looked after within two weeks of being referred to social services, indicating the "crisis intervention" nature of much social work with families and in particular ethnic minority families.[82] Equally, children of ethnic minority families were also found to be looked after by local authorities longer than children of white families.[83]

Local authorities are required to draw up a written care plan,[84] if possible before placing a child whom they are looking after, otherwise as soon afterwards as is reasonably practicable with a view to meeting the child's needs in a focused manner and avoiding drift. The plan should be drawn up in agreement with the child's family. It should be based upon a social work assessment of the child's needs, wishes and feelings, the wishes and feelings of the child's family, the advice of professionals and the range of options. It should identify what sort of accommodation and other services are needed, likely duration of the placement of the child and the arrangements for maintaining family links and promoting contact and reunification of the family.[85] In view of the importance of proper planning as a central aspect of the local authority's duty under the Children Act 1989 to safeguard and promote the welfare of children they are looking after,[86] it is regrettable that research evidence about the nature of social services provision for ethnic minority families under the Act has shown that almost a half of the accommodated/looked after children had no care plan and that a significantly greater proportion of children from ethnic minority families than from white families had no plan.[87] Care plans were not being prepared in a systematic way in two of the three local authorities sampled, with practitioners and some managers seeing them "as an administrative nuisance".[88]

---

[80] See Barn, Sinclair and Ferdinand, *op cit.* n. 23, p. 93. The Department has now declared an intention to introduce ethnic monitoring into routine statistical collections on children's services from 2000, see Department of Health, *The Children Act Report 1995–1999* (London: TSO, 2000) paras. 1.26–1.29.

[81] *Ibid.*, at 56–7.

[82] A greater proportion (68%) of African-Caribbean children became looked after within two weeks than any other group (59% of mixed parentage, 50% of Asian and 49% of white).

[83] With the exception of children of Asian origin of whom 8% had been in public care for more than 5 years compared with 10% of children of white origin, 24% per cent of children of mixed parentage and 36% of African-Caribbean children.

[84] In accordance with the Arrangements for Placement of Children (General) Regulations 1991, SI 1991/890. See especially Regs. 3–4 and Sched. 1–4. There is no prescribed format for a care plan but it should follow as far as possible the guidance in Department of Health, *Volume 3, op cit.* n. 22, para. 2.62; *Manchester City Council* v. *F* [1993] 1 FLR 419 and Local Authority Circular LAC (99) 29, "Care Plans and Care Proceedings under the Children Act 1989".

[85] Department of Health, *Volume 3, op cit.* n. 22, paras. 2.59–2.61.

[86] Children Act 1989, s. 22(3).

[87] In fact, 44% did not have a care plan while 69% of white children had a care plan as did 64% of African-Caribbean children: see Barn, Sinclair and Ferdinand, *op cit.* n. 23, p. 60. The figure fell to 40% of children of mixed parentage and 17% of Asian children: *loc cit.*

[88] *Ibid.*, at 61.

A Placement

The duty[89] owed by local authorities to "looked after" children to give due consideration to the child's religious persuasion, racial origin and cultural and linguistic background is of particular relevance in relation to the placement of the child. As Barn and others explain:

> Placement decisions are about finding the best available option to meet all the needs of a child. A holistic framework based on the Children Act and which addresses the needs of minority ethnic children in a comprehensive fashion, while taking account of individual emotional and psychological factors, is essential.[90]

Research shows that "trans-racial" placements expose ethnic minority children to overt and covert forms of racism and discrimination and have a detrimental effect on the child's development during and after being looked after.[91] Ethnic minority children also "encounter institutionalised as well as personally focused racism".[92] In order to avoid all such racism and discrimination there is a principle, but not a rule, for ensuring that a child's carers are of the same religious persuasion and ethnic background as the child, so that he or she is not confused as to their cultural identity. This is acknowledged in practice guidance:

> It may be taken as a guiding principle of good practice that, other things being equal and in the great majority of cases, placement with a family of similar ethnic origin and religion is most likely to meet a child's needs as fully as possible and to safeguard his or her welfare most effectively. Such a family is most likely to be able to provide a child with continuity in life and care and an environment which the child will find familiar and sympathetic and in which opportunities will naturally arise to share fully in the culture and way of life of the ethnic group to which he belongs . . . Families of similar ethnic origin are also usually best placed to prepare children for life as members of an ethnic minority group in a multi-racial society, where they may meet with racial prejudice and discrimination, and to help them with their development towards independent living and adult life.[93]

The *Guidance* acknowledges that this principle must not be applied rigidly but in accordance with the duty in the Children Act 1989, section 22(3) to safeguard and promote the welfare of the individual child, which may on occasions indicate to the contrary and which must not be obscured by the unquestioning application of any general social policy as was the tendency prior to the Children Act

---

[89] Children Act 1989, s. 22(5)(c).
[90] Barn, Sinclair and Ferdinand, *op cit*. n. 23, p. 73.
[91] See Ince, *op cit*. n. 1, p. 76, within the context of that research trans-racial placements referred to the placement of black children in white foster or adoptive families *or* in all-white residential homes.
[92] Utting, *op cit*. n.51, para. 10.19.
[93] See Department of Health, *Volume 3*, *op cit*. n. 22, para. 2.40. For fuller practice guidance see Local Authority Circular CI (90) 2, para. 7 which anticipated the implementation of the Children Act 1989.

1989.[94] The situation can be compared with that when the courts decide prospective adoption cases where there is a wish to move a child because the child has been placed with a family of different ethnic background. The courts have made it clear,[95] when deciding the child's future upbringing, that they are concerned with the welfare of the particular child, and the outcome will be determined in accordance with what is in that child's best interests.[96] The difference is that in those cases there is a challenge to an existing placement rather than the establishment of a placement. So the question turns on whether it is in the child's interests to be removed from his or her replacement family to an ethnically matched family in view of the emotional and psychological harm such further removal may cause to the child. The establishment of a placement does not involve the same removal, but rather a quest for continuity of cultural care and identity development with the child's ethnic home background.

The central issue, however, is still what is in the particular child's best interests. Hence, while same-race placements should be followed as a general principle, where there is a lack of ethnically matched placements that principle should not be upheld at the expense of the welfare of the child and planning for the child. Such a view has support in practice broadly in line with the Children Act guidance (although in the context of a "policy vacuum"[97] and absence of systematic placement monitoring). The evidence suggests that the majority of children were placed in a family setting rather than languishing in residential care due to non-availability of ethnically matched placements and most were in same-race placements.[98] Where a same-race placement does not occur, the

[94] See the same-race oriented placement policies criticised in *Re N (A Minor)(Adoption)* [1990] 1 FLR 58, *infra* n. 96. For an Australian comparator with respect to race oriented placement policies, see Dewar's chapter in this collection.

[95] Much of the relevant case law (see n. 96 *infra*) was decided before the Children Act 1989 when private law orders for upbringing were frequently made under the wardship (rather than statutory) jurisdiction. Nowadays, such cases would be resolved by a section 8 residence order. The principles applicable to such cases remain unchanged (although in adoption decisions the child's welfare is the first consideration (Adoption Act 1976, s. 6) rather than the paramount consideration in upbringing decisions (Children Act 1989, s. 1(1)). The inter-relationship of these differing principles is outside the scope of this essay, but for further analysis see Cromack and Parry, "Welfare of the Child— Conflicting Interests and Conflicting Principles" [1996] *Child and Family Law Quarterly* 72.

[96] See *Re N (A Minor)(Adoption)* [1990] 1 FLR 58. The case concerned a Nigerian child aged 3 weeks who was placed with white private foster parents who later sought adoption while the child's unmarried father sought care and control in wardship. Notwithstanding the difference in ethnic background between the foster parents and the child, to separate the child from the foster parents would be harmful to the child. As an adoption order was contrary to the Nigerian cultural pattern, the appropriate order was one of care and control in favour of the foster parents. In *Re P (A Minor)(Adoption)* [1990] 1 FLR 96 a mixed race child aged 5 days was placed by local authority with white foster parents who sought to adopt. The local authority (which had a policy following national guidelines that every child should be brought up by a family of the same-race and ethnic group) sought to place the child with a black or mixed race family. It was held to be in the child's best interests to be brought up in such a family. *Cf. Re JK (Adoption: Trans-racial Placement)* [1991] 2 FLR 340. See also *Re J (A Minor)(Wardship: Adoption: Custodianship)* [1987] 1 FLR 455; *R v. Lancashire County Council ex parte M* [1992] 1 FLR 109.

[97] See Ince, *op cit.* n. 1, p. 89; Barn, Sinclair and Ferdinand, *op cit.* n. 23, p. 29.

[98] Barn, Sinclair and Ferdinand, *op cit.* n. 23, p. 68. While that study found that the vast majority of African-Caribbean and Asian children were in ethnically suitable placements, the placement

child's ethnic needs should be met in other ways, for example by ensuring that the child has contact with his family in accordance with the statutory duty to promote contact,[99] if needs be, in cases of family financial hardship, by the local authority meeting the expenses of a visit.[100] As Frost and Stein acknowledge, contact may be particularly significant for ethnic minority children, especially black young people whose needs may not be met if they are cared for in predominantly white settings.[101] Where family contact is not possible, or is infrequent, consideration should be given to the appointment by the local authority of an appropriate independent visitor[102] who could provide a link with the child's ethnic background.[103]

As the Utting Report acknowledged, cultural needs "should be met in every setting in which a child is living".[104] The complexities in placement decisions of giving effect to all four factors in section 22 (5)(c) "requires a careful consideration of ethnic diversity and need"[105] to ensure that ethnic minority children do not lose their ethnic identity during placement and their ability to identify with their ethnic community after leaving local authority accommodation.

B Leaving Local Authority Accommodation

For most children leaving home is neither fixed in time nor irrevocable. It is part of the gradual transition from childhood to adulthood for which good parents, as part of their parental responsibility, prepare the child and offer support afterwards. The situation is often very different for children who have grown up being looked after by local authorities. The vulnerability of such children is well known, "they are over represented among homeless young people, young offenders, single parents and other indicators of social risk and deprivation".[106] Research findings before the Children Act 1989 showed that care leavers generally received little or no preparation for either leaving care or independent life

needs of children of mixed parentage and other minority ethnic backgrounds such as Chinese, were a cause for concern: *ibid.*, at 76.

[99] Children Act 1989, Sched. 2 para. 15 (which is applicable to all children being looked after by a local authority). Where the child is in local authority care, additional provisions in s. 34 apply.

[100] *Ibid.*, Sched. 2 para. 16.

[101] Frost and Stein, *Working with Young People Leaving Care* (London: HMSO, 1995).

[102] Children Act 1989, Sched. 2 para. 17(1). The duty upon local authorities is not generally discharged properly: see Utting, *op cit.* n. 51, paras. 10.13–10.16.

[103] See Department of Health, *Volume 3* and *Volume 4*, *op cit.* n. 22, paras. 7.15 and 6.15 respectively.

[104] Utting, *op cit.* n. 51, para. 10.22. See also *UK National Standards for Foster Care* (London: National Foster Care Association, 1999) pp. 14–5 and 20.

[105] Barn, Sinclair and Ferdinand, *op cit.* n. 23, p. 74. See also Freeman and Hunt, *Parental Perspectives on Care Proceedings* (London: TSO, 1998) pp. 63–5.

[106] Hoggett, *Parents and Children: The Law of Parental Responsibility* (London: Sweet & Maxwell, 1993) p. 156. For an overview of the literature on leaving care see Ince, *op cit.* n. 1, ch. 2. See also Children (Leaving Care) Bill [HL] implementing the proposals in Department of Health, *Me, Survive, Out There?—New Arrangements for Young People Living in and Leaving Care* (London: TSO, 1999).

after care,[107] particularly residential care.[108] In the context of ethnic minority children, the limited research evidence identified an additional problem of lack of cultural identity leading to isolation and loneliness.[109] Initial research since the Children Act 1989 indicates that the provision of after care services under the Act has been sparse[110] despite the duty placed upon local authorities to "advise assist and befriend" any child who is being looked after so as to promote his welfare when he stops being looked after.[111] The availability and quality of services has been described by Broad as a lottery in terms of local authority policies and implementation: "[l]eaving care work still remains unsafe in the hands of the Children Act 1989".[112]

While a child is being looked after by a local authority his or her progress and future must be monitored regularly by a process of statutory reviews,[113] the function of which is to consider the plan for the child's welfare and whether it fulfils the local authority's duty to safeguard and promote the child's welfare,[114] including whether it makes necessary provision for the child's religious and ethnic background.[115] The planning process for leaving care should begin well before the child leaves accommodation and should be addressed as soon as the care plan is drawn up. Practice guidance identifies three broad areas of after care preparation for all children in local authority accommodation. First, building and maintaining relationships with others; secondly, developing self-esteem and thirdly, teaching practical and financial skills and knowledge.[116] In respect of the needs of ethnic minority children when building and maintaining relationships, it is accepted that they "will need to have contact with adults and young people from their own cultural background",[117] which the youth service may well be able to facilitate. As Biehal and others have observed, "[e]nsuring that

---

[107] See, e.g., Kahan, *Growing up in Care* (Oxford: Blackwell, 1979); Stein and Carey, *Leaving Care* (Oxford: Blackwell, 1986); Garnett, *Leaving Care and After* (London: National Children's Bureau, 1992).

[108] Ince, *op cit.* n. 1, pp. 82–8.

[109] Morgan and Taylor, *op cit.* n. 61, pp. 5–6 and 10–12; Ince, *op cit.* n. 1. See also Marsh and Peal, *Leaving Care in Partnership* (London: TSO, 1999) pp. 34–6 and 52–3.

[110] See Broad, *Leaving Care in the 1990s: the Results of a National Survey* (Kent: Royal Philanthropic Society, 1994). On developing leaving care services see Biehal, Clayden, Stein and Wade, *Moving On: Young People and Leaving Care Schemes* (London: HMSO, 1995) ch. 23.

[111] Children Act 1989, s. 24. See also s. 61(1)(c) and s. 64(1)(c). The local authorities' duties under s. 24 will be amended and expanded on enactment of the Children (Leaving Care) Bill.

[112] Broad, *Young People Leaving Care: Life after the Children Act 1989* (London: Jessica Kingsley Publishers, 1998) p. 267. See also House of Commons Health Committee, Second Report, *Children Looked after by Local Authorities, Volume 1*, HC 319–1 (London: HMSO, 1998) paras. 304–16.

[113] See Children Act 1989, s. 26(1)(2) and the Review of Children's Cases Regulations SI 1991/895.

[114] *Ibid.*, s. 22(3). See also Local Authority Circular LAC (99) 29, "Care Plans and Care Proceedings under the Children Act 1989" para. 27

[115] See Department of Health, *Volume 3, op cit.* n. 22, para. 8.20 and Grimshaw and Sinclair, *Planning to Care* (London: National Children's Bureau, 1997) pp. 133–4.

[116] See Department of Health, *Volume 3* and *Volume 4, op cit.* n. 22, paras. 9.45 and 7.45 respectively.

[117] *Ibid.*, paras. 9.46 and 7.46.

black, Asian or mixed heritage children and young people have positive contact
with others of similar origin while they are 'looked after' would offer them the
opportunity to maintain some continuity with their ethnic background".[118] As
regards the development of self-esteem, it is recognised as helpful if young
people are told as much as possible—preferably from someone with the same
background—about all aspects of their cultural and individual identity[119] in a
positive way to enable them to take pride in their ethnic background.[120] As Ince
observes: "[i]n order that black young people do not suffer cultural deficits, adequate preparation for leaving care requires detailed attention to the role of culture"[121] which "should be included as a discrete category in all planning and
review systems for leaving care and transition to independence".[122] Local
authorities should also help ethnic minority children to deal with the discrimination and racism which, regrettably, they are likely to encounter in society.

In terms of after care support, local authorities will need to provide advice,
information, and assistance in cash or kind; continued interest in the child's welfare and support in education, training and accommodation.

IV CONCLUSION

Although the Children Act 1989 makes scant reference to ethnicity in its provisions relating to local authority support for children and families, it does partially address the issue. The practice guidance relating to local authorities'
responsibilities ameliorates the lacuna, but only incidentally. Submissions to the
Review of the Safeguards for Children Living Away from Home[123] contained
few references to racial issues beyond identifying black children as one group
particularly liable to abuse and harm when living away from home.[124] The limited research evidence since the implementation of the Act suggests, however,
that there have been significant improvements in local authority provision for
ethnic minority children and families[125] but there must be no complacency
regarding the need for further improvement[126] and further investigation. In particular, there is a need for the development of written policy guidance, available
to all staff, addressing equal opportunities in the various aspects of service provision, with effective procedures for policy implementation,[127] monitoring[128]

---

[118] Biehal *et al*, *op cit*. n. 110, p. 129.
[119] See Utting, *op cit*. n. 51, para. 10.20.
[120] Department of Health Volume 3 and Volume 4, *op cit*. n. 22, paras. 9.52–9.53 and 7.52–7.53.
[121] *Op cit.*, n. 1, p. 25.
[122] *Ibid.*, at 87, where the author presents a useful diagram showing the type and nature of work
required to achieve an integrated approach to leaving care with race and culture as an integral part.
[123] Utting, *op cit*. n. 51.
[124] *Ibid.*, para. 10.18.
[125] See Barn, Sinclair and Ferdinand, *op cit*. n. 23, p. 93.
[126] *Loc cit*, pp. 93–6.
[127] See Colton, Drury and Williams, *op cit*. n. 49, p. 196.
[128] Including ethnic monitoring, see *supra* p. 25.

and review. Service provision should include assessment and meeting of all needs, and not just placement needs, for the diverse ethnic groups, including children of mixed parentage.[129] Local authority staff need appropriate development and training[130] in ethnicity issues and awareness including anti-discriminatory practice and should be aware of the difficulties of working with clients whose ethnic backgrounds differ from their own. Research evaluating the Children Act 1989 suggests that:

> [w]hat emerges from the data from the families of minority ethnic origin is not so much the need for a set of guidelines about race or ethnicity for workers to follow, but a leap of imagination and extra sensitivity to be made in order to empathise with families.[131]

Suitable training should be provided, monitored and reviewed also for foster carers of ethnic minority children in view of the incidence of placement breakdown and disruption experienced by children from ethnic minority groups.[132] All this requires adequate and properly focused resources, without which all the legislation, practice guidance, good practice and goodwill are to little avail and service provision to ethnic minority children and their families is likely to remain "patchy and incremental".[133]

---

[129] See Hunt, Macleod and Thomas, *op cit*.n. 36 pp. 21–3 and generally pp. 29–30, 34–5, 42, 86–7, 103–4 and 383.

[130] See Colton, Drury and Williams, *op cit*. n. 49, p. 198.

[131] Brandon Thoburn, Lewis and Way, *op cit*. n. 66 p. 115 and see also pp. 32, 91–3, 111–5, 117–18, 171–2, 185–7 and 198.

[132] See Hunt and Macleod, *The Best-Laid Plans* (London: TSO, 1999) p. 51.

[133] See Barn, Sinclair and Ferdinand, *op cit*. n. 23, p. 86.

3

Child Welfare in Transracial Adoptions: Colour-blind Children and Colour-blind Law

JOHN MURPHY*

I INTRODUCTION

TRANSRACIAL ADOPTIONS, though often successful, are often vehemently
opposed as a means of finding alternative parents for minority children.
There are two principal bases for such opposition: first, it is thought that "children adopted in this way will suffer problems of 'identity' later in life" and secondly, "such adoptions represent the exploitation of the black community by
white society"[1] because blacks and Asians who were historically the servants of
whites continue to service them by providing them with children that they are
unable to provide for themselves.[2] Clearly, the first of these objections is related
to familiar welfarist concerns—albeit that, in this context, the adoptive child's
long-term rather than immediate interests are emphasised. By contrast, the second objection is concerned primarily with the interests of the minority community as a whole, rather than with those of the specific child.

Neither of these objections is concerned with matters that resonate exclusively in terms of legal impropriety. The concerns that go to their heart are of
equal social and political importance. Yet a number of distinctly legal questions
do arise in this context. For example, if a law were to be implemented that satisfied the proponents of the arguments just outlined, would that law be consistent with our existing laws on racial discrimination?[3] And even if it could

* University of Manchester.

[1] O. Gill and B. Jackson, *Adoption and Race: Black, Asian and Mixed Race Children in White Families* (London: British Agencies for Adoption and Fostering, 1983) p. 1. In the USA, where fees are paid to private adoption agencies by would-be adopters, the practice has even been described as the "re-commodification" of African Americans. The notion of "re-commodification" is intended to conjure memories of America's history of large-scale slave trading. See, R.A. Howe, "Race and Color Matters in Adoption: an American Dilemma" (1997) (revised, unpublished paper presented to a conference of the *Yale Journal of Law and Feminism* 9 November 1996) p. 3.

[2] See, e.g., M.K. Benet, *The Character of Adoption* (London: Jonathan Cape, 1976).

[3] See the Race Relations Act 1976.

ostensibly be justified in terms of affirmative action with, say, black community interests at its core,[4] ought it not ultimately to be rejected in favour of a law that made the familiar welfare principle[5] (or something akin to it[6]) the central issue? The methodology and objectives of most of the thoroughgoing studies in this area have been markedly sociological and for this reason they form an inappropriate basis on which to answer the kinds of questions just posed. They are characterised more by broad considerations of social policy[7] rather than by how, in dispositive terms, the courts ought to deal with individual cases of transracial adoption. They are equally unhelpful in relation to questions about how the relevant legislation and regulations ought to be framed. It is somewhat disheartening, then, that no major legal academic study of transracial adoption has been conducted in this country.[8]

This essay is designed in part to help fill that gap and to question, from a lawyer's viewpoint, the assumption prevalent among sociologists and others that, ideally, adoption should mirror biology; that matching genetic heritage is a fundamental determinant of successful adoptive placements for minority children. More particularly, it examines two legalistic questions. The first is whether adoption law founded upon a policy of "race-matching"[9] can be legitimated in terms of affirmative action. The second is whether arguments about black and Asian community rights simply miss the relevant legal point and whether, although sometimes pertinent, "identity" issues are the *paramount* concern, or simply one of a set of factors that ought to be considered in deciding whether any particular transracial adoption ought to take place. In the course of discussing this latter point, my central thesis will become clear: that, for the purposes of the law *in this country*, it is the child's welfare that ought to be the primary determinant in transracial adoptions.[10]

---

[4] See A. Howard *et al.*, "Trans-racial Adoption: The Black Community Perspective" (1977) 22 *Social Work* (USA)184.

[5] See the Children Act 1989, s. 1 making the child's welfare the court's "paramount consideration".

[6] In the adoption legislation currently in force, the child's welfare is only the first (but not paramount) consideration of the court or adoption agency: Adoption Act 1976, s. 6.

[7] See, L. Raynor, *Adoption of Non-white Children in Britain* (London: Allen & Unwin, 1970); B. Jackson, *Family Experiences of Inter-racial Adoption* (London: Association of British Adoption and Fostering, 1976) and O. Gill and B. Jackson, *op cit*. n. 1.

[8] The leading family and child law texts devote hardly any space to transracial adoption, and there is scarcely any discussion of it (as a purely national, as opposed to intercountry, issue) in the academic periodicals. See, e.g., A. Samuels, "Transracial Adoption: Adoption of the Black Child" (1978) 9 *Family Law* 237 (2½ pages in a practitioners' monthly journal!) and A.L. James *et al.*, "Court Welfare Work with Asian Families: Problems in Practice" (1992) 18 *New Community* 265, at 271 (half a paragraph!). Transracial adoption was only tangentially discussed (in the context of intercountry adoptions) in the *Review of Adoption Law* (London: HMSO, 1992): see *Discussion Paper No. 4: Intercountry Adoption* (London: HMSO, 1992).

[9] I have borrowed this phrase from E. Bartholet, "Where do Black Children Belong? The Politics of Race Matching in Adoption" (1991) 139 *University of Pennsylvania Law Review* 1163.

[10] A multiplicity of financial and other important factors weaken the case for a strong commitment to transracial adoption in the United States: see R.A. Howe, *op cit.*, n. 1. Similarly, in countries where entire communities' very survival might be threatened by the practice, it is less easy to be so firmly committed to the centrality of child welfare concerns. See Hollinger's account of the

The essay is structured as follows. In the next section I consider two things: the truth behind the popular supposition that minority children are better off being adopted by "ethnically compatible" adults, and the extent to which such same-race placements are consistent with the recognition and promotion of minority community interests. In Part III, I consider the particular legal improprieties of same-race placement policies. In Part IV I make a number of suggestions as to how a more acceptable approach to transracial adoptions might look. In Part V, I offer some conclusions based on the arguments made in the preceding three sections and add a number of cautionary remarks about those conclusions reached in the sociological literature which, it will become apparent, differ very considerably from my own.

II TWO URBAN MYTHS

As indicated at the outset, the two main arguments against transracial adoption are that it is thought to be contrary to the best interests of the child concerned, and that it is believed to be contrary to the interests of the (sub)community to which, in ethnic terms, that child "belongs". These contentions, if grounded, would certainly found a strong arguable case in favour of either proscribing transracial adoptions altogether, or at least in favour of making them available on only a "last resort" basis. But to what extent are these suppositions actually substantiated rather than merely groundless suspicions?

A Transracial Adoptions are Harmful?

A trawl of the relevant sociological reviews consistently reveals three main concerns about how a minority child adopted into a white household might suffer harm by comparison with another minority child adopted into a same-race household.[11] The first of these is that he or she will suffer in terms of personal development and academic achievement. The second is that the child may grow up with a confused sense of identity because of an inability wholeheartedly to identify himself or herself with either one racial group or another.[12] The third worry is that the child will grow up with low self-esteem by comparison with

Indian Child Welfare Act 1978 (USA) which only permits non-American Indian adults the right to adopt Indian children as a last resort since "[a] basic assumption of the Act is that Indian children are essential tribal resources": "Beyond the Best Interests of the Tribe: The Indian Child Welfare Act and the Adoption of Indian Children" (1989) 66 *University of Detroit Law Review* 451, at 456. See also Dewar's account of the similar concerns that apply with respect to Australian Indigenous populations in ch. 6 of this collection.

[11] From a UK perspective see those studies cited *supra* n. 7. For USA equivalents see the many sources cited in E. Bartholet, *op cit*. n. 9, at nn. 118–69.

[12] For an intriguing fictional account of this kind of identity crisis, see S. Alexei, *Indian Killer* (London: Vintage, 1998).

other children adopted into same-race households. Taken together, these three fears form the basis for two important *Practice Notes*, produced by the British Agencies for Adoption and Fostering,[13] which are frequently relied upon by both private and local authority adoption agencies.[14] In *Practice Note No. 13*, it states:

> We aim for a society in which all cultures and races are respected and accepted for what they are. Britain today is not yet such a society. Good child care practice is embedded in the society in which it operates and until Britain becomes a truly multiracial society there can be little place for transracial placements. It is essential for black children to be placed with families who can help them deal with the experience of being black in a racist society and can counteract the negative stereotypes of black people presented to children as a result of racism. Black families can provide this added dimension.[15]

Whether there is any *real* basis for the fears that prompted this policy statement seems highly doubtful. In relation to the personal development and academic achievement issues, much of the available empirical evidence reveals that, at least in respect of those children who were adopted as babies or infants,[16] there are likely to be no prejudicial effects of having been adopted by white parents.[17] According to Gill and Jackson's British study of thirty-six families in which the transracially adopted children had reached adolescence, there was "no general evidence of the children doing worse academically than their age-mates: if anything, the study children seemed to be doing better".[18] These findings have been widely echoed in the United States where, again, the general emphasis of the enquiries has been placed onto the potentially negative aspects of transracial adoption. Take for instance Shireman's study which revealed that: "transracially adopted children seem as well integrated into their families, seem to be doing well in school, and seem in general to be as well adjusted as other adopted children".[19] Furthermore, beyond merely performing well in school, those

[13]   British Agencies for Adoption and Fostering, *Practice Note 13: The Placement Needs of Black Children* (London: British Agencies for Adoption and Fostering, 1995) and *id*, *Practice Note 18: Recruiting Black Families* (London: British Agencies for Adoption and Fostering, 1991).

[14]   My own evidence of this widespread reliance is gleaned from correspondence with a number of private and local authority adoption agencies and from *Re N (A Minor) (Adoption)* [1990] 1 FLR 58, 62. McCallum's more extensive study, *Focus on Adoption* (London: British Agencies for Adoption and Fostering, 1997) indicates that only 24% of ethnic minority children are placed transracially: see para. 5.2.3.

[15]   *Op cit.*, n. 13, p. 4.

[16]   Age at placement rather than racial differences between adopters and adoptees seems to be the overwhelming explanation for problematic adoptions: see, Goodfield and Carson, "Predicting Adoption Disruption" (1988) 33 *Social Work* (USA) 227, at 231.

[17]   I am making the assumption here that the adoptive parents will be white because white-parent demand outstrips supply where white babies and infants are concerned. In addition, though there is no evidence cited for their claim, the British Agencies for Adoption and Fostering state in *Practice Note 13* that "transracial adoption of white children by black families is still unknown": British Agencies for Adoption and Fostering, *op cit.* n. 13, p. 2.

[18]   O. Gill and B. Jackson, *op cit.* n. 1, p. 130.

[19]   J. Shireman, *Growing up Adopted: An Examination of Major Issues* (1988) p. 24 (cited in E. Bartholet, *op cit.* n. 9, at 1180).

children adopted transracially at an early age seem perfectly able to develop well socially: "in spite of their often having very little contact with other children of the same racial background, we found the large majority of children were able to relate effectively to peers and adults outside the family".[20]

In respect of the fears about "identity crises" and low self-esteem, the evidence again seems to indicate that there is nothing, *per se*, problematic about transracial adoptions and that, in any event, even when problems of this kind do arise they are not perceived by the children concerned to be particularly significant. In one extensive study of four-hundred-and-six Korean adoptees in Tennessee, Kim found that, though the children had little to no Korean self-image, they nonetheless had developed high self-regard in comparison with other groups of adolescents.[21] These findings were echoed in another study of African Americans conducted by McRoy and others:

> This exploratory study indicated that there were no differences in overall self-esteem between the sampled transracially and inracially adopted children. Furthermore, the level of self-esteem of the adoptees was as high as that reported among individuals in the general population.[22]

Similar findings were revealed by Gill and Jackson's much less extensive survey in this country: "[t]here was no general evidence . . . that the absence of racial pride or identity was, at this stage, associated with low self-esteem or behavioural disorder".[23]

It seems fair to conclude, then, that whether it is a good thing or a bad thing that transracial adoptees are likely to grow up race-neutral *in attitudinal terms*[24] depends very much on one's political predisposition. If one believes that minority groups should live separately both from each other and from whites, but with mutual respect, then such transracial adoptions and their tendency to produce race-neutrality will be viewed in negative terms. If, however, one believes in a fully integrated society, as I do, there is nothing at all problematic about failing to identify oneself as a member of a particular minority group.[25] The perception of the child being harmed in identity terms by reason of the fact that he or she

---

[20] See O. Gill and B. Jackson, *loc cit*. See also, Womack and Fulton, "Transracial Adoption and the Black Preschool Child" (cited in E. Bartholet, *op cit*. n. 9, at n. 128).

[21] D.S. Kim, "Intercountry Adoptions: A Study of Self-concept of Adolescent Korean Children who were Adopted by American Families" (unpublished Ph.D. referred to in H.S. Maas, *Social Service Research* (Washington, DC: National Association of Social Workers, 1978).

[22] R. McRoy *et al.*, "Self-esteem and Racial Identity in Transracial and Inracial Adoptees" (1982) 27 *Social Work* (USA) 522, at 524–6.

[23] O. Gill and B. Jackson, *op cit*. n. 1, p. 130. Similar findings as to successful placements exist in the more recent study of J. Thoburn *et al.*, *Permanent Family Placement for Children of Ethnic Minority Origins* (London: Whitaker, 1998).

[24] There is an important difference between racial attitude and racial self-image. It is one thing to be cognisant of one's physical appearance and racial attributes, but quite another to hold certain racial prejudices or assumptions: see further, E. Bartholet *op cit*. n. 9, at 1218.

[25] *Cf.* the Australian approach which endeavours to ensure Aboriginal placements for Aboriginal adoptees on the basis that failure to do so can be seen as posing a significant threat to the survival of Aboriginal communities. See Dewar, *op cit*. n. 10.

was transracially adopted will seldom be held by the child concerned. Nor will it be held by those committed to the integrationist ideal.

B Transracial Adoptions Damage Minority Community Interests?

In this section of the essay, I want to assess the extent to which minority community interests are adversely affected by the absence of same-race placement strategies. For those who advocate such strategies, there are perceived to be two main benefits. To begin with, they help to remove the image of exploitation we saw earlier which views blacks (and other minorities) as continuing to be the servants of whites who are unable to produce their own children.[26] Secondly, they preserve and help to perpetuate certain attitudes about racial differences: preponderantly, that society is profoundly divided along racial lines and that, therefore, certain kinds of survival mechanism—which can only be learnt in a same-race household—must be acquired. As Chestang has put it:

> there are certain social survival techniques that white parents just cannot teach their black children and experiences that they cannot share. Their child will need to look to other black adults or black friends in order to learn these skills. This is not possible for a child cut off from his own community.[27]

As regards the first of these supposed benefits, it is simply not true that there is a pervasive image of black exploitation in Millennial Britain. The idea that there is such an image has been imported by a select pocket of academics relying on studies conducted on the other side of the Atlantic where the history of race relations has been a good deal more torrid, and of considerably more recent vintage than in this country.[28] Race riots in this country, such as those in Brixton and Toxteth in the early 1980s, have not only been the exception rather than the rule, they have also tended to have been sparked more by perceptions of racist policing—in particular, indiscriminate stopping and searching of black youths—than by any notion of there being general, institutional racism.[29]

In relation to the contention that transracial adoption is harmful in that it denies the adoptee the chance to acquire the survival skills that he or she will need in later life, it is important to make two points. The first is that empirical evidence suggests that such children will grow up better able to cope in a racially differentiated society than inracially adopted children. They seem more positive

[26] See R.A. Howe, op cit. n. 1.

[27] See M. James, "Finding the Families" (1981) 103 Adoption and Fostering 10, at 15–16. See also L. Chestang, "The Dilemma of Biracial Adoption" (1972) 17 Social Work (USA) 100, at 103–4 and British Agencies for Adoption and Fostering, Practice Note 13, op cit. n. 13, at p. 2.

[28] For judicial castigation of experts making such claims in court, see Re N, supra n. 14, at 61–2 (per Bush J).

[29] See, e.g., Lord Scarman, The Brixton Disorders 10–12 April 1981: Report of an Inquiry (1981) Cm 8427 and, for a briefer account, E. Stockdale and S. Casale, Criminal Justice under Stress (London: Blackstone Press Ltd, 1992) pp. 13–17. Even the more recent disquiet surrounding the Stephen Lawrence case can be attributed only to racism within the Metropolitan Police force rather than to any pandemic racism.

about relationships with whites than those raised in same-race households, they are also more at ease in those relationships, and more interested in generally living an integrated lifestyle.[30] The second is that it is by no means clear that minority communities' *best* interests are served by adoption placement policies that assist in maintaining racial divisions. If, as the evidence suggests, transracial adoptions are conducive to proper racial integration—in which direction, thankfully, we are ineluctably moving[31]—then it might be argued that the relevant minority groups' interests lie more in taking measures that expedite this process and obviate the need for survival skills in the first place. If we are to take the integrationist ideal seriously, we ought to take heed of Elizabeth Bartholet's cautionary reminder that, "[h]ow we deal with race in the intimate context of the family says a lot about how we think about and deal with race in every other context of our social lives",[32] and Alec Samuels' contention that, "[a] harmonious multi-racial plural society can only be promoted and improved by transracial contact in the family setting, a mark of maturity in society".[33]

A final reason why minority communities, and society generally, ought to oppose the avid pursuit of same-race policies by adoption agencies is the cost involved. There are at least two aspects to this cost. The first and most obvious relates to the fact that local authority adoption agencies are funded by increasingly limited public monies. The cost of making strenuous efforts to find same-race homes for minority would-be-adoptees is very considerable indeed. This is partly because making assiduous efforts to identify potential black and Asian adoptive parents is expensive,[34] but mainly because of the costs associated with keeping many of the children concerned in local authority accommodation.[35] The second cost of adhering to race-matching strategies is an opportunity cost[36] borne by the children themselves. For they lose the (early) chance of what the evidence suggests would be a perfectly satisfactory home with white adoptive parents. This cost impacts on all potential minority adoptees whether they are currently being looked after by a local authority or a voluntary adoption agency (so long as the agency in question adheres to a race-matching policy).

[30] See R.J. Simon and H. Alstein, *Transracial Adoption* (London: John Wiley, 1977) pp. 59–68 and 80–3.
[31] Many examples of this move could be given. Let us focus, however, on just the integrationist achievements of the television companies since, probably more than any other medium television influences our perception of what is acceptable and normal. For more than a decade, programmes for very young viewers have been made involving dolls that reflect a broad range of different races and creeds. For slightly older viewers, there has been a marked move in favour of black children's TV presenters. And as regards programmes designed for adult audiences, the popular soap operas abound with mixed race marriages (and cohabitation) while the racist sit-coms of the 1970s—such as *Love Thy Neighbour*—appear to have left our screens for good.
[32] E. Bartholet, *op cit.* n. 9, at 1174.
[33] A. Samuels, *op cit.* n. 8, at 237.
[34] For example, the cost of advertising in the national media.
[35] I have been unable to find any figures on the precise additional cost of current same-race placement policies, but personal conversations with several local adoption agencies about delays in finding placements suggest that these are considerable.
[36] I have borrowed this term from economics: it represents the cost of the opportunity forgone.

III LEGAL IMPROPRIETIES OF RACE-MATCHING

In this part of the essay I want to consider two ways in which the application of same-race placement policies can be challenged in juridical terms. The first centres on the fact that such policies are probably racially discriminatory and therefore contrary to extant legislation in this field. The second concerns the fact that when race-matching policies become the primary touchstone of adoption practice, they fail to give the requisite weight to the welfare of the child under section 6 of the Adoption Act 1976.

A Race-matching as Racial Discrimination

The norm in most spheres of our daily lives is that decision making on the basis of racial or ethnic considerations is unlawful under the Race Relations Act 1976. In the present context, section 20(1)(b) is apposite. There, it is provided that:

> It is unlawful for any person concerned with the provision (for payment or not) of goods, facilities or services to the public or a section of the public to discriminate against a person who seeks to obtain those goods, facilities or services . . . by refusing or deliberately omitting to provide [those services] . . . in the like manner and on the like terms as are normal . . . in relation to other members of the public . . .[37]

This provision lends weighty support to the contention that race-matching policies are unlawful. Moreover, this support is amplified by reference to section 23(2) of the 1976 Act which specifically excepts from the general provisions of the Act those local authority foster parents who seek to provide a home for minority children,[38] but, importantly, does not except the local authority itself. To treat white would-be adopters less favourably than their black or Asian counterparts is almost certainly discriminatory.[39] It is also difficult, if not impossible, to justify such a practice in terms of affirmative action. Although affirmative action is unlawful only if it results in someone becoming the victim of discrimination specifically proscribed by the legislation, it seems tolerably clear that race-matching policies satisfy this test. They are not designed primarily to provide equality of opportunity to otherwise under-represented minority adopters—which is broadly the basis of many acceptable forms of affirmative (a.k.a., *positive*) action[40]—but, rather, to screen out the possibility of white adopters. In other words, their objective is negative rather than positive!

---

[37] It is clear that this provision applies to local authority (adoption agency) services since s. 20(2)(g) of the Act makes specific provision to this effect.

[38] The subsection states: "[s]ection 20(1) does not apply to anything done by a person as a participant in arrangements under which he (for reward or not) takes into his home, and treats as if they were members of his family, children . . . requiring a special degree of care and attention".

[39] Race Relations Act 1976, s. 1(a).

[40] See R.J. Townshend-Smith, *Discrimination Law: Text, Cases and Materials* (London: Cavendish, 1998) pp. 541–51.

In addition to discriminating against white would-be adopters, further reflection also reveals that such same-race policies are of only spurious or partial benefit to minority communities. While they may advantage those potential minority adopters who would not otherwise satisfy the stringent criteria normally applied to assess the suitability of white adopters, they most certainly do not benefit the adoptees who may, in consequence, find themselves in an economically challenged household which is situated in a run-down or otherwise undesirable location.[41] Commenting on the effect of such policies in the United States, Elizabeth Bartholet has noted that:

> the pool of black adopters looks very different in socio-economic terms from the pool of white parents. Black adoptive parents are significantly older, poorer, and more likely to be single than their white adoptive counterparts [and yet] . . . those at the bottom of the black list are generally preferred over all those on the white list.[42]

As such, only some of the adopters among the minority group benefit by adherence to such policies. But this benefit is obtained only at the expense of the adoptees, who are both more likely to end up in socially disadvantaged homes and more likely to remain unadopted, in agency accommodation, for longer than would have been the case if there had been no objections to a transracial adoption.[43] Furthermore, the fact that race-matching policies are by nature segregationist (rather than integrationist) raises serious doubts as to whether, ultimately, they can be seen as a form of *positive action* at all. In short, integration and measures conducive to racial harmony must surely be in the interests of minority (sub)communities, so long as those measures do not threaten the viability of those (sub)communities.[44]

Against this background what can be made of section 22(5)(c) of the Children Act 1989 which imposes upon local authorities making decisions with respect to children accommodated by them an obligation to "give due consideration . . . to the child's religious persuasion, racial origin and cultural and linguistic background"? To begin with, it is clear that this subsection applies in respect of placement decisions concerning children currently accommodated by a local authority adoption agency. Secondly, it should be noted that this provision is also designed to be beneficial to the relevant child. It therefore stands in stark contrast to the overt race-matching policies proposed by the British Agencies for Adoption and Fostering that we saw earlier.[45] For these latter, when examined,

---

[41] Note here that the British Agencies for Adoption and Fostering *Practice Note 18* recommends targeting just such areas in which English is not the first language as potential sources of would-be adopters: *op cit.* n. 13, p. 2. But if a child grows up in this country unable to speak English, it is difficult to see how any placement that carried this risk could be seen to be in the long-term interests of that child.

[42] E. Bartholet, *op cit.* n. 9, at 1199–200. Similar effects were observed by Gill and Jackson: see O. Gill and B. Jackson, *op cit.* n. 1.

[43] I have been unable to obtain any reliable evidence as to the extent of the delays in this country but for the American position, which is broadly analogous in most other respects: see E. Bartholet, *loc cit.*

[44] *Cf.* the Australian experience recounted in Dewar, *op cit.* n. 10.

[45] See *op cit.*, n. 13.

seem primarily designed to discriminate against white prospective adopters (with potentially undesirable consequences for would-be adoptees). Thirdly, the significance of section 22(5) in this context would appear to be limited: it is plainly of decreasing importance the younger and less well developed the child happens to be. The reason for this, as we have already seen, is that the evidence suggests that transracial placements may be as good as, or better than, inracial placements where the adoptee is a baby or very young infant. It is only where the child has passed beyond infancy and begun to acquire a particular cultural self-image that the virtues of a race-matching policy start to become apparent. Yet even here, there is nothing in section 22(5) which necessarily impinges upon the welfare principle embodied in section 6 of the Adoption Act. It merely highlights what might be a relevant consideration in judging how best that welfare can be safeguarded and promoted.

In short, there is nothing in section 22(5) of the Children Act which is ineluctably inconsistent with the commitment to anti-discriminatory principles embodied in the Race Relations Act or the version of the welfare principle contained in the Adoption Act. It is only where considerations that are overtly racist are taken into account that the anti-discrimination statute will be abrogated, giving rise to the possibility of judicial review of such decisions.

B The Centrality of Child Welfare

The second way in which race-matching policies can be thought of in terms of legal impropriety concerns their tendency to undermine the welfare requirements of section 6 of the Adoption Act 1976. In diverting attention away from the centrality of the child's welfare in favour of considerations of minority community interests, same-race placement policies place a higher premium on third party interests than on those of the specific child. Such policies often thereby ignore the empirically borne-out fact that it can be better for a minority child to be placed in a loving, white-parent home than not placed at all. And it is clear that there are fewer potential minority adopters than there are minority children waiting to be adopted.[46] This means that, after considerable delay, many such children either end up being placed with white families after all, or they remain with (a series of) foster parents or in local authority care. As regards local authority care, the *Cleveland Report* bears ample testimony to the fact that such accommodation is often only a lesser of two evils rather than a genuine solution to a child's plight and something that is positively beneficial to the child concerned.[47] Accordingly, such accommodation ought not to be thought of in terms of a viable, long-term option. Equally, serial foster placements deny the child the

---

[46] See O. Gill and B. Jackson, *op cit*. n. 1, p. 138.

[47] Recall, for example, the worrying account of life in care provided by "Samantha" in that *Report*: see the *Report of the Inquiry into Child Abuse in Cleveland 1987* (1988) Cm 412, pp. 244–54.

continuity that is widely accepted to be desirable for growing children.[48] And as a worst case scenario, the child may never be placed at all, because the older he or she gets, the less desirable he or she becomes as a potential adoptee.

In the absence of comparable evidence for this country, I return again to research in the United States which reveals details of holding policies that commonly specify a minimum period for which a child who cannot be placed with same-race adopters must be held before a transracial adoption can even be considered.[49] Summarising the research findings, Bartholet notes: "large numbers of minority children who could be placed for adoption with waiting white families spend months or years waiting in foster-care for a same-race placement" and "[s]ome will wait for their entire childhood".[50] There is no reason to suppose that the same is not true of this country. And the irony is, those minority children who remain in care are probably preponderantly in contact with, and grow up beside, white children.

Even where minority adopters can be found, there is still a risk that a *willingness* to adopt will be mistaken for, or treated as an equivalent to, a *genuine desire* to adopt. The photograph of a parentless child in a Sunday supplement might inspire sympathy and maybe even guilt. But these feelings should not be equated with a genuine, pre-existing commitment to adoptive parenting. For parenting for the wrong reasons is highly unlikely to conduce to the child's best interests. What the child needs is loving parents, not reluctant, or guilty, or merely willing parents. In short, two primary factors in assessing parental suitability must be their commitment to parenting and their motives. As Owen Gill and Barbara Jackson concluded: "[t]he most obvious reason for the successful outcome of these [transracial] adoptions is the commitment and caring of the adoptive parents" and "[a]lthough we came across families living in different settings and developing different family styles, we were impressed by the *natural and continuing dedication* [my italics] to make *this* child part of *this* family".[51]

By focusing on parental dedication, a great deal can be assured by way of the child's future welfare (always assuming that other factors such as relative youthfulness, good health and so on are present). By contrast, race-matching—at least when it is argued to be designed with the child's best interests in mind—may be taken implicitly to assert the primacy of a same-race placement as a guarantor of child welfare.[52] And as we have seen, there is little to nothing in the empirical research findings to support this view. Furthermore, beyond the *personal*

---

[48] A series of foster placements, recall, was one of the key bases for the negligence action brought against the local authority in *Barrret* v. *Enfield London Borough Council* [1999] 3 All ER 193.

[49] See the several studies cited in E. Bartholet, *op cit.* n. 1, at 1193–6.

[50] *Ibid.*, at 1172.

[51] O. Gill and B. Jackson, *op cit.* n. 1, p. 134.

[52] The British Agencies for Adoption and Fostering *Practice Note 13* contains such a suggestion: "all black families, whatever their ethnicity, share the common experience of racism. They are likely, therefore, to be better able than white families to combat the subtle messages of racism . . . and can provide the child with a positive role model as 'good' black parents": *op cit.* n. 13, p. 4 (emphasis in the original).

qualities of the potential adopters (including their motivation), agency staff should take into account the broader context of the proposed same-race home. It might, for example, be located in an area renowned for racial tension which clearly could not be seen to be conducive to the child's welfare. Additionally, or alternatively, that home may be situated in an area that boasts few if any recreational facilities for children such as public parks and vibrant youth clubs. All such facilities can help the child to develop his or her socialisation skills for later life by providing the necessary interaction with other children. Yet often, ethnic minorities find themselves clustered in run-down areas riven with racial tensions and woefully short of the kinds of good, safe, healthy recreational facilities just outlined.[53]

The problem of agencies placing the greatest amount of emphasis on the prospective parents' racial background means that the only corrective to the deployment of this strategy lies with the courts. And while the courts are typically committed to giving primacy to the child's welfare,[54] the problem remains that decisions in isolated pockets of litigation tend not to get reflected in day-to-day agency practice. Naturally, there is a limit to what any one court in any one private law case can do to influence general adoption agency practice.[55] The *Practice Notes* produced by the British Agencies for Adoption and Fostering that we saw earlier have a far greater impact in this respect. Accordingly, in the next section of this essay, I want to suggest a range of measures that might help to remove the need to pursue a legal challenge through the courts in order to ensure that the child's welfare, properly construed, should form the central plank of adoption placement decisions.

IV REFORM MEASURES

In this penultimate section, I want to advocate a number of measures—some practical and some legal—that I consider have the potential significantly to improve the adoption prospects of many minority children.

A Practical Measures

While I do not accept that same-race households *must* be found for all minority would-be adoptees—the empirical evidence clearly suggests that very young

[53] See David Cowan's essay in this collection, at ch. 9.

[54] See *Re N, supra* n. 14, at 68 (*per* Bush J); *Re P (A Minor) (Adoption)* [1990] 1 FLR 96, 98 (*per* Balcombe LJ) (noted: S.P. de Cruz, "Transracial Adoption and the Child's Best Interests" [1990] *Journal of Child Law* 51); *Re K (A Minor) (Wardship: Adoption)* [1991] 1 FLR 57, 64 (*per* Butler-Sloss LJ).

[55] The impact of a case might be significantly greater if the local authority's decision were to be challenged successfully by way of judicial review. For such a challenge might result in a change of policy in much the same way as happens in the context of public law challenges to health authority decisions: see D. Longley, *Public Law and Health Service Accountability* (Buckingham: Open University Press, 1993).

children and babies can quite successfully be adopted by white parents—I nonetheless acknowledge that transracial adoptions can be problematic in respect of older children who may have already formed, or begun to form, a clear cultural or racial sense of themselves. For the benefit of these older children, we should, rather than adhere to overtly discriminatory race-matching policies, seek instead to change the conditions that discourage otherwise enthusiastic minority adults from adopting. For a start, there might be a conscious effort on the part of adoption agencies to recruit more ethnic minority staff. Such recruitment policies would not only be acceptable under existing race relations law—under-representation of minorities in a particular job or profession is one of the circumstances in which positive action is permissible[56]—but they also diminish the possibility "that the cultural bias of white-oriented adoption agencies and workers" will continue to be responsible for the evident "unwillingness of black parents to submit themselves to the investigations of a white bureaucracy".[57] The point is a simple one: minority parents who seek to adopt same-race children have been empirically shown to be wary of approaching what they perceive to be predominantly white adoption agency staff. A more racially mixed staff might therefore be expected to yield greater numbers of suitable would-be minority adopters.

In addition to this, advertisements in newspapers that highlight the need for minority parents for older children should, of course, continue to be used. But as a *caveat* to this, it is imperative that such advertising is not used solely as a means of finding homes for difficult-to-place minority children. They must also be backed up with thorough and proper assessments by adoption workers to ensure that the same general criteria are applied to the new-found minority adopters as are applied to white adopters seeking to adopt white children. In short, the child's welfare must remain the key determinant of a placement decision.

As regards younger children and babies who have yet to form any fixed self-image, the present resistance to transracial adoption among adoption workers and the British Agencies for Adoption and Fostering must be discouraged. This could perhaps be achieved to some extent by further research, the emphasis of which is markedly different from that which has permeated the sociological literature thus far. To date, the leading studies have been dominated by investigations into suspected problem issues. None of them particularly look to the potential strengths of transracial adoption, such as its ability to produce children who are "colour-blind" in the sense that they grow up free from internalised racial prejudices and stereotypes. Instead of seeking to confirm the very worst suspicions about identity crises and the like, future research might instead investigate the ways in which transracial adoption might help to reduce the overall number of unadopted minority children and contribute in some

[56] Race Relations Act 1976, s. 37(1)(a), (b).
[57] O. Gill and B. Jackson, *op cit*. n. 1, p. 3.

measured way to the attainment of a more racially integrated society. By changing the accepted wisdom about transracial adoption, and by filtering the new
research findings into the education of future generations of adoption workers,
the stage would be set for a radically new approach (at the level of agency
practice, at any rate).

B Legal Steps

It is often suggested that it is anomalous that the child's welfare—normally the
court's paramount consideration in child law matters—should be only its first
consideration in adoption law.[58] In the interests of congruence with the
Children Act 1989,[59] it is sometimes argued that adoption law should place the
very same premium on the child's welfare. The difficulty with this approach,
however, is that where the paramountcy principle dictates not just whether any
particular adoption order ought to be made, but also whether the requirement
of parental agreement ought to be dispensed with, it has the potential to undermine the right to family life provided for by Article 8 of the European
Convention on Human Rights and now embodied in English law by virtue of the
Human Rights Act 1998.[60] Nonetheless, the legislation could be drafted so as to
ensure that the paramountcy principle applies in all cases where parental agreement has been granted, and a variant of the present Adoption Act test applied in
the absence of any such agreement. A suitable variant of the welfare test (for just
such cases) was suggested in the adoption law *Review* of 1992.[61] There it was
proposed that the court should be satisfied:

> that the advantages to a child of becoming part of a new family and having a new sta-
> tus are so significantly greater than the advantages to the child of any alternative
> option as to justify overriding the wishes of a parent or guardian.[62]

This combination of welfare tests—one designed for the straightforward case,
one designed for the case involving parental objection—coupled with a checklist akin to the one in section 1 of the Children Act[63] (which would allow
the older adoptee a say in the matter) would have two main advantages. First,
where parents have agreed unconditionally to their child being adopted, the

[58] See, e.g., Department of Health and Welsh Office, *Review of Adoption Law* (London: HMSO,
1992) para. 7.1 and E. Cooke, "Dispensing with Parental Consent to Adoption—A Choice of
Welfare Tests" [1995] *Journal of Child Law* 259, 261–2.
[59] See B. Lindley and N. Wylde, "The Children Act and the Draft Adoption Bill—Diverging
Principles" [1996] *Child and Family Law Quarterly* 327.
[60] For further discussion of the potential for adoption law to undermine this right see J. Murphy,
"Aids, Human Rights and Familial Responsibilities" in M. Brazier *et al.* (eds.), *Aids, Europe and
Human Rights* (Oxford: OUP, 2000) and B. Lindley and N. Wylde, *loc cit.*, at 330.
[61] *Op cit.*, n. 58.
[62] *Ibid.*, para. 12.6
[63] The Draft Adoption Bill of 1996 contained such provision: see Department of Health and
Welsh Office, *Adoption—A Service for Children: Adoption Bill—A Consultative Document*
(London: HMSO, 1996), cl. 1.

application of the paramountcy principle would remove any prospect of "minority community" arguments—in my view, a distraction—from influencing the court or adoption agency.[64] Secondly, the more explicit variant welfare test would make it more difficult for minority natural parents to stymie the transracial adoption of their child even before he or she has begun to develop any kind of racial or cultural self-image (without denying those parents at least some say in the matter). Although, on occasion, the case-law has held such refusals to be reasonable, it is less likely that those objections based on preventing "the [birth] father and the whole of his family losing face"[65] would continue to hold sway under the variant welfare test. It is difficult to see how being placed in a loving home is not significantly better than the very young child remaining in the limbo of care or foster homes just to save the birth family's image.

As regards older children, we have already seen that the drafting of section 22(5) of the Children Act is consistent with the arguments made in this essay for greater recognition of the potential virtues of transracial adoption. It is submitted that this provision might usefully be replicated in the Adoption Agency Regulations 1983, which are currently silent on the matter in terms of the duties they impose on agencies in respect of proposed placements.[66] The main reasons for this proposed extension are, first, that these regulations apply as much to voluntary adoption societies as they do to local authority agencies, and secondly, that specific provision to this effect might help to mitigate the influence of the British Agencies for Adoption and Fostering's *Practice Notes* which advocate race-matching policies in what I have argued to be discriminatory terms.[67]

Another suggestion, but only in relation to older transracial adoptees, is that there might usefully be a presumption in favour of open adoption. Such a presumption, allowing some maintenance of contact with the birth family, where possible, might help to overcome some of the difficulties associated with placing a minority child with white parents (assuming that minority adopters cannot be found). The transition from having one set of parents to the acquisition of a second set is hard enough by itself, and the problems associated with this transition may easily be compounded where the child in question has already developed a strong cultural or racial self-image. Open adoption could reasonably be expected to facilitate such transitions.

[64] The Adoption Act, s. 6 currently applies with respect to both the decisions of the courts, and to those of adoption agencies.

[65] See *Re N, supra* n. 14, at 63 (*per* Bush J). The judge somewhat spuriously tried to justify this preservation of the birth family's interests thus: "it clearly would not be in N's interests for her father to feel the shame and distress that in his culture an adoption order would bring": *ibid.* But why when N was only three at the time and her birth father lived in the USA with only minimal future contact between the two envisaged?

[66] See Reg. 9.

[67] Clearly, though not discriminatory, section 22(5) is not a "colour-blind" provision. Its tenor is that, where race and culture will matter, it would be pointless to pretend to the contrary. In respect of very young children, its effect may be nugatory in which case the law can be applied in a colour-blind fashion, but there would be enormous pretence if a child who had grown up in a particular culture *and language* were to be placed in a white, English-speaking home.

V CONCLUSIONS

In this essay, I have explored the extent to which current adoption law and practice affords the welfare of children the same degree of importance in transracial and inracial (white) adoptions. I have argued that, though the law could be improved in some minor respects, the main problems lie with adoption practice where a combination of distractions,[68] misconceptions,[69] misdirected research[70] and a failure properly to distinguish the younger and older transracial adoptee have conspired to produce a discriminatory approach to transracial adoption. In addition, I have proposed a number of reform measures that might reasonably be expected to achieve a non-discriminatory legal and practice framework that places welfarism at the centre of decision making and, simultaneously, holds true to the ideal of achieving, or at least moving inexorably towards, a properly and fully integrated society.

[68] E.g., the concern with so-called minority community interests.

[69] E.g., that transracial adoptions are almost certain to give rise to identity problems.

[70] I.e., research that looks to the confirmation of negative assumptions about transracial adoption rather than to its potentially positive aspects (such as the probability of producing young adults who are genuinely neutral in terms of racial issues). In Gill and Jackson's study (*op cit*. n. 1)—the most comprehensive to date in this country—chapters 2 to 11 (of a 12 chapter book) explore the extent to which problems arise with transracial adoptions. But, apart from showing that assumptions about the frequency and magnitude of these problems are grossly over-stated, and that such adoptions are generally successful, they present no basis on which to assume that similar problems to the ones that they do identify would not arise in same-race placements. And as Bartholet concluded about the American research, "[t]he studies in fact provide *no basis* for concluding that placement of black children with white rather than black families has any negative impact on the children's welfare": E. Bartholet, *op cit*. n. 9, at 1210.

PART II
International Issues

4

Recognition of Foreign Divorces: Unwarrantable Ethnocentrism

I INTRODUCTION

PROCEEDINGS, IN WHICH the recognition of foreign matrimonial decrees[1] are sought, are a familiar occurrence in English private international law. Indeed, the ease of international travel, combined with the plurality of cultures, has meant that the English courts are increasingly faced with proceedings of this nature. Although in Christian countries divorces are granted mainly by a court of civil jurisdiction,[2] the means by which marriages are dissolved vary widely across the world. Alternatives frequently centre upon processes prescribed by traditional and religious customs, resulting in many divorces being obtained "extra-judicially". Such processes may involve a religious court, as does the Jewish *ghet*;[3] they may merely embody a mutual agreement between the spouses and their respective families, as exemplified by customary divorces in many African countries;[4] they may involve the act of just one spouse, such as a "bare *talaq*" under Muslim law; or they may entail a combination of a religious process and procedures set out by a civil authority, like the decrees obtained under the Pakistan Muslim Family Laws Ordinance 1961.[5] These various systems pose a range of problems for the recognition rules in English private international law.[6] Chief among these is the question of when recognition should be

---

* Lecturer in Law, University of Liverpool.

[1] Note that "matrimonial decrees" refer not only to divorces, but also to legal separations and nullity decrees. This essay, however, considers only divorces, for foreign legal separations and nullity decrees are seldom granted informally and do not appear to present problems in terms of recognition.

[2] Albeit that in some instances divorces may be obtained by way of administrative decisions.

[3] A consensual divorce in the form of the delivery, by the husband, to the wife of a written document before a rabbinical court.

[4] See S. Poulter, *English Law and Ethnic Minority Customs* (London: Butterworths, 1986) pp. 98–100.

[5] In this case the husband, having pronounced the "*talaq*", must give written notice to this effect both to the chairman of an administrative council and to his wife. The divorce becomes effective only after the expiry of 90 days, during which an attempt at reconciliation is made.

[6] See, e.g., S. Poulter, *op cit*. n. 4, pp. 98–127.

afforded to avoid the problem of "limping" marriages, which are "recognised in one country but not recognised in another with the unhappy results that may flow therefrom—namely bigamous remarriage, illegitimate children and uncertainty or confusion over status and property rights".[7]

On the one hand, it may be argued that ethnic communities living in the United Kingdom should forego their customs and conform to this country's law and practice ("when in Rome, do as the Romans do"). On the other, however, many of the ethnic customs are deeply rooted in moral and religious beliefs, and to be expected to relinquish them would be perceived as surrendering cultural identity and therefore unacceptable. Clearly, any satisfactory solution must be based on a balanced compromise between these principles.[8] Hence, the purpose of this essay is to assess the adequacy of the law in this respect, and to examine whether such a compromise has been achieved or whether the law leads to an unwarrantable ethnocentrism.[9] That is to say, this essay explores the legal and judicial attitudes towards the recognition of foreign divorces and the extent to which their approach is capable of accommodating ethnic customs and traditions. In order to appreciate more fully the impact of the law on ethnic groups, a brief historical overview of the recognition rules, tracing the gradual change in attitude, must form the starting point.

II HISTORICAL OVERVIEW

Historically the recognition of foreign divorces was a matter regulated exclusively by the common law. Although initially they were hesitant to recognise the validity of overseas divorces, over time, the English judiciary became increasingly willing to afford such recognition,[10] irrespective of both the nature of the divorce and the country in which it was obtained.[11] They did so according to four criteria only,[12] any one or more of which would satisfy the courts. First, if the parties were, at the commencement of the proceedings, domiciled in the foreign country whose courts granted the decree;[13] secondly, if the divorce would

---

[7] *Quazi* v. *Quazi* [1980] AC 744 at 766.

[8] Poulter, *op cit.* n. 4, ch. 5.

[9] See J. Young, "The Recognition of Extra-judicial Divorces in the United Kingdom" (1987) 7 *Legal Studies* 78, who advocates that the recognition rules, discriminating against informal divorces, suggest an unacceptable ethnocentrism.

[10] Note that *Harvey* v. *Farnie* (1882) 8 AC 43 was the first case in which the English courts recognised the validity of a foreign divorce. Prior to this case, even a divorce obtained in Scotland would not be recognised in England: see D. McClean, *Morris: The Conflict of Laws* (London: Sweet & Maxwell, 4th ed, 1993) pp. 186–90.

[11] Note that *Har-Shefi* v. *Har-Shefi* (No. 2) [1953] P 20 was the first case in which the validity of an extra-judicial divorce (a Jewish *ghet*) effected in England was upheld; and *El-Riyami* v. *El-Riyami* [1958] CLY 497 was the first case in which recognition was afforded to an extra-judicial divorce (a Muslim *talaq*) obtained abroad. For further discussion see S. Poulter, *op cit.* n. 4, pp. 110–23.

[12] Note that both the basis on which the foreign court had assumed jurisdiction and the grounds on which the decree had been granted were considered irrelevant.

[13] *Harvey* v. *Farnie* (1882) 8 AC 43; *Ratanachai* v. *Ratanachai* [1960] CLY 480; *Lee* v. *Lau* [1967] P 14.

be recognised by the courts of the parties' domicile;[14] thirdly, if the English court would have had jurisdiction to grant the divorce;[15] and fourthly, if there was a real and substantial connection between either party to the proceedings and the country where the divorce was obtained.[16]

Eventually, the legislature intervened by way of the Recognition of Divorces and Legal Separations Act 1971, which was designed to give effect to the Hague Convention on Recognition of Divorces and Legal Separations 1968.[17] Importantly, the 1971 Act[18] drew a distinction between divorces obtained in courts in any part of the British Isles[19] and those obtained elsewhere.[20] In the former case, recognition was virtually automatic, but only in respect of divorces obtained after the Act came into force. By contrast, the Act applied to foreign divorces obtained both before and after that date.[21] Additionally, the 1971 Act placed foreign divorces into two further categories: "overseas" divorces, and divorces "obtained in a country outside the British Isles". An "overseas" divorce was one obtained in a country outside the British Isles by means of "judicial or other proceedings",[22] whereas a divorce obtained "outside the British Isles" was one that was obtained without proceedings.[23] This dichotomy resulted in the application of separate recognition rules. The recognition of an "overseas" divorce depended on two jurisdictional bases: either habitual residence of either spouse in the country in which the divorce was obtained, or nationality of either spouse of that country.[24] By contrast, the recognition of a divorcee obtained "outside the British Isles" depended on section 6 of the Act, which preserved the common law rule in *Armitage* v. *Att-Gen*[25] that a divorce would be recognised if it was valid by the law of the domicile of each spouse.

While less liberal than the common law, the 1971 Act restored some degree of clarity to the law. Nonetheless, the statute was far from perfect, and this led the Law Commission in 1984 to propose that essentially one set of rules should govern all foreign divorces. As a result, it was concluded that the 1971 Act should be replaced by new legislation by virtue of which the rules in the 1971 Act would

---

[14] *Armitage* v. *Att-Gen* [1906] P 135; *Russ* v. *Russ* [1964] P 315.

[15] *Travers* v. *Holley* [1953] P 246.

[16] *Indyka* v. *Indyka* [1969] 1 AC 33.

[17] The full text of the Convention, together with a commentary, can be found in Law Commission Report No. 34, *Hague Convention on Recognition of Divorces and Legal Separations* (London: HMSO, 1970).

[18] As amended by the Domicile and Matrimonial Proceedings Act 1973.

[19] Recognition of Divorces and Legal Separations Act 1971, s. 1 (hereafter, "the 1971 Act"), as amended by the Domicile and Matrimonial Proceedings Act 1973.

[20] *Ibid.*, ss. 2 and 6.

[21] This was subject to certain transitional and safeguard provisions set out in s. 10(4) of the 1971 Act.

[22] *Ibid.*, s. 2.

[23] *Ibid.*, s. 6.

[24] *Ibid.*, s. 3. Note that habitual residence in this context included domicile where the country in which the divorce was obtained applied this concept.

[25] [1906] P 135.

be simplified and clarified.[26] These recommendations were implemented in Part II of the Family Law Act 1986.

III   THE SCHEME OF THE CURRENT LAW

The 1986 Act, which to some extent re-enacted the 1971 legislation, also went further and, subject to certain savings discussed below, replaced all the pre-existing statutory and common law rules in this context.[27] The 1986 Act now covers divorces obtained at any time.[28] It also removed the distinction between "overseas" divorces and divorces obtained "outside the British Isles" while retaining the distinction between divorces granted in any part of the British Isles and those granted elsewhere. It is the significance of the distinction between domestic and overseas divorces as well as the subdivision of the latter category into "proceedings" and "non-proceedings" divorces that forms the subject matter of this essay.

A Divorces Obtained Within the British Isles

Divorces granted by courts of the British Isles are recognised in England in accordance with the provisions of section 44 of the Family Law Act 1986. This permits the almost automatic recognition of divorces granted by courts in any part of the British Isles.[29] Only if the divorce is obtained otherwise than from a court of civil jurisdiction will it not generally be recognised. This means that extra-judicial divorces obtained in the British Isles will presumptively be denied recognition. So, for example, a husband cannot normally pronounce a *talaq* within these territories and consider himself to be validly divorced.[30] Only exceptionally will recognition be granted to such divorces within the British Isles; and then only if they were obtained before 1 January 1974 and would have been recognised as valid under the common law rules applicable before that date.[31]

It is noteworthy that divorces granted by a court of civil jurisdiction within the British Isles will be recognised throughout the United Kingdom and cannot be questioned on any ground of lack of jurisdiction.[32] Apart from two excep-

---

[26] Law Commission Report No. 137, *Recognition of Foreign Nullity Decrees and Related Matters* (London: HMSO, 1984) Part VI.

[27] Family Law Act 1986, s. 45 (hereafter, "FLA 1986").

[28] *Ibid.*, ss. 44(2), 52(1)(a) and 52(3).

[29] *Ibid.*, s. 52(1)(a) and (3).

[30] This contrasts with the common law rule in *Armitage* v. *Att-Gen* [1906] P 135, whereby divorces recognised as valid under the law of the spouses' common domicile would be recognised in England. See, e.g., *Har-Shefi* v. *Har-Shefi (No. 2)* [1953] P 20 and *Qureshi* v. *Qureshi* [1972] Fam 173.

[31] FLA 1986, s. 52(4), (5)(a).

[32] *Ibid.*, s. 44(2).

tional cases covered by section 51 of the Act which concern the validity of the marriage in the first place, British divorces cannot be denied recognition anywhere in the United Kingdom, despite the fact that they may be, for example, contrary to public policy or natural justice (which factors are relevant in respect of overseas divorces). This approach was avowedly justified on the basis that "in such circumstances the complaining party should seek to have the divorce decree set aside by the court which granted it, or on appeal from that court, and that it would be objectionable to allow a court in another part of the British Isles, to refuse to recognise the decree".[33] This is in stark and not immediately comprehensible contrast to the recognition of the validity of foreign divorces.

B Overseas Divorces

As indicated earlier, the 1986 Act forges a crucial distinction between those divorces obtained by means of proceedings and those obtained otherwise. We now consider each in turn.

(1) *Divorces Obtained by Means of Proceedings*

Where a divorce obtained by means of proceedings is granted outside the British Isles, section 46(1) sets out the grounds for recognition as follows:

The validity of an overseas divorce . . . obtained by means of proceedings shall be recognised if:

(a) the divorce . . . is effective under the law of the country in which it was obtained; and
(b) at the relevant date either party to the marriage-
  (i) was habitually resident in the country where the divorce . . . was obtained; or
  (ii) was domiciled in that country; or
  (iii) was a national of that country.

This provision, complex though it may appear, has considerably simplified the previous law. As a general rule, it enables the recognition of an overseas divorce in England so long as it is effective in the country where it was obtained,[34] provided that, at the relevant time, one of three jurisdictional requirements is satisfied; namely, habitual residence, domicile or nationality of either party to the marriage. So, for example, where the domestic court has no competence to grant a divorce, the fact that it is ineffective abroad means that it will be denied recognition in the United Kingdom. This is so even where competence was lost purely

---

[33] Law Commission, *op cit*. n. 26, para. 4.7.
[34] Dicey and Morris suggest that "effective" in this context is likely to mean "effective to dissolve the marriage": Dicey and Morris, *The Conflict of Laws* (London: Sweet & Maxwell, 13th ed, 2000) Rule 79, at 737.

for procedural reasons. Take, for example, the case of *D* v. *D*,[35] where the husband, unbeknown to the wife, initiated divorce proceedings before the Customary Arbitration Tribunal in Ghana with the wife's mother standing as defendant. The latter protested that she could not deal with the matter without her daughter being either present or notified. The husband obtained the divorce and sought a declaration from the English court that it was entitled to recognition under section 46(1) of the Act. Having been satisfied that the divorce was obtained by means of proceedings, Wall J refused to recognise it because, among other reasons,[36] it was not effective under Ghanaian law. This conclusion was reached on the basis that the failure to notify the wife and the mother's protest meant that the tribunal did not meet its obligation to arrive at their decision after hearing both parties in a judicial manner. The burden of proof had lain with the husband to establish that there had been voluntary submission by that other party to the jurisdiction of the tribunal. On the facts, he had failed to do so, and accordingly, the divorce was ineffective under Ghanaian law.[37]

Of practical importance in this context is deciding what types of divorces fall within the phrase "other proceedings", since the recognition of a foreign divorce, obtained without proceedings (judicial or otherwise), is subject to the more stringent provisions of section 46(2) of the Act. To be afforded recognition under that subsection, the divorce must be obtained either in the country of the spouses' common domicile, or in the country of the domicile of one spouse and recognised as valid in the country of domicile of the other spouse.[38] It will not be sufficient if the divorce was recognised in both countries, but obtained in neither.

Meaning of "Proceedings"

As we have already remarked, a number of foreign legal systems permit divorces to be obtained extra-judicially. These may take a variety of forms, such as a unilateral divorce by the husband, a consensual divorce, or a family consultation and conciliation process.[39] Examples of the first two forms can be found under Muslim law. In the Sudan, parts of East Africa and some Arab States, a husband can divorce his wife simply by pronouncing the word *talaq* three times. No rea-

---

[35] [1994] 1 FLR 38. See also *Adams* v. *Adams* [1971] P 188, where a divorce obtained in Southern Rhodesia was denied recognition in England on the ground that the judge had not taken the judicial oath in the prescribed manner.

[36] Wall J went beyond section 46(1) and held that even if the divorce was effective, it would still be denied recognition on the ground of section 51(3)(a)(i) for want of notice of the proceedings. See *infra* for discussion of this ground.

[37] For a useful analysis of Wall J's decision in this case, see J. Murphy, "The Recognition of Overseas Marriages and Divorces in the United Kingdom" (1996) 47 *Northern Ireland Legal Quarterly* 35, 44–9.

[38] Provided that neither party to the marriage was habitually resident in the UK throughout the period of one year preceding the date of the commencement of the proceedings: FLA 1986, s. 46(2)(c).

[39] See, e.g., P. North, "Recognition of Extra-Judicial Divorces" (1975) 91 *Law Quarterly Review* 36; and A. Jaffey, "Recognition of Extra-Judicial Divorces" (1975) 91 *Law Quarterly Review* 320.

sons need be given, the wife in some instances need not be present, and no further formality is required. This type of divorce is known as a *bare talaq*.[40] Equally, Muslim law permits a divorce by *khula*, which is a divorce by mutual consent, instigated by the wife's suggestion.[41] In some jurisdictions, such as Egypt, the divorce would usually be registered with a court, notwithstanding that this is not an essential requirement for its validity.[42] By contrast, in Pakistan, under the Muslim Family Laws Ordinance 1961, the effect of the *talaq* is suspended for a certain period of time to allow for conciliation proceedings to take place.[43] The Jewish *ghet* is another kind of extra-judicial divorce obtained by a religious process. Again, it is a consensual divorce, instituted by the husband in a document, which is approved by the Beth Din in a rabbinical court, and delivered to the wife in the presence of witnesses.[44] The multiplicity of extra-judicial means by which a divorce may be obtained each raise the question of whether they would qualify for recognition in England in accordance with the jurisdictional criteria contained in section 46(1), irrespective of the nature and extent of the formalities involved. The crucial issue is what is meant by "proceedings".

Section 54(1) of the 1986 Act states that the term *"proceedings"* means *"judicial or other proceedings"*. No further guidance or elaboration is provided. Its interpretation has therefore caused considerable difficulty and judicial disagreement.[45] The Law Commission, while accepting that the distinction between divorces obtained by means of proceedings and those obtained otherwise should remain in place, recommended that the scope of the former should be broadly interpreted.[46] Accordingly, it should cover "acts which constitute the means by which a divorce, annulment or legal separation may be obtained in [the foreign] country and are done in compliance with the procedure required by the law of that country", including bare *talaq*s.[47] In the Commission's view, this did not mean that all extra-judicial divorces would be recognised in the United Kingdom: where necessary, they might still be denied recognition on the basis of, for example, public policy, or any of the other grounds then contained in section 8 of the 1971 Act.[48] Had this broad approach been adopted, it would have meant that non-proceedings divorces were those involving only the most

[40] See, e.g., *Sharif* v. *Sharif* [1980] *Family Law* 216 and *Zaal* v. *Zaal* [1982] 4 FLR 284.

[41] *Quazi* v. *Quazi* [1980] AC 744.

[42] See the expert evidence given in *Russ* v. *Russ* [1963] P 87 at 95 [1964] P 315 at 321–2. For a case involving a *talaq* pronounced in a court in Bahrain see *Z* v. *Z* [1992] 2 FLR 291.

[43] See *Qureshi* v. *Qureshi* [1971] 1 All ER 325; *R* v. *Registrar General of Births, Deaths and Marriages, ex p. Minhas* [1977] QB 1; and *Quazi* v. *Quazi* [1980] AC 744. Note that section 1(2) of the Ordinance states that it applies to all Muslim Pakistani nationals, wherever they may be.

[44] See *Berkovits* v. *Grinberg* [1995] Fam 142.

[45] See A. Jaffey, *op cit.* n. 39 and P. Smart, "Recognition of Extra-Judicial Divorces" (1985) 34 *International and Comparative Law Quarterly* 392, who also advocates the need to revert back to the common law principles whose application did not distinguish between judicial and extra-judicial divorces.

[46] Law Commission, *op cit.* n. 26, paras. 6.7–6.11.

[47] *Ibid.*, para. 6.11.

[48] Now replaced by FLA 1986, s. 51.

informal type of dissolution of marriage by consent.[49] Regrettably, however, this recommendation was rejected by the government for three reasons.[50] First, it was argued that such a liberal approach would create problems of proof in respect of informal "proceedings" divorces: that is, it would be difficult to ascertain whether what was alleged to have taken place had actually taken place. On close examination, this argument appears unconvincing since the government's solution was merely to permit recognition according only to more stringent grounds of jurisdiction.[51] Furthermore, this objection is equally difficult to sustain in the light of section 51(3) of the 1986 Act which provides that in respect of a divorce obtained otherwise than by means of proceedings, the non-availability of an official document certifying that the divorce is effective in the country where it was obtained grants a discretionary power to the English courts to deny recognition. An equivalent provision relating to extra-judicial proceedings divorces could easily have been inserted into the Act. The second reason for rejecting the Law Commission's recommendation was avowedly that since most informal divorces were obtained by men, they discriminated against women. But again, this objection seems unsustainable in view of the fact that the legislature, instead of denying their recognition altogether, elected to permit them on the strength of restricted jurisdictional grounds.[52] In respect of both these contentions, it is difficult to understand how simply satisfying a jurisdictional requirement as to domicile removes a concern centred on informality. The final reason for rejecting the Law Commission's proposal was stated to be that such divorces often provide little to no financial support for dependent family members. Yet, the force of this argument was significantly undermined after Part III of the Matrimonial and Family Proceedings Act 1984 was implemented. For that Act enabled English courts to grant financial relief following an overseas divorce,[53] only where that divorce was obtained by means of proceedings.[54] If

---

[49] See P. North, "Private International Law of Matrimonial Causes" (1990) I *Hague Recueil* 9, 125–6.

[50] HL Deb (1986) vol 473, cols 1082 and 1103.

[51] These are set out in s. 46(2) of the Act which states that:

The validity of an overseas divorce, annulment or legal separation obtained otherwise than by means of proceedings shall be recognised if:

(a) the divorce, annulment or legal separation is effective under the law of the country in which it was obtained;

(b) at the relevant date:

    (i) either party to the marriage was domiciled in that country; or

    (ii) either party to the marriage was domiciled in that country and the other party was domiciled in a country under whose law the divorce, annulment or legal separation is recognised as valid; and

(c) neither party to the marriage was habitually resident in the United Kingdom throughout the period of one year immediately preceding that date.

[52] Indeed, if either, or both, of these arguments were to stand, all such divorces should have been denied recognition.

[53] That is a divorce obtained outside the British Isles.

[54] Note that s. 12(1) of the 1984 Act excludes informal divorces from the scope of the Act. Hence, it was all the more reason for the Government to have adopted a more liberal approach to ensure that problems of this type would not arise.

the United Kingdom legislature deliberately saw fit to give preferential treatment to those divorced by way of proceedings, it could hardly object that foreign jurisdictions did the same.

As things stand, the recognition of extra-judicial divorces provisions in Part II of the 1986 Act are, in essence, very similar to those contained in the 1971 Act. Hence, cases decided under the earlier Act remain relevant when interpreting "proceedings". In *Quazi* v. *Quazi*,[55] the House of Lords interpreted the phrase "other proceedings" liberally. The husband and wife were both Muslims and Pakistani nationals. While living in Thailand, they made a consensual *khula* divorce. Later, the husband, who was unsure of the validity of the *khula*, went to Pakistan where he pronounced *"talaq"* three times. Notice of the *talaq* was given to the wife and to the chairman of an arbitration council as required by the Pakistan Muslim Family Laws Ordinance 1961, which postponed its effect for ninety days during which time reconciliation attempts should take place. On the question of whether either of the purported dissolutions would be recognised in England under section 2 of the 1971 Act, Wood J held that the *khula* could not be considered a valid divorce obtained by way of "other proceedings" since, although there was official recognition by the State Councillor for Muslim Affairs in Thailand, there was no procedure which led, or took place prior, to this recognition.[56] Conversely, the *talaq* obtained in Pakistan could be classed as a divorce obtained by way of other proceedings. Restricting their consideration to the latter issue, the House of Lords confirmed this classification but held that the phrase "other proceedings" was not limited to quasi-judicial proceedings, but also extended to any proceedings which were officially recognised in the country in which they took place.

The meaning of "other proceedings", in the opinions of both Lord Fraser and Lord Scarman in *Quazi* v. *Quazi*, ought not to be restricted to proceedings in which the state, or some official organisation recognised by the state, must have played some part in the divorce process, possessing the power to prevent the parties from dissolving the marriage tie as of right.[57] While Lord Fraser took the view that proceedings covered a divorce which, after some form of procedure, was officially recognised in the country in question,[58] Lord Scarman went further and opined that proceedings meant "any act or acts, officially recognised as leading to divorce in the country where the divorce was obtained, and which itself is recognised by the law of the country as an effective divorce".[59] In *Zaal* v. *Zaal*,[60] Bush J, following Lord Scarman's wider view, stated that the notion "other proceedings" was sufficiently broad to embrace a bare *talaq* pronounced

---

[55] [1980] AC 744.

[56] See also *Sharif* v. *Sharif* [1980] *Fam Law* 216, where Wood J decided that a bare *talaq* pronounced in Iraq did not fall within the meaning of "other proceedings".

[57] *Quazi* v. *Quazi* [1980] AC 744 at 814 and 823 respectively (thereby rejecting the Court of Appeal's interpretation of this point).

[58] *Ibid.*, at 814.

[59] *Ibid.*, at 824.

[60] [1983] 4 FLR 284.

in Dubai, provided that it was recognised as effective therein. In his view, the Muslim *talaq* was a ceremony of religious significance, involving the process of pronouncing *"talaq"* by the husband three times, thereby constituting proceedings.[61] It was immaterial that the husband did so with or without witnesses, and with or without a document to support it, provided that the spouses were regarded as validly divorced under the law of that country.[62]

This liberal approach is what prompted the Law Commission to recommend the ascription of a wide interpretation of the phrase "judicial or other proceedings".[63] Yet, as we saw earlier, this recommendation was not implemented in the Family Law Act 1986. Subsequent cases have also revealed a judicial preference for a narrower interpretation. In *Chaudhary* v. *Chaudhary*,[64] for example, the Court of Appeal rejected the more liberal approach in favour of a restrictive meaning, and held that a bare *talaq* obtained in Kashmir was no more than a pronouncement which could fairly be described as a procedure or ritual, but did not constitute "proceedings". This restrictive meaning, in the court's view, was clearly to be preferred to one which would render the whole phrase otiose.[65] The court interpreted *Quazi* v. *Quazi*[66] as requiring the word "proceedings" to involve a degree of formality and at least the involvement of some agency of the state, or recognised by the state (whether lay or religious). This interpretation was based on what has been described as a dubious ground,[67] for the House of Lords, while reversing the decision of the Court of Appeal in *Quazi*, did not actually disapprove of Ormond LJ's interpretation to this effect.[68] Accordingly, it would seem that whereas a Jewish *ghet* and a Pakistani *talaq* fall within the scope of "judicial or other proceedings" and, therefore, their recognition in England is covered by the more liberal provisions of section 46(1) of the 1986 Act, bare *talaq*s (and similar forms of divorce obtained by consensus) fall outside its scope,[69] even though, to both partners concerned, they may be viewed as an acceptable means of divorce, both legally and morally.

---

[61] Bush J also disagreed with the decision of Wood J in *Sharif* v. *Sharif* [1980] *Fam Law* 216, that a bare *talaq* was not within the meaning of "other proceedings". In *R* v. *Immigration Appeal Tribunal and Seada Bi, ex parte Secretary of State for the Home Department* [1984] FLR 147, Taylor J stated that he preferred Bush J's view over that of Wood J.

[62] Note, however, that the divorce was ultimately denied recognition under section 8 of the 1971 Act as contrary to public policy.

[63] Law Commission, *op cit.* n. 26, para. 6.11, and clause 12(1) of the Draft Bill at p122.

[64] [1985] FLR 476. For criticism see P. Smart, *op cit.* n. 45.

[65] *Ibid.,* at 483.

[66] [1980] AC 744.

[67] Dicey and Morris, *op cit.* n. 34, Rule 80 at 746.

[68] *Quazi* v. *Quazi* [1980] AC 744, 788. The material text reads as follows: "The inclusion of these words must be intended as a limitation on the scope of the section. . . . Some forms of divorce must, therefore, be excluded and the filter is the phrase 'judicial or other proceedings' . . . the phrase must be intended to exclude those divorces which depend for their legal efficacy solely on the act or acts of the parties to the marriage or one of them. In such cases, although certain formalities or procedures have to be complied with, there is nothing which can properly be regarded as 'proceedings' ".

[69] For example, Thai divorces of the type in *Ratanachai* v. *Ratanachai* [1960] CLY 480; and *Varanand* v. *Varanand* (1964) 108 SJ 693.

The situs *of an extra-judicial divorce*

A second difficulty that arises in relation to "proceedings" divorces concerns the *situs* of the divorce, though only where the proceedings in question are extrajudicial in nature. This is especially true of transnational divorces where a certain act is performed in one country but the divorce is completed by a further act in another country.[70] And, at a practical level, transnational divorces have presented substantial problems for divorcees living in the UK. The decision in *R v. Secretary of State for the Home Department, ex parte Fatima*[71] provides a useful illustration. The husband in that case, a Pakistani Muslim, married in Pakistan in 1968, then immediately came to live in England. In 1978, he purported to divorce his wife by *talaq*. He pronounced the *talaq* and made a statutory declaration to that effect before a solicitor in England. In accordance with the Pakistan Ordinance of 1961, copies of the document were sent both to the wife and to the chairman of the Union Council in Pakistan. No reconciliation took place and, thus, the marriage was dissolved effectively under Pakistani law on the expiry of ninety days. In 1982, he wished to marry a Pakistani national living in Pakistan, but the woman was refused leave to enter the UK by an immigration officer on the ground that the *talaq* obtained in 1978 would not be recognised under English law. Accordingly, the husband was not free to remarry in England.

The essential question before the House of Lords was to determine the country in which the divorce was obtained. Undoubtedly, if it was obtained in Pakistan where it was effective under the 1961 Ordinance, it would be capable of recognition under section 2 of the 1971 Act. If, on the other hand, it was obtained in England, where the *talaq* was pronounced, it would be denied recognition under section 16(1) of the Domicile and Matrimonial Proceedings Act 1973. Lord Ackner concluded that the pronouncement of the *talaq* by the husband was the first step in the proceedings which led to the divorce. As such, the proceedings had taken place partly in England and partly in Pakistan. Since the notion of judicial or other proceedings in section 2 of the 1971 Act only referred to overseas divorces obtained by a single set of proceedings initiated and completed in the same country, the divorce could not be recognised in England.

It follows that where an extra-judicial divorce is obtained by means of proceedings, such as those required under the law of Pakistan, it can only be recognised in England if the entirety of the proceedings is completed abroad. This is in line with the policy of denying recognition to divorces obtained within the British Isles unless granted by a court of civil jurisdiction.[72] The decision in

---

[70] It would appear that a bare *talaq* is located where the husband pronounces the required formula.

[71] [1986] 2 All ER 32, [1986] AC 527. See also D. Gordon, "Extra-Judicial Divorces Revisited—A Radical Approach" (1986) 37 *Northern Ireland Legal Quarterly* 151; and *id*, "Extra-Judicial Divorces Revisited—The Lords' Approach" (1986) 37 *Northern Ireland legal Quarterly* 293.

[72] FLA 1986, s. 44(1).

Fatima demonstrates the importance attached by the legislature and the judiciary to the place where the divorce is obtained. But, as North and Fawcett[73] point out, if the dissolution of the marriage is informal, "[this] is likely to be perceived by the lay man to be irrelevant".[74] A major defect in this decision is that it resulted in a limping marriage, the very thing the legislation had been designed to avoid. If the husband in this case had been advised, or had the financial means, to go to Pakistan to pronounce the *talaq*, the divorce would have been recognised in England, and to this extent it might be thought to be unjust in favouring the wealthier members of the UK's ethnic minority population over their rather more impecunious counterparts.

Shortly after the adoption of the 1986 Act,[75] a number of academics,[76] while criticising the implications of the *Fatima* decision, argued that it would not necessarily be followed in cases falling for consideration under this Act, on the basis that the latter is drafted in terms slightly different from its predecessor. Since section 46(1) of the 1986 Act states that a divorce obtained by means of proceedings must be effective in the country where it was obtained, without any express requirement that such proceedings must take place in that country, it has been argued that a divorce obtained under circumstances similar to those in *ex parte Fatima* ought now to be recognised, provided that the part of the proceedings which effected the divorce took place in that overseas country. Unfortunately, this very argument was unsuccessfully raised recently before Wall J in *Berkovits* v. *Grinberg*,[77] who was driven by the language of the Act to conclude that a divorce of this type would continue to be denied recognition in England.

The case concerned a Jewish *ghet* which had been written by the husband, an English domiciliary in London, in accordance with the formalities required by Jewish law, and delivered to the wife in Israel. The *ghet* was effective as a divorce in Israel, the country of the spouses' nationality. In 1992, the husband, who had been informed by the office of the Registrar-General that his divorce would not be recognised in England, sought an authorisation from Dayan Berkovits, a Jewish ecclesiastical judge, to remarry in a synagogue in accordance with Jewish law and as permitted under the English Marriage Act 1949. Berkovits, who had three other similar applications, applied to the English court for a declaration as to the husband's marital status. Wall J, while deciding that the criteria laid down in section 46(1) were met, in the sense that the divorce was

---

[73] North and Fawcett, *Cheshire and North's Private International Law* (London: Butterworths, 13th ed, 1999) pp. 800–2.

[74] *Ibid.*, at 801.

[75] Note that the Law Commission found the law in respect of transnational divorces satisfactory and recommended no changes: see Law Commission, *op cit.* n. 26, para. 6–11.

[76] See, for example, M. Pilkington, "Transnational Divorces Under the Family Law Act 1986" (1988) 37 *International and Comparative Law Quarterly* 130, pp. 132–6; J. Young, *op cit.* n. 9, at 87; and B. Berkovits, "Transnational Divorces: The *Fatima* Decision" (1988) 104 *Law Quarterly Review* 60, pp. 79–80.

[77] [1995] 1 FLR 477.

effective under the law of Israel and that at the relevant time the jurisdictional link required was satisfied, nonetheless thought that the question on which the outcome of this case hinged was whether the *ghet* could be classed as an overseas divorce. In his view, the answer to this question turned on whether or not *ex parte Fatima* remained good law in the light of the changes made by the 1986 Act. While accepting that the wording of this Act was different from that of the 1971 Act, he concluded that the result was not. Reviewing the process involved in a *ghet* divorce, he held that although it was difficult to think of policy reasons for denying recognition to such divorces, especially since the policy considerations underlying the decision in *ex parte Fatima* were themselves doubtful— because a rich applicant could avoid its effects by flying to Pakistan to pronounce the *talaq* while a poor applicant could not—found that the statute did not permit an interpretation which gave effect to the recognition of a transnational divorce. Such policy considerations, he stated, were properly a matter for Parliament and not for the courts.[78]

Following *Berkovits*, then, the current position on transnational extra-judicial divorces is that where the proceedings are initiated in one county but completed in another, the resulting divorce will not be recognised under section 46(1). This subsection applies only to divorces obtained by means of a single set of proceedings in a country outside the British Isles. I would argue that the implications of this decision may be reluctantly understandable when part of the divorce process takes place in England, in view of the provision of section 44 which denies recognition to all decrees obtained in the British Isles unless granted by courts of civil jurisdiction. However, it is undesirable and unsatisfactory, when the first part of the process takes place in one overseas country while the second takes place in another such country and the divorce is effective in both countries.[79] Suppose that, at the crucial time, a Pakistani married couple were habitually resident in Malaysia and the husband pronounced a *talaq* and notified the chairman of an administrative council in Pakistan (as required by the Pakistan Muslim Family Laws Ordinance 1961). In such a case, even though the divorce would be valid in both Malaysia and Pakistan, it would not be recognised in England under section 46(1) of the Act, simply because the divorce was not obtained in a single set of proceedings. Accordingly, if either party was later to become domiciled in this country, they would not be permitted to re-marry. Surely comity demands that, where possible, all overseas divorces should be recognised; and practicality suggests that we should be less hesitant in relation to divorces in respect of which there is no proof of possible injustices.

[78] He stated that "the question as to whether or not in an increasingly multi-racial and multi-ethnic society the refusal to recognise the transnational divorce can or should continue" was a matter for Parliament, *ibid.*, at 493–4.

[79] See also D. McClean, "The Non-Recognition of Transnational Divorces" (1996) 112 *Law Quarterly Review* 230; and A. Reed, "Extra-Judicial Divorces Since *Berkovits*" [1996] *Family Law* 100.

(2) *Overseas Divorces Obtained Otherwise than by way of Proceedings*

Section 46(2) of the 1986 Act limits the jurisdictional ground for the recognition of divorces obtained otherwise than by proceedings to domicile. In two broad circumstances, such divorces will be recognised in the UK. First, where the divorce is obtained and effective in the country of the common domicile of the parties, and secondly where either spouse is domiciled in that country, and the other is domiciled in a different country, but the divorce is effective in the country where it was obtained and valid in the other country.[80] Furthermore, section 46(2) lays down an anti-evasion criterion: the habitual residence of either party in the UK throughout one year immediately preceding the date on which the divorce was alleged to take place. Failure to satisfy this habitual residence requirement precludes the recognition of the divorce.[81] The purpose of this criterion is to prevent a spouse habitually resident in the UK from, for example, effecting a bare *talaq* in the country of his domicile, and then claiming that it should be entitled to recognition in England because the divorce is valid in the country of the other spouse's domicile.[82]

In one important respect, the jurisdictional basis of domicile in section 46(2) is narrower than that laid down in the 1971 Act: an overseas divorce which is obtained in a country where neither party is domiciled, albeit recognised either in the country of the parties' common domicile or the respective countries of their separate domiciles, and which would have been eligible for recognition under section 6(3) of the 1971 Act, can no longer be recognised under the 1986 Act.[83] There seems little basis for this change in the law and it is regrettable that it should have occurred.

(3) *Grounds for Non-recognition*

Even when an overseas divorce meets the requirements of section 44 or section 46 of the 1986 Act, it may still be denied recognition by virtue of one or more of the policy grounds set out in section 51 of the 1986 Act, all of which are discretionary. So far as is material, section 51 provides that recognition of an overseas divorce may be refused in three cases. First, where such recognition would be irreconcilable with an earlier court ruling that the marriage did not validly subsist.[84] Secondly, where the marriage would not attract recognition according to

---

[80] FLA 1986, s. 46(2). Domicile under this provision has two alternative meanings: that of English law or that of the foreign country in question.

[81] FLA 1986, s. 46(2)(c).

[82] Note that this prohibition does not operate in the context of extra-judicial divorces obtained by means of proceedings which are governed by section 46(1). So, habitual residence for longer than a year or even domicile in England cannot operate to prevent the recognition of such divorces.

[83] But note that a divorce of this type, obtained prior to the coming into force of Part II of the 1986 Act, will not be deprived of recognition: FLA 1986, s. 52(5)(b).

[84] *Ibid.*, s. 51(1).

English law.[85] Finally, where recognition would offend any one or more of four specified policy reasons.[86] In all there are six distinct grounds for refusal of recognition, but we are here only concerned with those grounds which betray ethnocentrism within the legislation.

Want of notice

Section 51(3)(a)(i) of the 1986 Act provides that an overseas divorce, obtained by judicial or other proceedings, may be denied recognition if it was obtained "without such steps having been taken for giving notice of the proceedings to a party to the marriage as, having regard to the nature of the proceedings and all the circumstances, should reasonably have been taken".

In order to determine whether recognition should be denied for want of notice, regard must be had to the nature of the proceedings and all the surrounding circumstances, and the question which must be addressed by the courts is one of reasonableness assessed in accordance with general principles of English law. In practice, problems arise mainly in deciding whether adequate notice has been given in cases dealing with extra-judicial divorces obtained by means of proceedings, such as *ghets* and Pakistani *talaqs*. Although the English courts clearly cannot require that such proceedings be of the same length and form as judicial proceedings, they might nonetheless consider whether it would be wrong in principle to recognise the divorce where insufficient effort to bring notice of the proceedings to the attention of the "aggrieved" party had been made. Compliance with the procedures required by Jewish *ghets* and Pakistani *talaqs* is likely to be regarded as affording adequate notice, so long as there is strict and full compliance with such procedures. But the English courts' insistence upon such compliance may in some cases be unwarrantably harsh. The point may again be illustrated by *D* v. *D*.[87] Unquestionably, the divorce in that case was one obtained by way of proceedings, albeit that there was extreme doubt as to its effectiveness under Ghanaian law.[88] Nonetheless, Wall J held *obiter* that even if the divorce had been effective under Ghanaian law—and therefore presumptively entitled to recognition under section 46(1)—the court might still exercise its discretion to deny recognition under section 51(3)(a)(i), since no reasonable steps had been taken to notify the wife of the proceedings. His Lordship accepted the argument that under Ghanaian law such proceedings depended on the participation of the families rather than the spouses, and that it was not necessary for either of them formally to be notified of the proceedings. Yet he still concluded that, as the wife's mother had voiced an objection to defending the case without her daughter being either present or notified, she

---

[85] *Ibid.*, s. 51(2).

[86] *Ibid.*, s. 51(3).

[87] [1994] 1 FLR 38.

[88] This doubt was based on the court's finding that if the matter were to be placed before the High Court of Ghana, the decision of the Tribunal would have been set aside on the ground that both sides had not been heard in a judicial manner. See the earlier discussion on FLA 1986, 46(1).

could not be regarded as a valid participant. Accordingly, since the wife had had no actual knowledge of the proceedings, coupled with the fact that the mother was not a proxy defendant, the divorce would have been denied recognition for want of proper notice of the proceedings, in any event.

In addition, it appears that recognition may also be denied for want of notice, notwithstanding that the local rules were complied with in all respects. As Balcombe J has stated,[89] "it cannot be sufficient merely to comply with local procedure, otherwise the provisions of the Act would be nugatory".[90] The local procedure itself may seem to the court to be unreasonable or contrary to natural justice.[91] While the availability of this discretionary ground to deny recognition may be legitimate, its actual *application* by the courts appears to have unnecessarily introduced "a further threshold requirement to the recognition of overseas decrees".[92] Assuming that the divorce was effective in the country where it was obtained, what useful purpose would be served if recognition was to be denied in the UK? Clearly, where the marriage has broken down irretrievably and neither spouse wishes to remain married to the other, the court's reluctance to afford recognition would not only create a limping marriage, but also prejudice the aggrieved party in terms of financial relief.[93]

Official documentation

By virtue of section 51(3)(b), an extra-judicial divorce, obtained otherwise than by way of proceedings, may be denied recognition for the non-availability of an official document certifying its effectiveness under the law of the country in which it was obtained. And where either spouse was domiciled in another country, recognition may be denied in the absence of an additional document certifying the validity of the decree under the law of that other country. As such, where an overseas divorce of this type satisfies the jurisdictional basis of domicile laid down in section 46(2) and is effective in the relevant country, it may still be denied recognition on the ground of the absence of the requisite "official document". Section 51(4) defines "official document" as one issued by a person or body appointed or recognised for that purpose under the relevant law. This requirement was neither discussed nor recommended by the Law Commission. While it is clear that it serves an evidential purpose, it is difficult to understand the policy considerations behind it. Of necessity, non-proceedings divorces will appear informal by comparison with judicial or other proceedings divorces. Yet if the government—presumably motivated by a sense of comity—accept *in principle* the notion of recognising such informal divorces, why should they at one stroke be capable of recognition despite their informality, but confer, at the

[89] *Sabbagh* v. *Sabbagh* [1985] FLR 29.
[90] *Ibid.*, at 33.
[91] See *Ingra* v. *Ingra* [1951] P 404; *Wood* v. *Wood* [1957] P 254, 296; *Hornett* v. *Hornett* [1971] P 255.
[92] See J. Murphy, *op cit.* n. 37, 44–9.
[93] *Ibid.*

same time, a discretion upon the courts to refuse their recognition simply because of the absence of formality (in the form of official documentation)? It makes no discernible sense.

Public policy

According to section 51(3)(c), any overseas divorce may be refused recognition in the UK if its recognition would be "manifestly contrary to public policy". Since both the common law and the 1971 Act had encompassed a similar discretionary basis for denying recognition on public policy grounds, the pre-1986 case-law remains instructive and influential to present-day courts. It should be emphasised that the word "manifestly" in section 51(3)(c) was included so that the courts would refuse recognition only sparingly. In so doing, the Act merely reaffirms the attitude taken at common law.[94] As Wood J explained in *Sharif* v. *Sharif*:[95] "English courts had always reserved to themselves a residual discretion whether or not to recognise foreign decrees. The principles of common law as they affected the residual discretion [were] unaffected by the provisions of the 1971 Act".[96]

The operation of public policy can best be illustrated by *Kendall* v. *Kendall*,[97] which appears to be the only reported case in which an overseas divorce was refused recognition solely on the ground of public policy. In this case, both spouses lived in Bolivia when in June 1974 the wife decided to return to Cyprus with their children for reasons connected with their education. Before leaving Bolivia, she signed certain documents at the husband's request which, he stated, related to the removal of the children from Bolivia. The documents were in Spanish, a language the wife hardly spoke. She never contemplated divorce, nor did the husband ever mention it. In 1975, the Bolivian Family Court pronounced a decree which purported to dissolve the marriage, and on the face of which, she appeared to be the petitioner. The decree also contained other falsehoods: *viz*, that there were no children to the marriage; that the wife worked; that neither spouse owned property. As it transpired, the documents that the wife signed were a power of attorney enabling the Bolivian court to grant the divorce without her being present. Consequently, she sought a declaration from the English court that the divorce was invalid and should, therefore, be denied recognition under the relevant provision of the 1971 Act. Since the wife was the apparent

---

[94] North and Fawcett: *op cit.* n. 73, p. 816; see also the view of Dicey and Morris, *op cit.* n. 34, who argue (at 757) that although the 1986 Act appears to have abolished the common law residual discretion to refuse recognition to decrees which offended the judges' sense of justice, and that such decrees could only now be refused recognition on public policy grounds, the difference in the language may be rather more illusory than real. For discussion on the application of this residual discretion, see P. Carter, "Rejection of Foreign Law: Some Private International Law Inhibitions" (1984) 55 *British Yearbook of International Law* 111, pp. 126–31; and P. Smart, "Public Policy in the Conflict of Laws" (1983) 99 *Law Quarterly Review* 24.

[95] [1980] *Fam Law* 216.

[96] *Ibid.*, at 217–18.

[97] [1977] 3 All ER 471.

petitioner in the Bolivian proceedings, the divorce could not be denied recognition for want of notice, for only respondents could avail themselves of that exception. Nevertheless, Hollins J exercised his discretion in favour of denying recognition on the ground that the decree was manifestly contrary to public policy. Emphasising the principles of comity—that is, observing and accepting decisions of foreign courts in so far as they do not cause injustice—he concluded that the fact that the Bolivian court had clearly been deceived, and that if it had been aware of such deception it would itself have invalidated the decree, rendered the divorce manifestly contrary to public policy.

Issues relating to public policy are particularly problematic in the context of the recognition of extra-judicial divorces. It has been suggested that the ground of public policy might be invoked in cases of *talaq* divorces, obtained by means of proceedings, where the husband travels to, and obtains the divorce in, the country of his nationality in an attempt to avoid the financial consequences attached to a divorce obtained in the UK.[98] Since the enactment of Part III of the Matrimonial and Family Proceedings Act 1984, which empowers English courts to grant financial relief following the recognition of an overseas decree obtained by way of proceedings, the circumstances in which such a ground may be invoked should now be rare. However, previous case-law is not encouraging. In *Zaal* v. *Zaal*,[99] Bush J denied recognition to a *talaq* pronounced in Dubai, even though the wife was reasonably secured financially. He stated:

> I have come to the conclusion on the restricted ground that what was done, though properly done according to the husband's own customary laws, was done in secrecy so far as the wife was concerned, The first this wife knew of it the deed was done and she was divorced in fact and in law and it was irrecoverable and binding according to the law of the husband's state . . . Common justice requires that some notice other than a casual threat ought to be given for so solemn a proceedings. It is this that in this case offends one's sense of justice and jars upon the conscience.[100]

Fortunately, the Scottish courts appear to adopt the correct approach. In the recent case of *Tahir* v. *Tahir*,[101] it was held that following the enactment of Part III of the 1984 Act, there could no longer be a public policy objection to the recognition of an overseas divorce obtained by way of proceedings based on the deprivation of the respondent's rights to claim financial provision. It is hoped that English courts will follow suit.

IV CONCLUSIONS

There is no denying that attitudes towards the recognition of foreign divorces in England have undergone major development. However, as the law has

[98] See *Chaudhary* v. *Chaudhary* [1985] FLR 476; and *Quazi* v. *Quazi* [1980] AC 744, 782–3 *per*Wood J.
[99] [1983] 4 FLR 284.
[100] *Ibid.*, at 289.
[101] 1993, SLT 194.

developed, it has widened the gap between divorces pronounced by a court of civil jurisdiction in the British Isles and overseas divorces.[102] While those within the former category enjoy virtually automatic recognition, those within the latter remain subject to a number of requirements which must be satisfied before recognition is allowed. Furthermore, the recognition rules applicable to overseas divorces continue to employ a troublesome distinction between divorces obtained by means of proceedings and those obtained otherwise.[103] This marks a significant departure from the common law rules, and its impact is acutely apparent in respect of extra-judicial divorces.[104] As Smart has argued, this area of the law would be placed on a more logical, as well as a fairer, foundation if the requirement of proceedings was deleted from the legislation.[105] It will also affirm the approach advocated by the Law Commission that "our courts recognise any divorce, whatever the form, methods or grounds, provided that the court in the State of origin has jurisdiction in our eyes. It would be a retrograde step to resile from this".[106]

Perhaps the single most important issue to require attention is the unsatisfactory judicial treatment of transnational divorces, the majority of which are of scriptural divine authority that must be respected by members of the same sect wherever they are. The restrictive decisions in *Fatima* and *Berkovits* have serious consequences which are socially damaging to the parties: as well as having created limping marriages, they appear biased in favour of those wealthy enough to be able to travel to the foreign country in question to pronounce the *talaq* or deliver the *ghet* to the wife. More importantly, a party to a limping marriage has to bear the uncertainty surrounding his or her status; it may disturb a relationship entered into in reliance on the validity of the divorce; it may cause problems in connection with immigration, inheritance, legitimacy, and tax-related issues. It is, thus, self-evident that the recognition rules, at least in this respect, have not achieved the required compromise: "the evils of a limping marriage are far greater than those resulting from the recognition of a broken down marriage (which, presumably, the wife entered into being fully aware of her husband's customs and religion)".[107]

---

[102] This gap will have even wider implications once the Brussels II Convention on Jurisdiction and the Recognition and Enforcement of Judgments in Matrimonial Matters 1998 comes into force. Pursuant to Article 14 thereof, a matrimonial judgment obtained in an EC Member State is automatically recognised in the other Member States. By virtue of Article 13, "judgment" means, *inter alia*, a divorce, legal separation or annulment pronounced by a court of a Member State.

[103] See D. McClean, *op cit.* n. 10, p. 191; M. Pilkington, *op cit.* n. 76, 132–6; J. Young, *op cit.* n. 9, at 87; and B. Berkovits, "Transnational divorces: The *Fatima* Decision" (1988) 104 *Law Quarterly Review* 60, 79–80.

[104] This is because whenever an overseas divorce is obtained in a foreign court, this will invariably have involved proceedings. See S. Poulter, *op cit.* n. 4, pp. 110–23.

[105] P. Smart, *op cit.* n. 45, at 397; see also J. Young, *op cit.* n. 9.

[106] Law Commission, *op cit.* n. 17, para.18

[107] D. Gordon, "Extra-Judicial Divorces Revisited—A Radical Approach" (1986) 37 *Northern Ireland Legal Quarterly* 151, 165–6. See also A. Reed, *op cit.* n. 79.

With similarly objectionable consequences, the legislative inconsistency in respect of the discretionary grounds for refusing recognition to certain overseas divorces call, also, for radical revision if not wholesale removal from the statute book. As things stand, the legislation bears all too often deep shades of unwarrantable ethnocentrism.

5

The Discretionary Refusal of Recognition of Foreign Marriages

JOHN MURPHY*

I INTRODUCTION

THIS ESSAY attempts to unpick and evaluate the bases on which the English courts exercise their discretion to refuse to recognise foreign marriages[1] whose *formal validity*[2] is beyond question and whose *essential validity*[3] is probably also satisfied.[4] It has been widely stated that this discretionary veto is to be wielded in accordance with the dictates of "public policy". As far back as 1945, Lord Greene MR said that such matters were to be resolved "with due regard to common sense and *some attention to reasonable policy*".[5] Nearly forty years later, Lord Simon, similarly minded and speaking in the House of Lords, was a good deal more emphatic. He said: "[t]here is abundant authority that an

---

* University of Manchester. This essay is based on an earlier article published in the *ICLQ*. It has benefited from comments made upon it by my colleagues Margot Brazier and David Booton.

[1] I use the term "foreign marriages" to depict marriages that take place outside the United Kingdom and involve at least one foreign domiciliary. I deliberately exclude, for reasons that will become obvious, marriages abroad involving two English domiciliaries even if they are both members of ethnic minority groups.

[2] Formal validity is determined unerringly by reference to the *lex loci celebrationis*: see, e.g., *Berthiaume* v. *Dastous* [1930] AC 79; *Ogden* v. *Ogden* [1908] P 46; *Simonin* v. *Mallac* (1860) 2 Sw & Tr 67.

[3] The essential validity of marriage concerns the capacity of each of the parties both to marry in general terms, and their capacity to marry one another.

[4] Doubts as to essential validity may always be raised because the test for essential validity is uncertain and tends to fluctuate between the (most prominent) "dual domicile test"—which amounts to a presumption against recognition unless both parties had capacity according to the law of their pre-nuptial domicile—and the rival "intended matrimonial home test" which stipulates that a single law should govern capacity: the law of the country in which the parties intend to establish their matrimonial home. For academic discussion of these (and other less well supported tests) see R. Fentiman, "The Validity of Marriage and the Proper Law" [1985] *Cambridge Law Journal* 256; A.J.E. Jaffey, "The Essential Validity of Marriage in the English Conflict of Laws" (1978) 41 *Modern Law Review* 38. See also Law Commission Working Paper No. 89, *Private International Law: Choice of Law Rules in Marriage* (London: HMSO, 1985).

[5] [1946] P 122, 129 (emphasis added). Approved and re-stated by Lord Parker CJ in *Alhaji Mohamed* v. *Knott* [1969] 1 QB 1, 13.

English court will decline to recognise or apply what would otherwise be the appropriate foreign rule of law when to do so would be against English public policy".[6] Perhaps surprisingly, this policy-based discretionary veto has commanded virtually no academic attention.[7] It is my intention to address that anomaly. It is wholly inadequate, as is sometimes done, both by the courts (as we have seen) and academics, simply to refer glibly to "public policy" as though its contents were somehow self-evident and its meaning plain.[8] It is also signally unenlightening merely to state, as Jaffey has done, that "[t]he premise should be that an invalidating rule of a domestic system, whether English or foreign, should only be applied to a given international marriage if there is a *good reason* for its application".[9] So doing merely recasts one nebulous term, "public policy", as another, "a good reason". Judicial synonyms have been scarcely any more illuminating. Take for example Lord Simon's famous enjoinder to have recourse to "common sense, good manners and a reasonable degree of tolerance".[10] A number of familiar criticisms can be made of the opacity of such broad terms as "common sense", "good manners" and "a reasonable degree of tolerance": they deny the common law the clarity, consistency and objectivity that are frequently (and correctly, in my view) thought to be necessary in order to legitimate and constrain the adjudicative function.[11] But beyond these objections, two further, more particular criticisms can be made in respect of the invocation of "public policy" to deny recognition to "offensive" foreign marriages.

The first of these criticisms centres on the capacity for the mask of "public policy" to be seen as judicial cultural imperialism rather than as adherence to some widely accepted social value or norm.[12] The second is that, in any event, the compendious term "public policy" conceals a series of particular concerns, only some of which are relevant to the adjudicative process, depending on context. For example, to present the denial of recognition to a bigamous marriage simply in terms of "public policy" disguises the fact that it is the preservation of the institution of monogamy within the country of recognition that is at stake in

---

[6] *Vervaeke* v. *Smith* [1983] 1 AC 145, 164. For other instances of judges acknowledging the role of "public policy" in this context see *Russ* v. *Russ* [1964] P 315, 327–8 (*per* Willmer LJ); *Cheni* v. *Cheni* [1965] P 65, 97g (*per* Simon P).

[7] It seems to have been accepted but not rigorously examined by a number of writers. See, e.g., A.J.E. Jaffey, *op cit*. n. 4, at 50; S. Poulter, *English Law and Ethnic Minority Customs* (London: Butterworths, 1986) p. 21; P.M. North and J.J. Fawcett, *Cheshire and North's Private International Law* (London: Butterworth's, 1992) p. 626 and J. O'Brien, *Smith's Conflict of Laws* (London: Cavendish, 1999) p. 462.

[8] See, e.g., S. Poulter, *loc cit*, ch. 3; A.J.E. Jaffey, *loc cit*, at 49–50.

[9] A.J.E. Jaffey, *op cit*. n. 4, at 38 (emphasis added).

[10] *Cheni* v. *Cheni* [1965] P 65, 99.

[11] See, e.g., L. Fuller, "The Forms and Limits of Adjudication" (1978) 92 *Harvard Law Review* 353, at 369; N. Duxbury, "Faith in Reason: The Process Tradition in American Jurisprudence" (1993) 15 *Cardozo Law Review* 601, at 610–32 and also the wealth of literature referenced therein.

[12] The recognition of foreign marriages is an arena particularly susceptible to accusations of cultural imperialism because of the wide diversity of religious and cultural traditions discernible among Britain's ethnic communities.

such cases.[13] Similarly, in the context of forced and arranged marriages it is the potential for the absence of consent to the marriage that vexes the court rather than some vague, ill-defined "policy" consideration. As Cumming-Bruce J cautioned in *Radwan* v. *Radwan (No 2)*:[14]

> [I]t is an over-simplification of the common law to assume that the same test . . . applies to every kind of incapacity—non-age, affinity, prohibition of monogamous contract by virtue of an existing spouse, and capacity for polygamy. Different public and social factors are relevant to each of these.[15]

In view of this, in part IV of this essay, I shall attempt to disinter the kinds of policy concern that arise in connection with only one type of problematic marriage: child marriage. Similar analysis could, of course, be applied to other controversial marriage types such as, non-monogamous marriages,[16] marriages involving a transfer of money or property—such as bridewealth—in consideration of a betrothal and, as we have already seen, non-consensual marriages.[17] But the point of this essay is not to provide a blue-print for the resolution of all conceivable hard cases concerning the recognition of foreign marriages. The moderate amount of imagination that I possess coupled with the limitations of space both preclude such an endeavour.

Returning to the question of child marriages, once I have identified the various policy concerns that the litigants may seek to raise in seeking recognition,[18] I shall explore the weight that ought to be attached to each one. But first I should explain in greater depth the way in which the invocation of "public policy" can be perceived as culturally imperialistic.

---

[13] See further on this S. Poulter, "*Hyde* v. *Hyde*: A Re-appraisal" (1976) 25 *International and Comparative Law Quarterly* 475.

[14] [1972] 3 All ER 1026.

[15] *Ibid.*, at 1037.

[16] I use this term to avoid distinguishing between bigamous marriages, potentially polygamous marriages and actually polygamous marriages, the technical differences between which are unnecessary for present purposes. But for those interested, see S. Poulter, *op cit.* n. 13.

[17] In the present context, these include chiefly forced and (to a lesser extent) arranged marriages.

[18] Underlying this whole field there are a multiplicity of broader political issues. One such issue, for example, is whether recognition might be refused as part of the general failure to recognise a foreign state and all its domestic laws (see, e.g., the British refusal of foreign divorce decrees obtained from Rhodesia following the Universal Declaration of Independence in 1965: *Adams* v. *Adams* [1970] 3 All ER 572). Another such essentially political question surrounding this area of law is whether the rules governing the recognition of foreign marriages ought to be left to Parliament rather than the courts on the basis that the political process is more likely to produce a satisfactory solution to the problem of culture clashes. This has been the Australian approach in Part VA of the Marriage Act 1961. For analysis, see M. Neave, "The New Rules on Recognition of Foreign Marriages—Insomnia for Lawyers" (1990) 4 *Australian Journal of Family Law* 190; P.E. Nygh, *Conflict of Laws in Australia* (Sydney: Butterworths, 1995) pp. 375–89; E.I. Sykes and M.C. Pryles, *Australian Private International Law* (Sydney: Law Book Co. Ltd, 1991) pp. 444–50. Other examples of political issues that surround the recognition of foreign marriages can be found in Law Commission Working Paper No. 89, *op cit.* n. 4.

II.   PUBLIC POLICY AND CULTURAL IMPERIALISM

To suggest that "public policy" can adequately resolve questions concerning the validity of foreign marriages is arguably implicitly to suggest that there is some obvious and universal, yet unstated, notion "public policy", and further that it represents some sort of accepted, dominant ideology. This need not necessarily be the case. As Freeman has pithily pointed out elsewhere in this collection, "[o]ften an examination will reveal that the so-called dominant understanding is in reality the understanding of the dominant".[19] In a pluralistic society such as Britain's—especially when confronted with a question that tests the very nature and extent of that pluralism—any assumption that there exists any such universal ideology is without foundation. Only to some of Britain's population would, say, proxy marriages[20] be unconscionable.[21] To a significant minority, such marriages would be perfectly acceptable (as would polygamous and arranged marriages). There would certainly be no universal sense of impropriety or repugnance. As Lord Merriman P recognised in *Apt* v. *Apt*,[22] there is no single problem of general unconscionability associated with proxy marriages. At a purely pragmatic level, some may be inflamed because of a suspicion that the marriage was contracted purely as a mechanism to circumvent English immigration laws.[23] Others, less concerned with the immigration implications, may instead recoil at the absence of solemnity and sense of occasion that is often absent in proxy marriages.[24] Accordingly, as Lord Merriman pointedly remarked:

> the problem should be sub-divided into categories and the test of public policy be applied, if at all, to each category separately . . . I do not think it is necessary to pursue this topic further than to say that I am not satisfied that a single test of public policy can be applied to all proxy marriages indiscriminately.[25]

Of course, one might respond that the judges have recourse to obscurities such as "public policy" *precisely because* there would otherwise be profound disagreement over the appropriate basis for the denial of recognition. For example,

---

[19] Ch. 1. See also M. Loughlin, *Sword and Scales: An Introduction to Law & Politics* (Oxford: Hart Publishing, 2000) *passim*.

[20] That is, a marriage at which one or both parties was not present. See, e.g., *McCabe* v. *McCabe* [1994] 1 FLR 410 (discussed in J. Murphy, "The Recognition of Overseas Marriages and Divorces in the United Kingdom" (1996) 47 *Northern Ireland Legal Quarterly* 35).

[21] At one point in his famous judgment in *Cheni* v. *Cheni*, Simon P recast "public policy" in terms of unconscionability. He said: "[t]he courts of this country will exceptionally refuse to recognise [a marriage] . . . on the ground that to give it recognition and effect would be unconscionable in the circumstances": [1965] P 85, 98. See also Lord Parker CJ's equally crepuscular re-formulation in terms of "repugnance" occasioned to "decent-minded men or women": *Alhaji Mohamed* v. *Knott*, *supra* n. 5, at 15.

[22] [1947] P 127.

[23] See further F.O. Shyllon, "Immigration and the Criminal Courts" (1971) 34 *Modern Law Review* 135, esp. at 136–8.

[24] See, e.g., *McCabe* v. *McCabe* [1994] 1 FLR 410.

[25] [1947] P 127, 141.

Judge X may consider immigration concerns to be the crux of the case. She may also see such concerns to be a matter of public policy and, hence, be happy that "public policy" should be stated as the basis for a refusal of recognition. Judge Y may feel precisely the same way about the preservation of the institution of monogamy. Accordingly, the two judges can agree to refuse recognition on the basis of "public policy" although the policy concern that propels each of them towards their decision is different from the other. Sunstein has captured the point thus:

> [L]egal systems tend to adopt a special strategy for producing stability and agreement in the midst of social disagreement and pluralism: arbiters of legal controversies try to produce *incompletely theorized agreements* . . . [for] [t]hey are an important source of social stability and an important way for people to demonstrate mutual respect, in law especially but also in liberal democracy as a whole.[26]

In advocating recourse to incomplete theorization, Sunstein suggests that decision makers (including judges in multimember courts) should produce decisions on the basis of agreement over certain issues upon which consensus can be reached without supplying a grand, fully-articulated account of an over-arching background theory. As he contends, "incompletely theorized agreements are well-suited to a world—and especially a legal world—containing social dissensus on large-scale issues".[27] The decision—or agreement, to use Sunstein's word—"is incompletely theorized in the sense that it is *incompletely specified*".[28] The perceived virtue of such incompletely theorized decision making, especially in pluralistic societies,[29] is that "judges on multimember bodies . . . [can] find commonality and thus a common way of life without producing unnecessary antagonism" because "low-level principles[30] make it unnecessary to reach areas in which disagreement is fundamental".[31] He claims further that this allows mutual respect among differently minded society members to flourish, and that "judges, perhaps even more than ordinary people, should not challenge a litigant's or even another person's, *most defining commitments*".[32]

Yet silence on what for the litigant is a crucial and deeply held conviction can, on reflection, be perceived as insult rather than respect. To ignore the depth of the litigants' conviction on a particular matter in favour of some "low-level principle" about which each of the (English) judges on the multimember tribunal can agree may be seen by the litigants as utter disrespect for a core social

---

[26] C. Sunstein, *Legal Reasoning and Political Conflict* (New York: Oxford University Press, 1996) pp. 4–5 (emphasis added).

[27] *Ibid.*, at 39.

[28] *Ibid.*, at 35 (emphasis added).

[29] *Ibid.*, at 47.

[30] Sunstein states that commonality is reached at low levels of abstraction but it is more plausible that agreement is easier to reach at higher levels of abstraction: see N. Duxbury, "Ambition and Adjudication" (1997) 47 *University of Toronto Law Review* 161, at 166–7.

[31] C. Sunstein, *op cit.* n. 26, p. 39 (emphasis added).

[32] *Ibid.*, at 40 (emphasis added). The importance of highly-valued commitments to rational decision making are discussed below.

or cultural value that they hold. Take as an example one of the many African societies in which polygamous marriages are not only permitted, but in fact highly valued. This high regard for such marriages often stems not only from the socio-economic advantages that they can provide for the husband concerned, but also from the fact that they help to define his community standing and prestige.[33] Now suppose that in the Court of Appeal each of the three Lord Justices of Appeal called upon to decide the validity of a polygamous marriage has a different view about the morality of polygamous marriages generally. Suppose also that, on the facts, they can all agree that the marriage was, among other things, an attempt to circumvent restrictive immigration laws. They may then deny recognition to the marriage purely on the ground that it was contrary to public policy (as deduced from the relevant provisions of the immigration legislation). In eschewing any discussion of the defining qualities, or morality, of polygamous marriages, the judges may therefore expose themselves to the criticism that they treated such features of the case as "not even worth talking about". In other words, deliberate silence on the inherent values of polygamy (as they are perceived by the litigants) may appear tantamount to treating those values as "non-issues".[34] And to treat such deeply held convictions as non-issues may be argued to be culturally imperialistic. For the decision is reached only by reference to a value or norm prevalent among those in the cultural majority.

But let us be clear. The problem does *not* lie with the prioritisation of English cultural value X over foreign cultural value Y, since value Y is never even acknowledged to be a value in the first place. It is the failure to take cognisance of value Y and to acknowledge that it is a value at all that is the source of the *putative* offence. The emphasis in the last sentence is warranted because I am not suggesting that there will necessarily be any such cultural imperialism. Nor am I arguing that, whatever else is at stake, foreign cultural values should always play a part in judicial decisions. I am merely saying that non-explicit references to "public policy", or references to certain (but not all) of the cultural values at stake in hard cases, can be seen as derogatory. Implicit in this is the suggestion that regardless of whether there is consensus over any particular (foreign) cultural value, there is no need to dismiss that value cursorily. Often, as I shall argue below, it may harmlessly be acknowledged without it having to play any part in the formulation of the judge's final decision. A note of caution must, however, be sounded here: this suggestion must be distinguished from the assertion that, in all hard cases, the worth of (supposedly) dominant cultural value X should be compared with, and weighed against, that of minority cultural value Y. Such comparisons may often prove to be impossible. I suggest only—no more

[33] See, e.g., E. Hillman, *Polygamy Reconsidered* (New York: Orbis Books, 1975). For Muslims, for example, polygamy is only acceptable subject to the proviso that the man is able to provide adequately and equally for all his wives: see S. Poulter, *op cit*. n. 7, pp. 44–5. As such, the greater the number of wives, the greater the social statement about the husband's personal wealth.

[34] Sunstein views such silence in "constructive terms". His claim is that it can "help minimize conflict, allow the present to learn from the future, and save a great deal of time and expense": C. Sunstein, *op cit*. n. 26, p. 39.

and no less—that, as a minimum, explicit acknowledgement of (minority) cultural value Y ought to be provided if the decision is to *appear* both rational and non-ethnocentric.

But the foregoing begs the question: "why is *mere acknowledgement* of a minority cultural value any less derogatory than no acknowledgement at all?". After all, in both instances the minority cultural value plays no part in the formulation of the judge's decision. I address this issue in the next section of this essay.

III CULTURAL VALUES: REASONS AND NON-REASONS

Apart from its capacity to engender suspicions of cultural imperialism, the failure to acknowledge certain cultural values may lead to inadequate decision making in at least three ways. First, where value Y can and ought to be weighed against value X—even if, ultimately, value X were to hold sway—any decision based purely on the basis of consideration of value X might legitimately be condemned as irrational. The irrationality of a decision taken without due consideration of a pertinent factor is the very stuff of a significant body of administrative law.[35] Secondly—again where values X and Y ought to be weighed against one another—any decision taken without such a comparison being made will necessarily fail to reveal the extent of the decision maker's commitment to value X (the value that we will assume prevails).[36] Such a failure means, in turn, that future hard cases are rendered unnecessarily difficult to resolve because the reasons for, and the level of commitment to, value X were never made clear in the initial case.[37] Thirdly, in cases where values X and Y are incommensurable, it may only be by acknowledging that Y *is* only a background factor, and one that ought not to feature in the formulation of the final decision that a decision maker may become aware of the depth of his or her commitment to value X and, hence, the problem of incommensurability. The value in identifying the level of one's commitment to value X—especially where this commitment is absolute—is again that it helps remove the prospect of unnecessary future litigation.

What I shall attempt to do in the next section is to supply an example of the way in which I consider that the adjudicative function ought to be exercised in the context of foreign marriages that might be refused recognition despite their

[35] See Taylor, "Judicial Review: Improper Purposes and Irrelevant Considerations" [1976] *Cambridge Law Journal* 272.

[36] Deciding on the basis that "X is preferable to Y" compels the decision maker to question the depth of his or her commitment to X. In cases where only X is acknowledged to be stake, no such evaluation is necessary.

[37] The fact that I consider balancing exercises of this kind to be a vital part of the adjudicative process should not be seen as an attachment to Dworkian principle-based decision making. I am as happy for the decision maker to take account of policy considerations as principles, not least because, ultimately, the distinction between the two is unsustainable see, e.g., S. Fish, *Doing What Comes Naturally: Change, Rhetoric and the Practice of Theory in Literary and Legal Studies* (Oxford: Clarendon Press, 1989) pp. 369–70.

formal and essential validity. As indicated earlier, this example will involve the
hypothetical case of a child marriage. The purpose of this hypothetical is to
unearth the several policy considerations that would be likely to be raised by the
litigants in the case. I shall also endeavour to ascribe to each the status "commitment", "reason" or "non-reason". But before doing so, I must explain what
I mean by these terms.

It is often assumed (or, at least, seldom questioned) that the key to this particular branch of English conflicts law is "a proper balance" of "practicality,
commonsense, individual liberty, religious tolerance and the promotion of
racial harmony".[38] This list of considerations commands wide appeal, for it
appears to be an enumeration of precisely the kinds of "reasons" that most lib-
ertarian lawyers would consider relevant to deciding whether to afford or deny
recognition to a foreign marriage. In other words, these considerations can be
invoked to form all or part of the basis for a legal decision. But what seems to
go unquestioned is whether, on occasion, certain of these considerations are
legally irrelevant; whether, in other words, they may sometimes be *non-reasons*.
The point is this: if a consideration is, in legal terms, irrelevant to a decision, it
is a non-reason. It follows that if that consideration ultimately persuades the
judge in reaching his or her decision, that decision must, of necessity, be an irrational one. Again, this is this stuff of much administrative law.[39]

An example perhaps illustrates the point more clearly. Take the case of
arranged marriages. In Western societies the institution of marriage centres on
notions of love, compatibility and individual choice. Thus, the multilateral
Convention on Consent to Marriage (overwhelmingly ratified by Western
states) provides that:

> No marriage shall be legally entered into without the full and free consent of both par-
> ties, such consent to be expressed by them in person after due publicity and in the pres-
> ence of the authority competent to solemnise the marriage and of witnesses.[40]

Underpinning this provision is clearly a deep-seated respect both for human
individuality and for the highly cherished value of autonomous choice. By contrast, according to some African and Asian traditions and religions—notably
Sikhism and Islam—arranged marriages are regarded as perfectly acceptable.
This is largely because they are sanctioned and affirmed by patriarchal religious
doctrines. In Sikhism, for example, the subservience of women, and their
inequality within a marriage are justified by reference to the religious rewards
she is due to receive for her compliance. As Sharan-Jeet Shan explains in her
autobiography:

[38] See, e.g., S. Poulter, *op cit.* n. 7, p. *v.*
[39] For reported examples see *R* v. *Birmingham Licensing Planning Committee, ex p Kennedy*
[1972] 2 QB 140 and *Pilling* v. *Abergele UDC* [1950] 1 KB 636.
[40] Art. 1(1). Recall also that Art. 12 of the European Convention on Human Rights and
Fundamental Freedoms confers an equal right to "marry and found a family" upon all "men and
women of marriageable age".

A married woman must aspire to be a *pativarta istry* (one who worships her husband as God). In so doing she must observe *laaj* and *sharam* (chastity and honour). She must never raise her voice against her husband. His judgement in all decisions is superior . . . such an irreproachable wife secures a place in heaven for herself and her husband.[41]

Even beyond religious affirmation, some South Asian cultures make family honour, *Izzat*, depend in large part on arranged marriages. That is, such marriages can be of instrumental worth in a way that could not be guaranteed by consensual marriages. As Ballard's research reveals: "*Izzat* can be increased by overshadowing other families . . . [and by] contracting prestigious marriage alliances".[42] As such, simply to maintain this honour, or *Izzat*, "a family must send its daughters in marriage to families of equal status" and "[t]o enhance its *Izzat*, it must do better".[43]

On the one hand—always assuming the formal and essential validity of any particular arranged marriage—the court may be minded to afford recognition if each party's religious beliefs or cultural values accommodated such unions. On the other hand, the court may equally be "offended" if it found the marriage to be non-consensual in nature. It would be tempting to think that the judge could balance the potential offence to the court against the cultural tolerance that would point towards recognition of such a marriage. But in truth, it would be attempting the impossible. How, after all, does one compare the religious and cultural values that justify arranged marriages in parts of Africa and Asia with the wholly different cultural values that permeate Western thinking?[44] No judge brought up within one value-system is in a position to evaluate meaningfully the significance or centrality of doctrines and practices of another value system. It would therefore be irrational to suggest that one could reach a decision on the strength of a comparison between the two. What the judge must do in such a case, it is submitted, is identify *a commitment* to the value of personal freedom and, on this basis, exclude any evaluation of the relative merits of the foreign cultural tradition.[45]

In the context of the discretionary non-recognition of foreign marriages, many of the considerations that *might* be taken into account are, in truth,

---

[41] S. Shan, *In My Own Name* (London: The Women's Press Ltd, 1985) p. 24.

[42] C. Ballard, "Arranged Marriages in the British Context" [1978] *New Community* 181, at 184.

[43] *Loc cit.*

[44] As Catherine Ballard comments, "[t]here is an obvious contradiction between the South Asia view of marriage as a *contract between two families* which should be arranged by parents on their children's behalf, and the contemporary Western ideal that an intimate personal relationship should exist between a couple before *they* make a decision to marry: *ibid.*, at 181 (emphasis added).

[45] I am not suggesting here that all arranged marriages should be denied recognition. They are not all *ipso facto* non-consensual. Often, *both* spouses will accept the practice (albeit with some trepidation) because of their own commitment to the religious or cultural premise for such marriages. Rather, all that I am saying is that, where one spouse contests the validity of the marriage upon entry into this country, the court may legitimately exercise its discretion to deny recognition on the basis of a commitment to consensual marriages, regardless of the protestations of the other spouse.

incommensurable with one another. The cultural values—both domestic and foreign—that are ostensibly in binary opposition have intrinsic rather than instrumental worth and are therefore impossible to compare.[46] As such, any decision reached on the basis of *supposed* comparison must be irrational. It would be premised on a claim to have achieved the impossible.

What I suggest, then, is that such decisions take cognisance of the following three important things. To begin with, I reject (for the reasons given in Part II) Sunstein's notion of a "constructive use of silence" in this context, and require, as a minimum, that there be explicit *acknowledgement* of the diverse competing cultural values at stake in any particular case. Secondly, I suggest that the judges must also take note of the frequent incommensurability of these values. Finally, I consider it vital where incommensurabilities arise to decide those cases in terms of commitments and non-comparative exclusions of non-reasons. It is only by making such explicit exclusion of (legal) irrelevancies that decision making remains rational.

To be clear, what I have said so far should not be seen as the "be all and end all" of suitable decision making in this area. Naturally, in addition to what I have so far suggested, I consider, too, that a firm judicial commitment to cultural pluralism—which is necessarily guaranteed by what I have argued for[47]— to be critical. It is simply that I have not been centrally concerned with elucidating the preconditions for, and virtues of, such pluralism.[48] I have attempted *only* to make the case for the explicit acknowledgement of cultural values in all cases, and argued further, that they ought to be thought of in terms of "commitments", "reasons" (where comparison between competing values is possible) and "non-reasons".

IV.   CULTURAL VALUES IN THE NON-RECOGNITION OF CHILD MARRIAGES

Hitherto, I have mounted a case against both the glib use of the term "public policy" and the use of incompletely theorized judgments in order to deny recognition to foreign marriages that satisfy the usual rules concerning formal and essential validity. I have argued that in all instances specific (foreign) cultural values must

---

[46] Values of instrumental worth can normally be measured in financial terms; values of intrinsic worth cannot. Neil Duxbury has captured the point well. "Whereas fungible property has a purely economic or instrumental value, personal property is property that the owner is bound up with to such a degree that its loss would cause him or her pain that could not be relieved simply by replacing the object with other goods of equal market value. Thus, a credit card is likely to be fungible, whereas many items of jewellery [such as a wedding ring] will (for their owners) have more personal significance": see N. Duxbury, "Trading in Controversy" (1997) 45 *Buffalo Law Review* 615, at 616.

[47] Borrowing from, and extending the analysis of, Joseph Raz, the fact that the judges are able to acknowledge and choose between different cultural norms "inevitably upholds a pluralistic view" for "[i]t admits the value of a large number of greatly differing pursuits among which . . . [the judges] are free to choose": see J. Raz, *The Morality of Freedom* (Oxford: Oxford University Press, 1986) p. 399.

[48] On the virtues of pluralism (and its distinctiveness from relativism) see Michael Freeman's contribution to this collection in ch. 1.

at least be acknowledged even if, for reasons of pre-commitment to incommensurable (English) cultural values, they form no part of the rationale for any particular decision. What I now want to do, in the context of child marriages, is examine the kinds of values that are actually at stake and ascertain whether they should be afforded the label "commitment", "reason" or "non-reason".

Foreign marriages involving children (especially young girls) are prevalent in a number of African, Asian and Latin American Societies.[49] English domestic law, however, imposes a minimum age for marriage of sixteen years,[50] and it is generally thought (but not settled) that this minimum age applies even to foreign domiciliaries who seek to marry in this country.[51] But if foreign domiciliaries marry abroad and then seek to migrate to this country, will their marriage be recognised if it involves a pre-adolescent child? The answer is by no means clear. Suppose a man, A, and B (aged twelve) who are both from country X (which allows child marriages) were to marry in country X and set up home there intending to live there for good. Suppose further that one year later A was offered a job in the United Kingdom and decided to move here with his wife, B, in order to accept it. So long as the marriage met the formal requirements for marriage in X, it would be clear that, whether the dual domicile test or the intended matrimonial home test were applied, a strong case could be made for the recognition of A and B's marriage when they subsequently came to the United Kingdom. But reported authority confirms that non-age may sometimes be a suitable basis for the courts to exercise their discretionary veto on an overseas marriage.[52] What, then, are the considerations that might justify such a veto?

Before answering this question it is important to realise that three possible situations arise out of these facts. The first is the unlikely situation in which B alone seeks recognition of the marriage.[53] The second is where A alone seeks to have the validity of the marriage confirmed and the final case is where both A and B seek to have their marriage recognised. For the sake of the present analysis, we shall deal with the second and third situations together for, beyond those considerations that arise in connection with the "protection" of B (common to all three instances), the only pertinent additional factor to enter the frame, in the second and third instances, is the potential offence to A in failing to grant recognition to the marriage.[54]

---

[49] See S. Poulter, *op cit*. n. 7, pp. 16–17 and the sources there cited.

[50] The Marriage Act 1949, s. 2 provides: "A marriage solemnised between persons either of whom is under the age of sixteen shall be void".

[51] As to the existence and extent of any doubt, see S. Poulter, *op cit*. n. 7, p. 18.

[52] *Alhaji Mohamed* v. *Knott, supra* n. 5. Although the marriage of the 13–year-old in this case was recognised, it is clear from Parker CJ's judgment that the court reserved the right in other cases to refuse recognition.

[53] This might occur where A seeks to marry another person in this country and denies the validity of the foreign marriage. It might also occur where A has been permanently incapacitated so as not to be able to voice an opinion.

[54] Of course, the broader political considerations to which I adverted earlier (at n. 18) would also arise here. But for the purposes of disposing of *this* case, I am concerned only with those arguments that the litigants themselves would raise. For details of the kinds of political considerations that are likely to arise in connection with instances of corrective justice in hard cases, see M. Loughlin, *op cit*. n. 19, ch. 6.

Let us deal with the initial situation where B alone claims recognition of the marriage. Here, four considerations would obtain. First, the concern to protect vulnerable minors from the instability of premature marriages. As Ruth Deech, commenting on the marriage of a teenager in *Alhaji Mohamed* v. *Knott*,[55] explained:

> If the statistics on teenage brides are anything to go by the marriage seemed destined to break down and one can easily imagine the wife as a future deserted uneducated mother incapable of earning a living or bringing up her children.[56]

Secondly, a concern arises as to whether young children are able to give a genuine, free and informed consent to their marriage.[57] Thirdly, in addition to the socio-economic pitfalls that can often be associated with youthful marriages, there might also be psychological dangers for developmentally young children,[58] stemming from their involvement in sexual relationships at too early an age.[59] Finally, and counter to the first three concerns, B might argue that according to the culture in which she was brought up, there is nothing abhorrent or unnatural in a girl of her age marrying a gentleman who is considerably older, and that she should be allowed to do so if she so chooses. The question with which the court would have to grapple is: "how, if at all, may the first three factors—rooted in paternalism—be weighed against the claim to have the (culturally validated) practice of child marriage recognised?". The answer would depend on whether all of these concerns can be measured along any common metric. If they can, each could then be treated as a relevant (legal) reason which the judge must consider in formulating a judgment. I would contend that there is a common thread linking all four of these considerations which enables them meaningfully to be compared with one another. At bottom, they are all concerns that are relevant to the assessment of where a child's best interests lie.

John Eekelaar, writing in the mid-1980s, identified three kinds of children's interests in elaborating his account of children's rights.[60] These were what he termed the basic interest,[61] the development interest[62] and the autonomy

---

[55] *Supra*, n. 5.

[56] R. Deech, "Immigrants and Family Law" [1973] *New Law Journal* 110, at 111. For further recognition of the concerns associated with the instability of child-marriages, see S. Poulter, *op cit.* n. 7, p. 17 and A.J.E. Jaffey, *op cit.* n. 4, at 45.

[57] See S. Poulter, *loc cit.*

[58] There is little point in fixing an age for child marriages where the avowed reason for so doing is to protect the vulnerabilities of the child that stem from her immaturity. The better approach is to set a limit based upon the child's stage of intellectual development. It is implicit from his judgment in *Knott* (*supra* n. 5, at 15–16) that Parker CJ was sympathetic to this approach. *Cf.* I.G.F. Karsten, "Child Marriages" (1969) 32 *Modern Law Review* 212, esp at 215–16 (where a minimum age approach is preferred).

[59] It is just such dangers that prompted Mrs Victoria Gillick into litigation in the landmark case of *Gillick* v. *West Norfolk and Wisbech AHA* [1986] AC 112.

[60] J. Eekelaar, "The Emergence of Children's Rights" (1986) 6 *Oxford Journal of Legal Studies* 161.

[61] The basic interest was seen in terms of "[g]enral physical, emotional and intellectual care": *ibid.*, at 170.

[62] The developmental interest involves allowing a child's natural capacities to develop to full advantage in such a way "as to minimize the degree to which they enter adult life affected by avoidable prejudices incurred during childhood": *loc cit.*

interest.[63] The concern to protect the child from an unstable marriage (with all that that may entail for the future) and prohibition against consenting to marriage at a very young age may both be seen in terms of Eekelaar's developmental interests. Equally underpinned by protectionism is the concern to protect the child from sexual exploitation which might be seen in terms of Eekelaar's basic interest. By contrast, the child's claim to have her marriage recognised, because she wishes to be treated as a married person who is capable of making such a choice for herself, can be seen in terms of her autonomy interest. Clearly, in our instance, there is a conflict between the first two kinds of interest, and the autonomy interest. But as Eekelaar and others have convincingly argued, such conflicts *can* be resolved without treating the interests at stake to be incommensurable.[64] They are all simply different aspects of the same thing—the child's interests. Since there is an element of antipathy between the various goods in issue, the optimal outcome will be achieved by some measure of trade-off between each of the competing relevant reasons. Furthermore, it might be noted that not only can a meaningful decision be reached according to this analytical approach, it also has the virtue of eschewing recourse to cultural relativism (which would demand that we accept the practice of child marriage simply because it is thought to represent a cultural norm in country X derived from a particular custom practised there).[65]

The other problematic cases outlined earlier arise where A (either alone or together with B) claims that the marriage between A and B ought to be afforded recognition. In such instances, the key additional element to the case is the claim that A's cultural values (as evident in the practice of child marriage) ought to play a part in the judge's formulation of his or her decision. Here the judge must decide whether this contention should be rejected on the strength that it was incommensurable with the B's interests (which interests, as we have seen, would ultimately underscore any decision made in the first scenario). If we value the protection of children from exploitation so highly that we will never surrender our commitment to that protection, it follows that no countervailing consideration should figure in the ultimate decision of a judge called upon to decide whether a marriage involving a child (with its concomitant expectation of sexual relations within the marriage) should be afforded recognition. A would-be husband might contend that, on the one hand, the English courts might well value the protection of children, but on the other hand (and in this case), this factor must be weighed against the offence caused to him (and others culturally sympathetic) by failing to recognise a marriage celebrated and valid in the

---

[63] This is "the freedom to choose his own lifestyle and to enter social relations according to his own inclinations uncontrolled by the authority of the adult world": *ibid.*, at 171.

[64] Though a brief account of how this achievable is provided in "The Emergence of Children's Rights" (*op cit.* n. 60, at 171) a much fuller account is provided in J. Eekelaar, "The Interests of the Child and the Child's Wishes: The Role of Dynamic Self-Determinism" in P. Alston (ed.), *The Best Interests of the Child* (Oxford: Clarendon Press, 1994), p. 42, esp pp. 53–7. See also, M. Freeman, *The Rights and Wrongs of Children* (London: Frances Pinter, 1983) p. 57.

[65] For an account of the problems associated with relativism, see M. Freeman, *op cit.* n. 19.

country of the spouses' common domicile. Yet if the judge were to consider the offence to the husband (and others), he or she would at once surrender the absolute commitment to the protection of children from exploitative marriages. The only way in which the judge could maintain that commitment would be by discounting all other cultural considerations. Put bluntly, there would be no scope for comparing the welfare of the child with the (countervailing) good of showing cultural (and perhaps also religious) tolerance towards the husband. The two "goods" not only ought not to be compared, but cannot be compared. They are incommensurable. Comparison between the two is not susceptible to measurement along a single, common metric.[66] A commitment to one of these goods, the protection of children, necessarily requires that the other, religious tolerance, be excluded from the decision making process. Any attempt to evaluate the relative worth of a competing cultural value—even if this were possible—would be to abandon the absolute nature of one's commitment to the first such good. As Warner has put it:

> [t]o ignore the impossibility of comparison is to ignore the value and dignity of individual persons [in our case that of children]. Policy discourse which denies non-comparative exclusion [that is, the exclusion as *reasons* of those considerations which run-counter to an unassailable commitment that we hold] erases the value of individuals out of its policy making equations. What is at stake in the plea to recognize non-comparative exclusion is ourselves.[67]

Reaching a similar conclusion in relation to the question of whether the claims of parents to fair treatment in custody disputes should play a part in judicial decision making, Scott Altman has voiced the opinion that:

> [C]hild welfare is so important that, even after balancing other concerns, little else matters sufficiently to be worth discussing. The strongest reason for regarding welfare as the primary aim of custody rules is that children are extremely vulnerable. Physical and psychological trauma to young people, who cannot protect themselves can result in long-term disability and unhappiness. Adults have less to lose.[68]

Importantly, the interests of the parents are *acknowledged* here, but they are ultimately excluded from the decision because of their incommensurability with

---

[66] As Raz explains, "A and B are incommensurate if it is neither true that one is better than the other nor true that they are of equal value": see J. Raz, *op cit.* n. 47, p. 122.

[67] R. Warner, "Excluding Reasons: Impossible Comparisons and the Law" (1995) 15 *Oxford Journal of Legal Studies* 431, at 433.

[68] S. Altman, "Should Child Custody Rules be Fair?" (1996–97) 35 *Journal of Family Law* 325, at 353. Of course, it might be objected that this is not really an instance of incommensurability because Altman's conclusion appears to be premised upon a comparison between parental claims to fairness and the child's interest in having his or her welfare dealt with as the paramount consideration. But the truth is that he goes no further than acknowledging that the claim to fairness to parents is an incidental issue. So much is clear from the fact that he dismisses this claim as not worth discussing. It is therefore, an example of incommensurability and the parental claims play no part in the formulation of the ultimate decision on the basis of what Warner would call "non-comparative exclusion". It is an instance in which one value at stake (the claim to fair treatment for parents) is *acknowledged* but not included in the rationale for the final decision. And this is *precisely* what I am arguing for.

the child's welfare. This is not to deny that fairness to a parent is a "good", and that it might constitute a *reason* for a decision in another context where the paramountcy of a child's welfare was not in opposition to it. It is simply that, as Raz has explained:

> The existence of more goods than can be chosen by one person [or court], which are of widely different character, speaks of the existence of more virtues than can be perfected by one person [or court]. It tells of the existence of incompatible virtues [necessitating an element of sacrifice].[69]

Certainly, a strong argument can be made that English law is committed (in the sense discussed earlier) to the protection of the children if not the active advancement of their best interests. To begin with, recall that the United Kingdom has ratified the United Nations Convention on the Rights of the Child which requires, among other things, that states "take all appropriate . . . measures to protect the child from all forms of physical or mental violence, injury or abuse, neglect or negligent treatment, maltreatment or exploitation, including sexual abuse".[70] And although the provisions of the Convention do not form part of English law *directly*,[71] they nonetheless symbolise the kind of commitment to child protection I am suggesting exists. Echoing the Convention, the public law provisions of Parts III–V of the Children Act 1989 are further evidence of this commitment. And other legislative instruments (such as the Children and Young Persons Act 1933[72]) bear testimony to its existence. Against this backdrop, it would certainly be very difficult for a judge plausibly to deny the existence of strong commitment to child protection.

V CONCLUSION

In this essay I have sought to expose what I consider to be two fundamental flaws in the case-law governing the discretionary non-recognition of foreign marriages: the occasional willingness to decide cases in accordance with "public policy" concerns that are left unarticulated, and the (sometimes accompanying) tendency to fail to acknowledge certain cultural values that (for the immigrants concerned) are perceived to be at stake. I have argued that, as a minimum, there must be cognisance of any such values. But I have also stressed that this does not mean that those values need necessarily play a part in the formulation of any particular judgment. I have also suggested that where incommensurable cultural values exist and the courts (rightly or wrongly) are pre-committed to a domestic cultural value, that commitment necessitates the

---

[69] J. Raz, *op cit.* n. 47, p. 399.
[70] Art. 19.
[71] See G. Van Bueren, "The United Nations Convention on the Rights of the Child: The Necessity of Incorporation into United Kingdom Law" [1992] *Family Law* 373.
[72] See section 1.

non-comparative exclusion of the foreign value in the ultimate formulation of their judgment.

Finally, I have been at pains to stress the need that I see for the clear articulation of reasons for decisions. Such articulation, long since thought to be central to the common law tradition[73] has, in my view, a particular significance when dealing with competing cultural values. And while silence on such prickly matters, as Sunstein correctly observes,[74] conduces to functional, *ad hoc* decision making, this is by no means consistent with either pluralism or rational decision making.

[73] See the text associated with n. 11, *supra*, as well as the literature referenced therein.
[74] See n. 34, *supra*.

6

Indigenous Children in Australian Law

JOHN DEWAR*

I INTRODUCTION

THE INDIGENOUS INHABITANTS[1] of Australia account for about 2 per cent of what is an increasingly ethnically diverse population. Yet despite their relatively small numbers, the position of Indigenous Australians in law and in the wider framework of Australian politics and society, is a subject of intense public debate. Whether the issue is Indigenous land claims (native title),[2] or whether the government should apologise for past forcible removal of Indigenous children from their families, or the extent to which Indigenous communities should manage their own affairs in areas of health, housing and welfare, the question of the place of Indigenous peoples in the Australian polity remains unanswered.

In this chapter I do not offer a complete analysis of the position of Indigenous peoples in Australian family or child law. Instead, I focus on the legal and policy issues arising out of the legal position of Indigenous children in Australian law: the "public" law of child protection (which, in Australia, is primarily a matter for the States and Territories); and the "private" family law, administered by the Federal Family Court under the Family Law Act 1975. The reason for this rather selective treatment, apart from constraints of space, is that these topics provide a valuable starting point for understanding the tensions and possibilities entailed in seeking to create a tolerant and inclusive legal regime in societies characterised by racial diversity.

A number of factors combine to make Indigenous children an especially important focus for understanding the relationship between law and cultural diversity in family life. The first is that Indigenous understandings of kinship relations and of child-rearing practice are often fundamentally different from

* Griffith University, Brisbane, Australia. I would like to thank Tanya Denning and Frances Weekers for their research assistance.

[1] The term "Indigenous" refers to both Aboriginal and Torres Strait Islander peoples. "Aboriginal" itself is a blanket term encompassing many distinct groups of mainland Indigenous Australians.

[2] See *Mabo* v. *Queensland (No.2)* (1992) 175 CLR 1; *Wik Peoples* v. *Queensland* (1996) 134 ALR 637; Native Title Act 1993 (*Cth*). For discussion, see S Dorsett, "Land Law and Dispossession: Indigenous Rights to Land in Australia" in S. Bright and J. Dewar, *Land Law: Themes and Perspectives* (Oxford: OUP, 1998) ch. 11.

those accepted in the dominant white culture. Whereas white culture emphasises the nuclear family unit, and the importance of stability or the status quo in child care arrangements, those of Indigenous communities may instead emphasise flexibility and extensiveness of kinship ties and the importance of mobility in a child's development. To accommodate Indigenous values in this area requires the dominant culture to put aside its own values and to comprehend the sheer *otherness* of the practices, structures and values of a small minority. This will require fundamental rethinking about things that the dominant culture may take for granted, such as family structures, to avoid inadvertent discrimination against those minority cultures that do not conform to the dominant norm.

A second is that contemporary policy, especially regarding Indigenous inhabitants of territory seized by colonial invaders, must often bear the heavy weight of the past. In the case of Indigenous Australians, that past is dominated not only by a history of territorial dispossession, but also by the policies that produced the "stolen generations" of Indigenous children forcibly removed from their parents (see below). That historical legacy, and the powerful emotions generated by it, continues to suffuse Indigenous attitudes towards those state agencies that now seek to provide assistance or offer services, and creates for those agencies something approaching a paradox: namely, how to assist groups who regard the assistant as "part of the problem" and who, for that reason, may be reluctant to access the services provided at all, or who will be deeply suspicious of them when used.[3]

A third is that, from a legal point of view, the position of ethnic and Indigenous minorities is no longer exclusively within the legislative province of nation-states. Increasingly, human rights norms derived from international treaties are providing fertile ground as either sources for, or the interpretation of, domestic law as it applies to Indigenous peoples. This is particularly the case in Australia where, although treaties are not self-executing, both legislators and judges have at least declared that they take Australia's international human rights treaty obligations seriously. In the sphere of child law, this is evidenced by the incorporation of certain provisions of the UN Convention on the Rights of the Child into domestic legislation;[4] by the willingness of Australian judges to refer to the Convention in judicial reasoning;[5] and by the fact that the Convention has been treated as creating reviewable legitimate expectations of administrative action.[6]

---

[3] J. Litwin, "Child Protection Interventions within Indigenous Communities: An Anthroplogical Perspective" (1997) 32 *Australian Journal of Social Issues* 317. Evidence given to the National Inquiry into the Separation of Aboriginal and Torres Strait Islander Children from their Families (hereafter *Bringing them Home*) confirmed that "Indigenous families perceive any contact with welfare departments as threatening the removal of their child. Familes are reluctant to approach welfare departments when they need assistance": *Bringing them Home* (1997) p. 454.

[4] E.g., Family Law Act 1975 (*Cth*) s. 60B.

[5] B v. B: *Family Law Reform Act 1995* 21 Fam LR 676, at 737–7.

[6] *Minister of State for Immigration and Ethnic Affairs* v. *Ah Hin Teoh* 183 CLR 273. See M. Allars, "One Small Step for Legal Doctrine, One Giant Leap Towards Integrity in Government: *Teoh's* Case and the Internationalisation of Administrative Law" (1995) 17 *Sydney Law Review* 204.

In this chapter, I will suggest that the goal of legislative policy is increasingly, and ought to be, one of "self-determination" in the "public law" field of child protection, and of "multiculturalism" in the "private" field of family law. These terms, and the reasons for differentiating them along the public/private divide, will be explained in the next section. For the moment, I should explain that my intention is to use these labels both as (increasingly accepted) descriptions of the direction in which law and policy in these different areas appears currently to be shifting, and also as a yardstick by which to measure their success (or lack of it) in pursuing those objectives.

II SELF-DETERMINATION AND MULTICULTURALISM DEFINED

In liberal-democratic societies characterised by racial and ethnic diversity, two distinct approaches to the accommodation of cultural difference are encountered.[7] One, sometimes referred to as "self-determination" or "self-government", refers to a policy of ceding to a particular racial or ethnic group powers over the management of their own affairs. In the modern era, such policies may carry unfortunate associations with the policies of apartheid pursued in South Africa until the recent transition to democracy. But, unlike apartheid—which formed the basis of a racist, exploitative and oppressive regime—policies of self-government are designed to empower racial minorities, and to enhance rather than undermine respect for racial difference.[8] Self-determination is most frequently encountered in those states the population of which includes Indigenous groups whose presence pre-dated the arrival of white culture through colonisation.

"Multiculturalism", on the other hand, is associated with the conferment of rights that seek to ensure that ethnic (usually immigrant as opposed to Indigenous) communities are given full opportunity to participate in mainstream society. Multiculturalism is founded on equality of treatment of citizens, rather than difference, but recognises that there may be ways in which the dominant culture may inadvertently discriminate against ethnic minorities. A policy of multiculturalism seeks to be sensitive to ways in which this might happen, and may include conferment of "group-specific" rights as a way of combating inadvertent discrimination. Multiculturalism thus rests on a substantive, rather than formal, notion of equality. Translated into law and legal policy in an Australian context, "multiculturalism" means "a general amendment to Australian law to make it less narrowly monocultural and more flexible to accommodate individual differences".[9] "Multiculturalism" has been official

---

[7] See W. Kymlicka, *Multicultural Citizenship: A Liberal Theory of Minority Rights* (Oxford: Clarendon Press, 1995) ch. 2, for a valuable discussion.

[8] See R. Chisholm, *Black Children: White Welfare?*; *Aboriginal Child Welfare Law and Policy in New South Wales* (Social Welfare Research Unit Reports and Proceedings No. 52, April 1985) pp. 101–2.

[9] Australian Law Reform Commission, *Multiculturalism and the Law* (Report No. 57, 1992) para. 1.24 (hereafter *Multiculturalism*).

Australian government policy since 1989,[10] although the extent of the current conservative Government's commitment to it is questionable.[11]

As indicated, I will be suggesting in this chapter that, broadly speaking, self-determination represents an appropriate policy objective with respect to Indigenous communities in the "public" law of child protection, and that multiculturalism is an appropriate objective for "private" law of family law decision-making about residence and contact.[12] How these different policy objectives translate into practice, and the degree to which they are already realised in Australian law and practice (or not), will form the focus of much of this chapter. Before we get to that, however, some justification of this policy split between public and private is called for.

To begin with, I do not want to overemphasise the labels "public" and "private". They are merely ways of describing the different circumstances in which issues of cultural diversity are likely to arise, circumstances which, it seems to me, deserve different responses as a matter of legal policy. The chief difference I am seeking to elucidate is between those cases, on the one hand, in which the interests of the group loom large, such as where there is a real risk of a child being removed from the group and placed with carers fom a different racial or cultural group; and, on the other, those where the group interest *as such* is less prominent, either because the child enjoys a mixed-race heritage, or because both parents are from the same group. On this definition, there may be some cases arising under "private" family law that fall into the "public" category in this sense: for example, where the dispute is between a parent on the one hand, and a "private" or non-State substitute carer from a different cultural group from that of the parent, such as a privately-arranged foster parent, on the other.

The argument for self-determination for Indigenous groups[13] in child protection rests on the fact that decision making about removal of children from families, and making substitute placements, is likely to raise the question of the identity and survival of the group *as a group* in its most acute form. The removal of children from Indigenous parents and their subsequent placement with non-Indigenous carers could prevent the group reproducing itself socially and culturally through its children. This could threaten the viability of the group as a distinct cultural entity. This justifies group-specific rights, which might include a presumption that the child be placed with substitute carers in its own community, or a measure of participation by the community concerned in decision making about a child's future, or both. The precise extent of that participation

[10] Department of the Prime Minister and Cabinet, Office of Multicultural Affairs, *National Agenda for a Multicultural Australia: Sharing our future* (Canberra: AGPS, 1989).

[11] See H. McRae *et al.*, *Indigenous Legal Issues: Commentary and Materials* (North Ryde, NSW: LBC Informations Services, 1997) pp. 70–1 for a summary of the conservative Coalition Government's policies on Indigenous affairs since 1996.

[12] As we shall see, the divide may not always be clear-cut: for example, there may be some cases in which a presumption in favour of an Indigenous carer may be appropriate in private matters.

[13] The argument here is confined to Indigenous communities, and is not intended to be an argument against trans-racial placements more generally, which raise different issues.

may vary, from a right to be consulted (a very weak form of self-determination) through to the devolution of decision making authority to the group itself. The question of the extent to which the interests of the group should take precedence over other interests, such as those of a parent who wishes the child to be placed away from the group, are not easily resolved.[14] My point here is that where the interests of the group are in issue, then there should at least be a *presumption* that the decision about where the child will be placed should be made by the group, or at least with significant input from the group.

By contrast, where the issue is a "private" one, for example, which of two separated parents a child should live with, the interests of the group are less clear-cut. If both parents are of the same racial background, the group *as such* may have little interest in the outcome, since the impact on the group may be the same whichever decision is made. Alternatively, the child may be of mixed descent, in which case the child will have a mixed cultural heritage that deserves proper acknowledgement. In such cases, it would be reasonable for a decision-maker to have full regard to the Indigenous aspects of a child's background, without giving it the pre-eminent or presumptive weight that it would receive in "public" law.[15] Yet, consistently with a policy of multiculturalism, it is important that structures or values that seem obvious or taken-for-granted by the dominant culture, do not silently operate to exclude or devalue the weight to be attached to those cultural factors.

Both self-determination and multiculturalism as defined here would seem to be compatible with UNCROC, and specifically with Article 30. This requires states to ensure that an Indigenous child "not be denied the right, in community with other members of his or her group, to enjoy his or her own culture . . . or to use his or her own language". However, it could equally be argued that Article 30 is consistent with other policies less sympathetic to Indigenous communities: for example, that the State should have freedom to make whatever substitute care it considers necessary, provided only that *some* form of contact between the child and its Indigenous community is maintained. There is certainly nothing in Article 30 to mandate any sort of participation by Indigenous communities in child placement decisions.[16]

---

[14] On the potential for conflict between individual and group rights, see D. Goldsmith, "Individual vs. Collective Rights: The Indian Child Welfare Act" (1990) 13 *Harvard Women's Law Journal* 1, discussing the US Supreme Court's decision in *Mississippi Choctaw Band of Indians* v. *Holyfield* 109 S.Ct. 1597 (1989).

[15] As already noted, there may be some cases in which a private law version of the Aboriginal Child Placement Principle is justified: for example, where the dispute is between a parent on the one hand, and a "private" or non-State substitute carer, such as a privately-arranged foster parent, on the other. An example of such a case is *Re CP* (1997) 21 Fam LR 486, discussed later in this chapter.

[16] In its 1995 Report under the Convention, the Australian Government included the following matters as evidence of its compliance with Article 30: the passing of anti-discrimination legislation; the establishment of the Inquiry into the "stolen generations" (see above); the establishment of a programme to assist Indigenous families to reunite; and measures taken to preserve Aboriginal languages: pp. 409–19.

III CHILD PROTECTION AND CHILD PLACEMENT:

TOWARDS "SELF-DETERMINATION"?

A The "Stolen Generation"[17]

The experience of Indigenous communities since colonisation has been one of widespread forcible removal of Indigenous children. This became an official objective of government policy in the early twentieth century, as a response to concern at the growing numbers of children of mixed European and Indigenous descent. Beginning in the early 1900s, and using powers conferred by State "protectorate" legislation over Indigenous populations, Indigenous children were forcibly removed from their families and placed in dormitories. They were sent to work, or to settlements, when aged about fourteen. The objective was to merge, absorb or assimilate mixed-descent Indigenous children into the white population. Removals continued, in ever greater numbers, through the 1950s and 1960s, although by that time the legislative basis was not "protectorate" but general child welfare legislation.

By the late 1960s, however, it was clear that the policy of assimilation was not working; and the amendment of the Australian Constitution in 1967, to give the federal government legislative authority concurrently with the states over Indigenous populations, led to a shift in policy from assimilation to "integration". The election in 1972 of the reformist Labor Government of Gough Whitlam marked the beginning of the end of deliberate policies of removal.

The scale of removals between 1910 and 1970 is difficult to determine precisely. Estimates suggest that, during this period, anywhere between ten and fifty per cent of Indigenous persons experienced forcible removal from their families at some point in their lives. As *Bringing them Home* concludes, "most families have been affected, in one or more generations, by the forcible removal of one or more children".[18] The scale of human suffering caused by these polices is hard to imagine.[19]

B The Aboriginal Child Placement Principle (ACPP)

Beginning in the late 1970s, there was a gradual shift towards a more explicit policy of self-determination for Indigenous peoples in child care policy and

---

[17] See R. Chisholm, *op cit.* n. 8, ch. 1; *Bringing them Home, op cit.* n. 3, ch. 2; I. O'Connor, "Aboriginal Child Welfare Law, Policies and Practices in Queensland: 1865–1989" (1993) 46 *Australian Social Work* 11. Attempts to seek compensation for these policies have not so far been successful: see *Kruger* v. *Commonwealth of Australia* (1997) 146 ALR 126, on which see B. Cummings *et al.* "Lessons from the Stolen Generations Litigation" (1997) 19 *Adelaide Law Review* 25.

[18] Page 37.

[19] For a fictional account, see S. Morgan, *My Place* (Fremantle: Fremantle Arts Centre Press, 1988).

practice, inspired in part by the example of the United States in passing the Indian Child Welfare Act 1978. In this context, self-determination has been defined as "the right of Aboriginal people as a whole to have the opportunity to control their destiny, to consolidate, develop and adapt their laws, culture and traditions in a way that ensures their continuation as a viable and identifiable race".[20]

The importance of this to Australia's Indigenous communities is underlined by the fact that Indigenous children remain, even in the 1990s, statistically over-represented in the child care system—Indigenous children are twelve times more likely than non-Indigenous children to be involved in placement and support services.[21] One possible explanation for this is that it is a consequence of the application of standards and values of "white welfare" to black families, who may not share those values.[22] It has been said that:

[t]here is ample evidence that Aboriginal and Torres Strait Islanders experience adverse socioeconomic circumstances and are subject to many widely-held, if not often publicly-voiced, negative opinions—facts that may be reflected in the dispro-portionately high rates of maltreatment observed. Standards of education, health, hygiene and basic nutrition are derived from values essential to predominantly non-Aboriginal directed protective service authorities.[23]

It is for this reason that it is important that Indigenous child-rearing values are given full and proper, rather than token, weight in the decision making process, if the dispossessions of the past are not to be repeated. Indeed, as I shall explain later, there is a case for transforming altogether the nature of, and participants in, that process.

The growing acceptance of the policy of self-determination was associated with the introduction in all Australian States and Territories of an Aboriginal Child Placement Principle (ACPP) during the 1980s into either the legislation or policy governing substitute placements.[24] It was also

[20] R. Chisholm, *op cit.*, n. 8, p. 101.

[21] H. McRae *et al.*, *op cit.* n. 11, p. 425; see also the data collected in *Bringing them Home, op cit.* n. 3, ch. 21, showing that while Indigenous children represent 2% of the child population, they represent 20% of children in care: p. 430.

[22] R. Bailey-Harris and J. Wundersitz, "Over-representation of Aboriginal Children in Care Proceedings" (1985) 2 *Australian Journal of Family Law* 11, 25.

[23] P. Boss *et al.*, *Profile of Young Australians: Facts, Figures, Issues* (Melbourne: Churchill Livingstone, 1995) p. 143. The authors conclude that ATSI children "come to the attention of protection authorities . . . at a much higher rate than other children" and that they are particularly over-represented in cases of neglect.

[24] For a full history, see New South Wales Law Reform Commission (NSWLRC), Research Report 7, *The Aboriginal Child Placement Principle* (Sydney: NSWLRC, 1997) ch. 3. My discussion focuses on the principle in relation to fostering rather than adoption, because of the greater numer-ical importance of fostering as substitute placement. For a discussion of the principle in the context of adoption, see New South Wales Law Reform Commission, Report 81, *Review of the Adoption of Childen Act 1965 (NSW)* (Sydney: NSWLRC, 1997) and *Bringing them Home, op cit.* n. 3, ch. 22. There is currently only one statutory instance (in South Australia) of a separate Torres Strait Islander Placement Principle. Given cultural differences between Aboriginal and TSI peoples, espe-cially in the extent to which adoption is recognised, it has been suggested that a separate TSIPP be introduced: see NSWLRC, *The Aboriginal Child Placement Principle, op cit.*, pp. 234–8.

associated with the creation of specialist Aboriginal and Islander Child Care Agencies.[25]

Although the ACPP is now found in either the legislation or policy guidelines of all States and Territories, each jurisdiction displays its own peculiarities.[26] For the purposes of discussion, therefore, the State of New South Wales will be regarded as representative. In that State, the principle is enshrined in legislation for the purposes of foster placements,[27] and in a policy document for the purposes of adoption.[28] The legislative version of this principle lists a series of substitute care options, in descending order of preference, as follows:

An Aboriginal child shall not be placed in the custody or care of another person under this Part unless:

(a) *the child is placed in the care of a member of the child's extended family, as recognised by the Aboriginal community to which the child belongs,*

(b) *if it is not practicable for the child to be placed in accordance with paragraph (a) or it would be detrimental to the welfare of the child to be so placed the child is placed in the care of a member of the Aboriginal community to which the child belongs,*

(c) *if it is not practicable for the child to be placed in accordance with paragraph (a) or (b) or it would be detrimental to the welfare of the child to be so placed the child is placed in the care of a member of some other Aboriginal family residing in the vicinity of the child's usual place of residence, or*

(d) *if it is not practicable for the child to be placed in accordance with paragraph (a), (b) or (c) or it would be detrimental to the welfare of the child to be so placed the child is placed in the care of a suitable person approved by the Director-General after consultation with:*

(i) *members of the child's extended family, as recognised by the Aboriginal community to which the child belongs, and*

(ii) *such Aboriginal welfare organisations as are appropriate in relation to the child.*

Despite the almost universal adoption of the principle, or variants of it, throughout Australia, a number of criticisms have been levelled at it. First, there may be only a slender connection between an ACPP and self-determination in anything but a very weak sense. The principle usually requires only consultation by the relevant state agency with a relevant Aboriginal child care agency as a last

---

[25] *Bringing then Home, op cit.* n. 3, pp. 434–5.

[26] For an overview, see NSWLRC, *The Aboriginal Child Placement Principle, op cit.*, ch. 5. Successive official reports have recommended that the ACPP should be enshrined in legislation rather than left to policy guidelines: see Australian Law Reform Commission, *Recognition of Aboriginal Customary Law*, Vol. 1 (Canberra: AGPS, 1986) para. 366.

[27] Section 87 Children (Care and Protection) Act 1987 (NSW).

[28] NSW Department of Community Services, *Draft Policy Statement: The placement of Aboriginal children for adoption* (Sydney: DOCS, 1987).

resort, when all other specified options have been exhausted.[29] As *Bringing them Home* puts it:

> [t]he rhetoric of self-management has not been matched by practical measures. The administrative, executive and judicial decision-making about Indigenous children's welfare are controlled by child welfare authorities. Although Indigenous organisations have a right to be consulted, this typically occurs only at the final stages of decision-making about a child, when recommendations are being made for a placement in substitute care . . . Decision-making about Indigenous children's well-being falls well short of accepted notions of self-determination.[30]

An obligation to consult, where it exists, does little to shift control over resources or ultimate decision-making to Indigenous communities. In some States, such as Queensland, there is no obligation of consultation with Indigenous organisations at all.[31]

Second, the principle seems to have only limited practical effect. Since its introduction, there has been only a modest decline in the numbers of Aboriginal children in non-Aboriginal substitute care arrangements. In New South Wales, for example, the proportion of Aboriginal children in care in non-Aboriginal placements declined from 25.2 per cent to 17.1 per cent between 1990/1 and 1994/5.[32] This suggests that, despite the mandatory wording of the principle, there is a significant minority of cases in which it is being ignored. It has also been suggested that, because the principle applies only after a child has come into care by way of a court order, it "can do nothing to redress the over-representation of Aboriginal children dealt with informally by the State agencies".[33] In other words, the principle does not address the underlying problem of how and why Indigenous children are so much more likely than their non-Indigenous counterparts to come into contact with state agencies in the first place.[34]

Third, the principle does not resolve an underlying conflict of perception between Indigenous communities and welfare agencies concerning the nature of

[29] South Australia and Victoria are exceptions. Children Protection Act (*SA*), s. 5 requires consultation with a recognised Aboriginal or Torres Strait Islander Organisation *before* an Indigenous child is placed. Similarly, Children and Young Persons Act 1989 (*Vic*), s. 119 requires the involvement of the relevant Aboriginal community in planning for a child to be placed away from home.

[30] At pp. 436–7.

[31] Queensland Department of Families, Youth and Community Care, *Policy Statement in relation to Aboriginal and Torres Strait Islander fostering and adoption* set out in Appendix E to NSWLRC, *The Aboriginal Child Placement Principle*, *op cit*. Draft amending legislation in Queensland contains a statutory obligation of consultation with recognised ATSI Child Protection Agencies prior to decisions being made under the legislation, save in cases of emergency or impracticability: see Child Protection Bill 1998 (*Qld*), cl 6.

[32] See NSWLRC, *The Aboriginal Child Placement Principle*, *op cit*., Table 2, p. 99. The Northern Territory has a poorer record still, with 47% of all Aboriginal children in care being in non-Aboriginal placements: ibid, Table 8, p. 131. The pattern is similar for all States and Territories who keep records of their Indigenous population: ibid., ch. 5.

[33] NSW Department of Community Services, Legislation Review Unit, *Review of The Children (Care and Protection) Act 1987: Discussion Paper No. 1, Law and Policy in Child Protection* at p. 131.

[34] See n. 31 above for figures.

substitute care itself. The notion of foster or substitute care is linked to cultural assumptions about kinship relations, and in particular that children have only a limited set of consanguinal or affinitive relations; and that child care responsibilities rest primarily with the child's natural parents, and that it is this primary obligation that is being "substituted" or replaced. Indigenous groups may not share these assumptions, and may instead see kinship relations as encompassing a wider network of individuals, and obligations to care for children of the group as being widely distributed throughout the group itself (see further below). Against this background, the notion of substitute or foster care may make no sense at all.[35] Thus, to involve Indigenous groups in a process of consultation about substitute care may be to involve them in a process they do not recognise or understand in their own cultural terms.

Finally, a number of practical difficulties in implementing the principle have been identified. These include problems of defining and identifying those children who are "Aboriginal".[36] In addition, underfunding of Indigenous child care agencies has meant that there is a shortage of suitable Aboriginal substitute carers; and definitions of "suitability" are themselves derived from mainsteam assumptions of desirable child-rearing practice.[37] It is also said that the principle offers no guidance where either the child or its parent has specifically requested a non-Aboriginal placement,[38] or where the child has a relationship with two distinct Aboriginal communities.

C Towards greater self-determination?

The shortcomings of the ACPP, coupled with evidence of continuing high levels of removal of Indigenous children from their families, and the cultural insensitivity of much current welfare policy and practice, has led to a growing body of opinion favouring stronger forms of self-determination.[39] For example, *Bringing them Home* recommended the "eventual transfer of responsibility for children's well-being to Indigenous peoples" and "a framework for negotiating autonomy" on the basis that "existing systems have failed miserably".[40] In mak-

---

[35] ". . . the concept of foster care is not readily translated from mainstream to Aboriginal society. Aboriginal people do not think of themselves as foster carers for children of their own kinship or other Aboriginal children": West Australian Government submission to *Bringing them Home, op cit.* n. 3, cited at p. 436.

[36] There are various legislative definitions of "Aboriginal", which combine elements of descent, identification and acceptance by the Aboriginal community: see *Gibbs* v. *Capewell* (1995) 128 ALR 577.

[37] *Bringing them Home, op cit.* n. 3, p. 450.

[38] *Ibid.* at 132. Such cases raise, in an acute form, the question of how to balance the expressed wishes of the individual against the interests of the group: see D. Goldsmith, *op cit.* n. 14, discussing the US Supreme Court's decision in *Mississippi Choctaw Band of Indians* v. *Holyfield* 109 S.Ct. 1597 (1989).

[39] An early advocate of which was Richard Chisholm: see *Black children: White welfare?, op cit.*, n. 8.

[40] Page 560 and Recommendation 43.

ing this recommendation, the Inquiry was careful to avoid being prescriptive about the form and extent of self-determination, saying instead that "there are many possibilities from the exercise of local government style powers through to the development of State-like powers within a federal structure".[41]

The case for self-determination in child welfare rests mainly on its instrumental importance in the preservation of Indigenous communities and cultures. But it also receives some support from principles of international law, and from the seemingly successful implementation in other jurisdictions of strong forms of self-determination in the areas of child welfare.[42]

As far as international law is concerned, the case for self-determination rests primarily on Articles 1 and 27 of the International Covenant on Civil and Political Rights. Article 1 enshrines the principle of "sef-determination" for "all peoples". As far as Indigenous populations are concerned, it is increasingly argued that they are both "peoples" for these purposes, and that self-determination includes self-determination for Indigenous peoples within larger sovereign state entities.[43] Article 27 provides that "persons belonging to minorities . . . shall not be denied the right, in community with members of their group, to enjoy their own culture", which has been construed as offering support for self-government for Indigenous groups where necessary to preserve cultual distinctiveness.[44]

Any doubt about the principle of self-determination for Indigenous peoples would be resolved if the *Draft Declaration on the Rights of Indigenous Peoples* were adopted. Article 6 of the draft includes a "full guarantee against . . . the removal of Indigenous children from their families and communities under any pretext".[45] In contrast, as we have seen, Article 30 of the UN Convention on the Rights of the Child may not offer strong support for self-determination for Indigenous peoples over child welfare matters.

It remains to be seen what the response of Australian governments will be at state and federal level to the recommendations of *Bringing them Home*. The Report received a cool response from the conservative Government of Prime Minister John Howard, and few of its recommendations—including that the

---

[41] Page 575. There are already examples of varying levels of self-determination for Indigenous peoples in Australia, through the creation of local-government style councils for the delivery of basic services to Indigenous communities and, in some cases, limited control over policing and criminal courts. However, *Bringing them Home* described Australian instances of self-government as having been "established within paternalistic legislative frameworks in which limited powers are delegated and functions are performed with inadequate resources, often in adverse circumstances": *loc cit.*

[42] Particularly the Indian Child Welfare Act 1978, an Act of the Federal United States government. The Act confers jurisdiction, in certain circumstances, on tribal courts over child welfare matters. Children who live off-reservation are subject to the concurrent jurisdiction of tribal and State courts. For discussion, see R. Barsh, "The Indian Child Welfare Act of 1978: A critical analysis" (1980) 31 *Hastings Law Journal* 1287.

[43] S. Pritchard, "The right of Indigenous peoples to self-determination under International law" (1992) 2 (55) *Aboriginal Law Bulletin* 4.

[44] *Bringing them Home, op cit.* n. 3, p. 562.

[45] In many Indigenous communities, the terms "family" and "community" may be synonymous, so that the practical implications of this principle may not be as radical as they might first appear.

government of the day should apologise formally to Indigenous peoples of Australia for the policies that led to the "stolen generations"[46]—have so far been acted upon. Self-determination remains an aspiration rather than a realised objective.

IV FAMILY LAW: TOWARDS "MULTICULTURALISM"?[47]

So far, I have been discussing the State's child welfare functions, and the importance in that context of recognising the principle of self-determination as a way of protecting the legitimate claims of Indigenous groups to preserve their heritage and control their destinies. I want to turn now to consider cases where the question is which of two parents a child should live with following parental separation. As I have suggested, self-determination is less appropriate here, either because the Indigenous community may have less clearly defined interests at stake (for example, because both parents are from the same community); or, even if those interests are clear, it is less obvious that they should take precedence (for example, where the child is of mixed race). Instead, I have suggested that a policy of "multiculturalism" is more appropriate. Yet, as I will argue, Australian family law falls short of even this more limited benchmark.

As we have seen, it has been suggested that, when translated into legal policy, multiculturalism is best implemented, not by the development of special laws for particular groups, but rather through "a general amendment of Australian law to make it less narrowly monocultural and more flexible to accommodate individual differences".[48] In the particular context of children in family law, this becomes a question of the law's ability to recognise different conceptions of relationship or kinship, and to accommodate child-rearing practices that may differ from those considered desirable by the dominant culture. It will be suggested that, when viewed from the perspective of Australia's Indigenous communities, Australian family law is still some way from being "multicultural" in this sense; and that the barriers to achieving that sort of flexibility may be so close to the heart of the social practices of the dominant culture that they are almost invisible except from outside that culture. One consequence of this has been that "Indigenous families respond to the cultural inappropriateness of Australian family law by avoiding the Court and dealing with family disputes informally, or under traditional law".[49]

I am not suggesting that Australian family law has not sought to recognise and accommodate cultural factors in decision-making about children—far from

---

[46] Recommendation 3.

[47] This section is based on my "Indigenous children and family law" (1997) 19 *Adelaide Law Review* 217. I am grateful to the Editors and Trustees of the *Review* for granting permission for me to use that material here.

[48] *Multiculturalism and the law, op cit.* n. 9, at para. 1.24.

[49] *Bringing them Home, op cit.* n. 3, p. 486.

it. For example, in *B and R and the Separate Representative*[50] (a case involving a custody dispute of a part-Aboriginal child), the Full Court of the Family Court held that evidence concerning the history and effects of removal of Indigenous children to non-Indigenous environments was relevant to placement decisions under the Family Law Act 1975. It was held that the relevance of Aboriginality in child placement disputes went beyond the "right to know one's culture", and required a proper acknowledgment of "the effects on Aboriginal children of being raised in a white environment, in which the lack of reinforcement of their identity contributed to severe confusions of that identity and profound experiences of alienation".[51]

In addition, the Family Law Reform Act 1995, which came into force in 1996, after the decision in *B and R*, introduced a new item into the checklist of factors which a court must take into account in deciding where a child's best interests lie,[52] namely, a reference to the child's "background (including any need to maintain a connection with the lifestyle, culture and traditions of Aboriginal peoples or Torres Strait Islanders)".[53] Although it will be argued later that this provision needs to be strengthened, it represents for the first time a formal legislative acknowledgement of Aboriginality as a relevant factor in decision-making about children.

Yet in spite of these developments, I want to suggest that Australian law fails the test of flexibility and responsiveness to difference. This is because some of the structures and values are so deeply embedded in "white" thinking about kinship and good child-rearing practice, that they may almost be invisible except from a vantage point outside that culture.

A Family structures and family values

In defining kinship, or its conceptions of relationship, Australian family law reflects its Anglo-European heritage. So, when it comes to constructing legal relationships around children, family law tends to assume a nuclear model: that is, that a child will have two parents for legal purposes, generally those who are its biological mother and father.[54] These are the people who automatically have legal status with respect to the child, a status that they never technically lose. Thus, section 61C of the Family Law Act 1975 (*Cth*) states that each parent of a child has parental responsibility for it, and that this responsibility survives any

[50] (1995) Fam LR 594

[51] *B and R* at 601.

[52] FLA 1975 (*Cth*), s. 68F.

[53] *Ibid.*, s. 68F(2).

[54] "Parent" includes an adoptive parent, and anyone recognised as a parent under State, Territory and Commonwealth legislation dealing with assisted reproduction: FLA 1975 (*Cth*), ss. 60D(1), 60H. The FLA includes the concept of a "relative", which is elaborately defined in s. 60D(3), and is primarily relevant to the meaning of "family violence" in FLA 1975, s. 60D(1), s. 68F(i) and (j) and s. 68J.

changes in the relationship between the parents.[55] "Parental responsibility" for the child includes all powers, authority, rights and duties a parent might have in relation to a child.[56] The recent changes to the Family Law Act 1975, which introduced the concept of shared and continuing parental responsibility between biological parents have, if anything, served further to entrench this nuclear model in the law.[57] Thus, according to the principles underlying the new Part VII, contained in section 60B, children have a right to know and be cared for by both their parents,[58] but not by other significant figures in their lives; and parents (but not others) share duties and responsibilities for the care, welfare and development of their children, and should agree about their children's future.[59]

There are some notable exceptions to this nuclear model of kinship relations. For example, it is possible for someone who is not a parent to obtain parental responsibility for a child by applying for a "parenting order" under Part VII of the Family Law Act 1975. Any person concerned with the care, welfare or development of a child may apply for such an order.[60] There is in theory no limit to the number of people who may obtain parental responsibility in this way, although the extent to which a parenting order confers parental responsibility is determined by the order itself: there is no assumption that someone with a parenting order thereby acquires parental responsibility in full.[61] In that respect, the law still gives parents preferential treatment by automatically giving them (and only them) parental responsibility in full.

Other departures from the nuclear model can be found in the section 68F "best interests" checklist, which requires a court to take account of a child's relationships with persons other than its parents in making decisions about where the child's best interests lie. Thus, in addition to paragraph (f) already discussed, paragraph (b) refers to "the nature of the relationship of the child with each of the child's parents *and with other persons*"; paragraph (c)(ii) refers to "the likely effect of any changes in the child's circumstances, including the likely effect on the child of any separation from . . . any other child , or *other person with whom he or she has been living*"; and paragraph (e), which talks of "the capacity of each parent, *or of any other person*, to provide for the needs of the child, including emotional and intellectual needs".[62] Finally, the statement

---

[55] FLA 1975 (*Cth*), s. 61C.

[56] *Ibid.*, s. 61B.

[57] Although, ironically perhaps, the Australian Law Reform Commission (ALRC) supported the broad outline of these changes on the basis that continued parental responsibility after divorce or separation would allay the fears of some immigrant communities at their possible loss of parental status on divorce: ". . . depriving a parent of custody [sic] of a child may result in a major loss of status, honour and identity of that parent and deprive the parent of the opportunity to exercise a deeply felt sense of responsibility for a child" (*Multiculturalism*, at para. 6.29).

[58] FLA 1975, s. 60B(2)(a).

[59] *Ibid.*, s. 60B(2)(c) and (d).

[60] *Ibid.*, s. 65C(c).

[61] FLA 1975 (*Cth*), s. 61D(1).

[62] Emphasis added in each case.

of objects underlying Part VII talks of the child's right of contact with parents and with others "significant to their care, welfare or development".[63] However, each of these provisions has to be seen as qualifications of, or as exceptions to, a basically nuclear, two-parent, model of parent–child relations.

In general, then, Australian family law enshrines particular assumptions about relationships between children and parents. While these may seem natural to many members of the dominant European culture, they become, in the context of Indigenous cultures, a serious barrier to the sort of increased flexibility that the ALRC refers to. Yet it is the naturalness of these assumptions, and the powerful ideology of nuclear-familialism surrounding them,[64] that renders them invisible to many. From the point of view of the Indigenous community in particular, this nuclear model doesn't fit at all well with Indigenous child-rearing structures or practices.

Although practices vary between Indigenous groups, it seems generally true that conceptions of kinship and of good child-raising practice are significantly different from the nuclear model.[65] Kinship relations are constructed in different ways from Western kinship systems, with the term "mother", for example, often being used to cover a much wider group of people than the biological mother. Kinship systems among many Indigenous groups are classificatory, which means that a much larger proportion of the social group, perhaps all members of the group, are accounted for in terms of kinship.[66] Western kinship systems, by contrast, consist of a much narrower range of relations. As *Bringing them Home* states, "by privileging parents and relegating the rights of other family members, the Australian family law system conflicts with Aboriginal child-rearing values".[67] In addition, child-rearing practices often differ markedly: whereas white culture tends to emphasise permanence and stability as positives for children,[68] Indigenous culture sees movement of children, either geographically, or between or within kinship groups, as beneficial. As *Bringing them Home* argues, "by privileging stability of residence, the system entrenches

---

[63] FLA 1975 (*Cth*), s. 60B(2)(b).

[64] See "Is the myth of the Nuclear Family Dead?" in M. Bittman and J. Pixley, *The double life of the family: Myth, hope and experience* (Sydney: Allen & Unwin, 1997) ch. 1.

[65] E. Bourke and C. Bourke, "Aboriginal families in Australia" in R. Hartley (ed.), *Families and Cultural Diversity in Australia* (Sydney: Allen & Unwin/AIFS, 1995) ch. 3; D. Collard *et al.*, "The Contribution of Aboriginal Family Values to Australian Family Life" in J. Inglis and L. Rogan (eds.), *Flexible Families: New Directions in Australian Communities* (Sydney: Pluto, 1994) ch. 6.

[66] Kinship among the Mardu people of Western Australia studied by Tonkinson (*The Mardu Aborigines: Living the dream in Australia's desert*, 2nd ed. (Fort Worth: Holt, Rinehart and Winston, 1991)) extended "far beyond consanguinal and local group limits to include the most distant of kin and former strangers": discussed in M. Gilding, *Australian families: A comparative perspective* (Sydney: Longman, 1997) pp. 148–56.

[67] *Bringing them Home*, op cit. n. 3, p. 486.

[68] A good, and influential, example of this is the suggestion of J. Goldstein *et al.*, that a child's best interests lie in preserving the continuity of a child's relationship with one "psychological parent": *Beyond the Best Interests of the Child* (New York: Free Press, 1983). According to S. Parker *et al.*, "[p]reservation of the status quo appears to be the most significant determinant of custody disputes": see *Australian Family Law in Context: Commentary and Materials* (Sydney: LBC, 1994) p. 835.

a bias against the Aboriginal practice of mobility of children amongst responsible adults and their households".[69]

B *Re CP*: The Tiwi Island case

Many of these issues came into focus in a recent decision of the Full Court of the Family Court, *Re CP*.[70] This case concerned the residence of a four-year-old boy, C, whose parents were from the Tiwi Islands, a geographically remote group of islands eighty miles to the north of Darwin, on the north coast of Australia. C had been born on the Islands, but had been living since a very young age in Darwin with F, an Aboriginal woman from Thursday Island in the Torres Strait.[71] She had taken C to live with her in Darwin while working on a fishing boat around the Tiwi islands. C's biological mother lived on Melville Island, which is part of the Tiwi group. There was some dispute about the circumstances surrounding C's move to Darwin, especially over the expected duration of the arrangement. The litigation was initiated by F, who sought orders giving her joint guardianship and sole custody of C. This is now old terminology, but amounted to an application that C live with F, and that F and C's mother share responsibility for C's long term welfare and development. In many respects, the case was closer to a child welfare case (involving a contest between a parent and a substitute carer) than to an inter-parental dispute like *B and R*.

C's mother responded by seeking orders that C be "in the custody of his extended maternal and paternal family at Bathurst and Melville islands". Her application was supported by two sisters, and a cousin (that is, her father's brother's daughter, but someone who, in the Tiwi way, was also regarded as the mother's sister). According to Tiwi kinship thinking, all four women were C's mothers. The cousin was also co-ordinator of "Link-Up", a service which assists Indigenous parents to regain contact with children from whom they have been separated. Strictly speaking, the order sought by the mother was an order that it was not really possible for the court to make, since custody has to be vested in an individual, or individuals, rather than in a kinship group. In other words, while the order applied for may have reflected what was likely to happen if the child went back to the Tiwi islands—namely that responsibility for his care would be shared by his extended family—it could not be given expression by a Family Court order.

There was evidence before the trial judge concerning the child-rearing practices of the Tiwi people.[72] That evidence disclosed that it is common practice for

---

[69] *Bringing them Home, op cit*. n. 3, p. 486.

[70] (1997) 21 Fam LR 486.

[71] Torres Strait Islanders are considered a distinct cultural and ethnic group from mainland Aboriginals.

[72] The expert evidence is reproduced in greater detail by R. Davis and J. Dikstein, "It just doesn't fit: The Tiwi family and the Family Law Act—can the two be reconciled?" (1997) 22 *Alternative Law Journal* 64.

Tiwi children to be brought up by someone other than their biological mother and that "it is not uncommon for the children to locate themselves in several of the extended family households throughout their respective childhood years".[73] There was also evidence from an anthropologist appointed by the child's Separate Representative[74] concerning the differences between mainland and island Indigenous communities, and, more generally, on the importance of an Indigenous child remaining within their own community:

> [The] [d]isadvantages of not bringing up an Aboriginal child within his or her own community of kin and within at least frequent visiting distance of country with which he or she is identified might include: the loss of relations with a vast range of kin who will perform a wide variety of roles associated with social relations, emotional and physical support, educative knowledge, economic interactions and spiritual training; . . . loss of knowledge which stems from the social interactions mentioned above; . . . ambiguities in or loss of identity with one's own kin and country, features I understand as essential to identity from an indigenous point of view.[75]

The main issue in the case was whether the trial judge had properly taken account of the child's Aboriginal background, and specifically of his Tiwi background. The Full Court held that the judge had not given sufficient weight to the differences between the Indigenous culture of the Tiwi's as against F's Indigenous background as a Thursday islander (which, according to expert evidence in the case, were substantial). The judge, in short, had assumed that all Indigenous cultures were much the same, so that its weight as a factor was diminished in the judge's reasoning. As the Full Court put it, the judge "demonstrated an incorrect view of the homogeneity of aboriginal cultures".[76] The judge had also taken the view that the child's need to maintain "connection" with his lifestyle culture and traditions, as specified in section 68F(2)(f), would be satisfied by maintaining C's education about the Tiwi way of life and through regular visits to the Islands. This clearly conflicts with the Full Court's decision in *B and R*, and the Full Court in *Re CP* took this to be evidence of the judge's failure to appreciate the differences between, and specificity of, Indigenous cultures.

The case is of interest for a number of reasons. One is that, at least in cases of inter-Indigenous disputes over children's residence, the Family Court will be open to hearing evidence about differences in Indigenous cultures. It suggests that the rights contained in Article 30, and reflected in section 68F(2)(f), will be interpreted as a right to maintain connections with a *specific* Indigenous culture, rather than Indigenous culture in general. It also underlines the point that "connection" for the purposes of section 68F(2)(f) means more than education and occasional visits.

[73] At 65.
[74] A court may order that the child be separately represented in proceedings in which the child's best interests are the paramount, or a relevant, consideration: FLA 1975 (*Cth*), s. 68L.
[75] At 502.
[76] At 501.

For present purposes, though, my interest is in two other aspects of the case. The first is the Court's approach to Indigenous child-rearing practices, and especially to the practice of moving children around. The judge had regarded it as a factor favouring F that C's mother was not able to provide a clear picture of who would be looking after the child. The Full Court, however, quoted at length from the expert evidence of an anthropologist, Dr M:

> It is not at all unusual for Aboriginal children to move freely, even frequently, although the legal system tries to control and restrict this. Such movements, except for infants, are almost always with the willing consent of the child and are frequently initiated by the child who has a right to express their own desires with regard to residential arrangements. Moves can be occasioned by many factors, including the desire for change, to reside with paternal kin for some time, to move away from conflicts— in other words, many of the same reasons adults express as well for moving around. These movements between kin, and often between communities, are seen as important ways in which children acquire their understandings of the ways in which kinship and country relationships are lived out. They are thus not a sign of disruption as they might be interpreted by non-Aboriginal people but are an important factor in socialising children.[77]

The Court went on to suggest that the trial judge had failed to have regard to the importance of movement in an Indigenous child's social development and had therefore wrongly construed the mother's lack of clarity in future plans for the child adversely to her case.

This aspect of the case seems to be a very welcome development: it displays the sort of flexibility and openness to cultural practices that the ALRC was talking about. But it is striking how fragile the legal foundation for any such development might be. The case turns almost entirely on the weight given by the judge to the evidence before him: without the anthropologists' evidence, it might have been harder for the Full Court to have arrived at the conclusion it did. What flexibility there is, therefore, has to be fought for, and the cost reckoned in terms of gathering the necessary evidence. Indigenous parties, it seems, are always likely to be on the back foot when it comes to establishing the validity of cultural difference. This suggests that even the apparently progressive approach of the Full Court in *B and R* may leave something to be desired. As Lisa Young has argued, "asking every applicant to take responsibility for these issues [through the production of evidence] is the wrong solution . . . Caucasians are not put to proof of matters of such notoriety, why should Aboriginal . . . parents be?".[78]

The second important aspect of the case stems from the remarks made towards the end of the judgment about the problems of applying the legal framework of the Family Law Act to cases of this sort. As the Full Court put it:

---

[77] At 502–3.
[78] Quoted in *Bringing them Home, op cit.* n. 3, p. 486.

... this case has highlighted difficulties in the applicability of the Family Law Act to cultural systems of family care which, like the Tiwi way, contemplate circumstances where the child will live and be cared for within a kin network.[79]

The Court went on to talk about the limitations of what I have called the nuclear model of parent/child relations enshrined in Australian family law and that it led , in particular, to "the many non-biological mothers of a Tiwi child [being] invisible in the law".[80] Even the provisions about parenting orders, the Court suggests, are not sufficient to deal with the issue, because those in whose favour such orders are made still have to be identified in advance:

> ... the Act proceeds on the basis that orders will be made in favour of identified persons (who will usually be parties to the proceedings or have indicated their consent to orders being made in their favour). As the present case illustrates, the fluidity of indigenous care arrangements does not lend themselves [sic] to such a priori specificity and may give rise, as was again evident in this case, to criticisms about the uncertainty of arrangements for a child, which, depending on the facts found in a case, may be unwarranted. It appears to us that the legislative recognition of indigenous culture and heritage in section 68F may need to be complemented by provisions which take account of the kinship care systems of Aboriginal and Torres Strait Islander peoples.[81]

A solution proposed by the Court, but not discussed in detail, was that a Tribal elder could be nominated to accept responsibility for compliance.[82] While not providing a complete solution (not least because it leaves the underlying nuclear assumptions of the law unchallenged), such a creative approach to order-making by the Court could ameliorate the cultural blindness of basic family law structures.

C   Recuperating the "best interests" principle?

In the preceding discussion, I have suggested that there are real and often unintended barriers in the way of a full and formal acknowledgment of Indigenous child-rearing practices and values in Australian family law. In doing so, I have suggested that there are two main problems. The first is one of structure, and particularly the structure of the nuclear family that seems so deeply embedded in Australian law, and which is so far removed from the social practices of some Indigenous groups. The second is one of values, in particular the values concerned with what are good and bad ways of raising children. In this final section, I want to focus on the latter question, and to argue that the "best interests" principle may, unexpectedly perhaps, offer a way forward.

One way of resolving residence disputes involving Indigenous children would be to adopt a private law version of the Aboriginal Child Placement Principle.

[79] *Re CP* at 505.
[80] At 506.
[81] *Re CP* at 505.
[82] *Re CP* at 507.

This has been advocated by Davis and Dikstein in the context of cases like *Re CP*, in which the dispute is between a parent on the one hand and a non-parent substitute carer from a different racial group on the other.[83] Given the similarities with those child welfare cases in which ACPP is already operative, there seems to be a strong argument that the ACPP should extend into the realm of the Family Court's decision-making in such cases.[84] In cases involving disputes between parents of mixed-race children, however, the consensus has been that an ACPP would be inappropriate. It has been considered and rejected by those who have addressed the issue, either judicially[85] or as law reformers.[86] Further, it would run counter to the Family Court's reluctance to introduce presumptions of any sort into this area.[87] In view of this, it seems that the "best interests" principle will remain the yardstick for the foreseeable future.

The issue that then arises is whether the best interests principle, in the shape of a general, presumption-free and factor-driven standard, can be adapted so as to acknowledge the distinctive nature of Indigenous child-care practices, and the associated conceptions of where a child's best interests might lie. There are, I suggest, grounds for cautious optimism.

The historically conditioned and ideologically determined character of the best interests principle has properly been a pretext for criticism of it;[88] but, in this context, the malleability of the best interests principle, and its openness to inputs from other disciplines (such as anthropology), makes it potentially a suitable vehicle for a multicultural family law. Deployed sensitively, and with a consciousness of Indigenous child-rearing values, it might avoid the imposition of one set of values on another. But the success of the best interests principle in this area depends on a number of factors, such as the availability and admissibility of evidence and the sensitivity of the decision-maker to that evidence and its implications. *B and R* is a source for some optimism in this respect. It suggests that the Family Court is willing to admit the relevant evidence, on the basis of equality of respect, and that it has understood the distinction between a tokenistic acknowledgment of the relevance of cultural identity and background and a proper acknowledgment of Indigenous values and structures. However, *Re CP* itself is evidence that there is still some way to go: that not all Family Court judges at first instance may display the sensitivities of the judges of the Full Court who gave judgment in *B and R* and *Re CP*, and that having the evidence does not automatically mean that Indigenous practices will be given proper weight. More generally, there is the concern, already mentioned, that *B and R*

[83] Davis and Dickstein, "It just doesn't fit", *op cit.* n.70.

[84] This did not, in the end, occur in *Re CP* itself: when the case was re-heard by a different trial judge, the child was returned to the foster mother.

[85] *Per* Evatt CJ in *Goudge* (1984) FLC 91–534.

[86] ALRC No. 31, *Recognition of Aboriginal Customary Law* (Canberra: AGPS, 1986) p. 257; ALRC No. 57, *Multiculturalism, op cit.* n.9, at para. 6.39.

[87] B v.B: *Family Law Reform Act 1995* (1997) 21 Fam LR 676 at 734.

[88] R. Graycar and J. Morgan, *The Hidden Gender of Law* (Annandale, NSW: Federation Press, 1990) ch. 10.

places a heavy evidential burden on Indigenous parents and communities which non-Indigenous parents do not have to bear.

In the light of this, what can be done to ensure that the best interests standard achieves its potential for providing a flexible and inclusive basis for family law decision-making? There is no single answer, but there are a number of possible strategies. One of these is judicial education, so that Indigenous parties are not constantly under the evidential burden of proving the legitimacy of their difference. This is recommended by *Bringing them Home*;[89] and the Family Court has already started taking this seriously through the creation of its Indigenous and Torres Strait Islander Awareness Committee.[90]

Another would be further amendment of the Family Law Act 1975. This is also recommended by *Bringing them Home*, which suggests two changes.[91] The first is the addition of a new paragraph (ba) to section 60B(2), the subsection that sets out the objects and principles underlying Part VII of the Family Law Act 1975, which would incorporate Article 30 (see above) directly into Australian law.[92] The second is the amendment of section 68F(2)(f) to make it clear that the need of any Indigenous or Torres Strait Islander child to maintain contact with his or her culture must be taken into account in deciding a child's best interests, as opposed to the current drafting which appears to leave it to the discretion of the judge.[93] These changes would ensure that Indigenous parties would not have to establish the relevance of Indigenous culture, since a judge would have no option but to consider it. However, it could be argued that these changes would do little more than declare what, in the wake of *B and R*, is already the existing law. In *B and R*, as we have seen, the Court seemed to regard it as essential that the rights in Article 30 be vindicated where relevant.

I suggest that something more is needed. We have seen that one of the problems encountered by Indigenous parents is that child-rearing practices regarded as normal and desirable in Indigenous society, may be considered aberrant and harmful by dominant conceptions of children's best interests. The issue of mobility as against permanence, stability and the status quo is a central example. The changes proposed by *Bringing them Home* would not overcome that risk: the emphasis on connection with, or enjoyment of, their culture, however non-optional, may not be enough to persuade a judge to return a child to live in an environment which, on a non-Indigenous view of things, is going to be

---

[89] The Report recommends education for *all* Family Court officers involved in parenting disputes, including Registrars, counsellors and welfare officers: at 487.

[90] M. Harrison and D. Sandor, "News from the Family Court", *Family Matters* No. 44, Winter 1996; see also B. Smith, *Evaluation of the Alice Springs Counselling Service and of the engagement of Aboriginal Family Consultants in Alice Springs and Darwin* (Canberra: Family Court of Australia, 1997).

[91] At pp. 596–7; see also A. Nicholson, "Family Court Initiatives with Aboriginal and Torres Strait Islander Communities" (1995) 76 *Aboriginal Law Bulletin* 15.

[92] The new paragraph would read: "children of Indigenous origins have a right, in community with other members of their group, to enjoy their own culture, profess and practice their own religion, and use their own language".

[93] See above.

harmful to the child. I suggest, therefore, that the Full Court's suggestion in *Re CP*, that section 68F should be amended to "take account of the kinship care systems of Indigenous and Torres Strait islander peoples",[94] should be taken very seriously. I understand this to be a recommendation that judges should in future be directed to take account of the child-care practices and values of the Indigenous group concerned as a relevant factor in its decision-making.[95]

I am not suggesting that this would be an easy thing to do:[96] it would require extensive education of decision-makers, and a heavy reliance on evidence in each case as to what the values of a particular community are. Nor am I advocating a complete slide into cultural relativism, so that the values of the minority group are determinative no matter what. That would seem to run counter to the legal policy of multiculturalism as presently understood. I am suggesting, however, that those minority values should be accepted in the decision-making process as proper and legitimate, to be weighed as such in the process of balancing the other factors relevant to the child's best interests. In those family law cases in which an ACPP would not be appropriate (and they are likely to be a majority), factor-based decision-making of this sort, conscientiously exercised, is perhaps our best hope of achieving the flexibility and inclusiveness characteristic of a legal policy of multiculturalism.[97]

V   CONCLUSION

This chapter has attempted to summarise, in a very confined space, some of the issues arising from the legal treatment of Indigenous children in Australian law. It has been argued that an appropriate policy framework can be found in ideas of self-determination in the area of child protection, and of multiculturalism in the area of private family law decision-making. These frameworks have been advanced as both descriptions of current tendencies, and as yardsticks by which to measure the current state of Australian law. As things stand, it has been argued that in neither the public nor the private spheres does Australian law live up to the policy objectives that might fairly be expected of it.

Yet there are signs of a willingness to achieve a greater accommodation of cultural difference in family relations. The process of reconciliation between white and Indigenous Australians is still comparatively young, and it is remarkable

---

[94] *Re CP* at 506.

[95] This is not a suggestion that the Family Court should recognise and give effect to Indigenous customary laws concerning children, although any such laws would form part of the "practices and values" of which account should be taken. For a brief discussion, see McCrae *et al.*, *op cit.* n. 11, pp. 446–9.

[96] It is possible, for example, that parents may come from different groups whose practices differ.

[97] *Cf.* C. Sunstein, *Legal Reasoning and Political Conflict* (New York: OUP, 1996) who suggests that factor-based (as distinct from rule-based) decision-making is an essential technique in a society characterised by diversity and lack of consensus: see especially ch. 6.

how the landscape has been transformed over the last quarter century. Even so, the further accommodation of cultural difference with respect to children, of different conceptions of the good, remains one of the greatest challenges facing Australian law.

7

Rhetoric and Reality in Inter-Country Adoptions: Divergent Principles and Stratified Status

JOHN MURPHY*

I INTRODUCTION

THE YEARLY NUMBER of inter-country adoptions in Britain was relatively insignificant until about 1990.[1] At about this time, however, harrowing revelations about the appalling conditions under which orphaned and abandoned children were living in a number of countries in eastern Europe—most notably Romania—and South and Central America aroused considerable interest in the prospect of inter-country adoptions among many childless British couples. This desire to adopt from abroad was fuelled not merely by sympathy for the plight of these children, but also by the dire shortage of babies and infants available for adoption domestically. Alarmingly, in their clamour to overcome childlessness, many of these couples removed children from their State of origin with little or no formality,[2] while others obtained highly dubious foreign adoption orders that were not recognised as valid under English law.[3] Neither approach was at all satisfactory from the perspective of either English law or the parties concerned.

As a result, the growth in inter-country adoption,[4] the absence of any

---

* University of Manchester. A version of this essay was presented as a paper at the Faculty of Law, University of Western Australia. I am grateful to all those who commented helpfully on that occasion.

[1] According to one account, there were as few as 50 per annum: see the White Paper, *Adoption: The Future* Cm 2288 (London: HMSO, 1993) para. 6.2. By contrast, the estimate in the *Adoption Law Review* of 1992 was of roughly 100–20 per year: see Department of Health and Welsh Office, *Review of Adoption Law*, Discussion Paper No. 4 (London: HMSO, 1992) para. 27.

[2] See C. Bridge, "Reforming Intercountry Adoption" [1992] *Journal of Child Law* 116 and the sources cited therein at nn. 1–3.

[3] See, e.g., *Re C (Adoption: Legality)* [1999] 1 FLR 370 where a Guatemalan adoption order was not recognised under English Law, and *Re Adoption Application (Non-Patrial: Breach of Procedures)* [1993] 2 WLR 110 where an order obtained in El Salvador was held invalid.

[4] There was evidence in *Re C, supra* n. 3, at 376, that there are now roughly 400 inter-country adoptions per year. Of these, approximately a quarter are made in disregard of the proper procedures by persons who have been rejected as suitable adopters of British children.

satisfactory international standard practice,[5] and the problems associated with the frequent abrogation of extant immigration rules made it plain that a proper system of regulation was required. And since Britain was not alone in experiencing this phenomenon, it was widely accepted that international co-operation over the regulation and recognition of inter-country adoptions was desirable. A conference at the Hague on Private International Law on Inter-country Adoption was duly convened in 1993 and, by May of that year, a Convention to *regulate*[6] inter-country adoption had been drawn up. (This Convention has now been incorporated into English law via the Adoption (Intercountry Aspects) Act 1999.)[7] It is clear from the preamble to the Convention that it is intended to be consistent with the principles embodied in both United Nations Convention on the Rights of the Child and the United Nations Declaration on Social and Legal Principles relating to the Protection and Welfare of Children with special reference to Foster Placement and Adoption Nationally and Internationally. This means that the Hague Convention is seemingly committed to the best interests of the child.[8] And these interests, as we shall see, are presumed to be better served by a State of origin placement than by an inter-country adoption. Yet the actual degree of commitment to the best interests of the child, and the extent to which the assumption that these are best secured by a State of origin placement are highly questionable. As we shall see, notwithstanding the 1993 Convention, a number of factors combine to make the premium placed upon the child's welfare in inter-country adoptions markedly lower than that applied in domestic adoptions. In particular, this is attributable to the practical ineffectuality of a range of statutory safeguards against procedural improprieties in inter-country adoption. In addition, it will also be seen that, even once adopted, the status of the inter-country adoptee is far from equivalent to that of the domestic adoptee.

In short, this essay will make the argument that there is a two-tier system of adoption in operation: one for domestic adoptees and one for inter-country

---

[5] The Hague Convention on the Adoption of Children 1965, having only three signatories, has been of nugatory effect in this context.

[6] It is important to note that the Convention was designed to be regulatory in nature rather than simply a means of facilitating inter-country adoptions. As such, in the preamble to the 1993 Convention there is a clear statement that the emphasis should lie with finding acceptable homes for children rather than with finding children for childless couples. It signals "the necessity to take measures to ensure that intercountry adoptions are made in the best interests of the child . . . and to prevent the abduction, the sale of, or traffic in children". See also the applicable Art. 20 of the UN Convention on the Rights of the Child which stipulates that States Parties must "ensure that the best interests of the child should be the paramount consideration".

[7] At the time of writing, the 1999 Act still requires to be brought into force by statutory instrument. For this reason, and for the benefit of non-British readers, I shall make reference in this essay only to Articles in the Hague Convention.

[8] UN Convention on the Rights of the Child, Art. 21; Hague Convention Arts. 1(a), 4(b). *Cf.* the parent-centric view of Judge Heald that "foreign adoptions should be encouraged to help those childless couples who want as near to normal a child as possible": "W(h)ither Adoption: Present and Future Developments" [1992] *Family Law* 29, at 30.

adoptees. More particularly it will be contended first, that the 1993 Convention (and hence the 1999 Act) places an uncertain and confusing emphasis on the best interests of the child, secondly, that by dint of irony, those adopters whose suitability has been rejected for the purposes of domestic applications may nonetheless circumvent or abrogate the Convention's provisions and adopt from abroad with virtually certain impunity, and thirdly, that the Convention's provisions with respect to the recognition of inter-country adoptions are far from adequate.

II THE WELFARE OF THE CHILD IN INTER-COUNTRY ADOPTIONS

Despite the formal incorporation of the provisions of the Hague Convention into English law, it remains necessary to consider the welfare of the child in inter-country adoptions under two heads: those that take place in accordance with the provisions of the Convention (hereafter, "Convention adoptions") and those that involve either children adopted from States not Party to the Convention, or children adopted from States Party to the Convention, but in respect of whom there has been a disregard of the appropriate Convention procedures (hereafter, "other adoptions").

A Convention Adoptions

In respect of domestic adoptees, the weight to be attached to the welfare of the child is clear: it is to be the court's first (but not paramount) consideration.[9] By contrast, as we have already seen, inter-country adoptions under the Hague Convention must "take place in the best interests of the child".[10] But the way in which the child's best interests are to be evaluated for these purposes is qualified by two important provisions. One of these exists in the Convention itself; the other is to be found in the United Nations Convention on the Rights of the Child.

Under Article 4(b) of the Hague Convention, a Convention adoption "shall take place only if the competent authorities[11] of the State of origin . . . have determined, *after possibilities for placement of the child within the State of origin have been given due consideration,* that an intercountry adoption is in the

---

[9] Adoption Act 1976, s. 6. The way in which the first and paramount considerations differ has been authoritatively settled by the House of Lords: the first consideration means that it will outweigh any other consideration, but not all others: see *Re D (An Infant) (Adoption: Parent's Consent)* [1977] AC 602, 632 (*per* Lord Simon). A pertinent example of a second relevant consideration is immigration policy: see *Re H (A Minor) (Adoption: Non-Patrial)* [1997] 1 WLR 791.

[10] Art. 1(a).

[11] In practice, these will be local authority and approved voluntary adoption agencies. For further details, see N. Lowe and G. Douglas, *Bromley's Family Law* (London: Butterworths, 1998) pp. 681–2.

child's best interests".[12] Several comments are warranted in connection with this rather cryptic provision. First, it is clear that the possibility of a State of origin placement is made the *first consideration* in a Convention adoption. This arguably contrasts with the principle enshrined in the Adoption Act 1976 that makes the child's welfare the first consideration.[13] Secondly, it is also implicit in Article 4(b) that, beyond being simply the first consideration, State of origin placements are regarded as being necessarily preferable to inter-county alternatives. This implication arises partly from the wording of Article 4(b) and partly by reference to the second of the two provisions just referred to—Article 21(b) of the United Nations Convention on the Rights of the Child. The relevance of this latter provision to the interpretation of Article 4(b) derives from the fact that the preamble to the Hague Convention makes it clear that its several chapters are designed to "establish common provisions" with "the principles set forth in international instruments, in particular the United Nations Convention on the Rights of the child". As such, Article 21(b) of the UN Convention is relevant to the interpretation of Article 4(b) of the 1993 Convention, stating as it does, that Member States are required to consider inter-country adoption only "if the child cannot be placed in a foster or an adoptive family or cannot be cared for in the child's country of origin".

The combined effect of the two provisions of the respective Conventions is this: the child's best interests will hold sway only once it has been established that a State of origin placement cannot be made. Of course, it could be argued that, for reasons analogous to those often made in favour of same-race placements in the context of the domestic adoption of minority children,[14] there is no inconsistency between the prioritisation of State of origin placements and the child's best interests. The argument would hang on the assumption that the child will always be better off if he or she is placed with carers of the same race and culture in the country of origin. But the trouble with this argument is that it underplays or ignores the significance of the deplorable conditions from which many inter-country adoptees typically come in their State of origin, and under which they might reasonably be expected to continue to live in the absence of an inter-country adoption. As Johnson J noted in *Re C*,[15] a case involving a Mayan Indian adoptee from Guatemala:

> Anyone who has seen the conditions in which some children are brought up in some Central and South American countries, in the shanty towns and favelas alongside the great cities, will feel an urgent desire that [these] children be given the opportunities represented by adoption into an English family.[16]

Much more plausible than any necessary or obvious link between the best interests of a child and an adoptive or foster placement in his or her State of ori-

---

[12] Emphasis added.
[13] As to why, see *infra*.
[14] See my other contribution to this collection at ch. 3.
[15] *Supra*, n. 3.
[16] *Ibid.*, at 376–7.

gin, is the political explanation for Article 4(b)'s inclusion in the Convention: namely, that Article 4(b) was included to ensure that the Convention would not become an instrument to *facilitate* inter-country adoptions, but rather one to *regulate* the practice and encourage the establishment of better child care services in the developing nations from which inter-country adoptees normally emanate. William Duncan has explained the anti-exploitative nature of this provision in the following terms:

> [I]n intercountry adoptions, there is concern lest the principle of giving priority to the child's interests be used as an excuse for social engineering, that is to justify a more generalised transfer of children from poor to wealthy parents or from developing to rich economies.[17]

In terms of housing quality, sanitation, educational opportunities, back-up State support systems, access to health care, quality of health care and a myriad of other amenities and facilities not generally associated with developing nations, it is difficult to see how the child's best interests can, *ipso facto*, normally best be served by a State of origin placement.[18] As such, it seems fair to conclude that under the 1993 Convention there is a serious limitation to the extent to which the child's best interests will genuinely be a central guiding principle.

B Other Adoptions

In cases where the procedures specified by the 1993 Convention have been evaded, or in cases where the State of origin is not a Party to the Convention, it is equally the case that a lower standard of welfare will be afforded to the inter-country adoptee. More particularly, despite official Department of Health policy to the contrary,[19] this will occur because the courts are usually less rigorous in their insistence on the suitability of the adopters once the child in question has already been brought to the United Kingdom. Indeed, according to the personal experience of one judge, nearly all of those who had applied to him to adopt a child from overseas in contumacious disregard for the proper procedures had

---

[17] W. Duncan, "Regulating Intercountry Adoption—an International Perspective" in A. Bainham *et al.* (eds.), *Frontiers of Family Law* (Chichester: John Wiley & Co, 1995) p. 42.

[18] This is not to deny, of course, that this may well, on occasion, be possible. For, of course, State of origin adoptions could easily be preferable where the child concerned is no longer an infant, has acquired a particular cultural identity, has learnt to speak a language other than English or formed a close bond with individuals living in his or her country of birth.

[19] In the DoH's *A Guide to Inter-Country Adoption Practice and Procedure* it states that "there can be no question of operating a two-tier adoption service, applying a lower standard to overseas adoption. A person who cannot be recommended as suitable to adopt a child living in the United Kingdom cannot be recommended to adopt a child living overseas": cited in the judgment of Johnson J in *Re C*, *supra* n. 3, at 375.

previously been rejected as suitable prospective domestic adopters.[20] And according to another High Court judge:

> There are between 75 and 100 applications which are made after disregard of those [overseas adoption] procedures. Most of those will be by parents who have been previously rejected as suitable for the adoption of a British child.[21]

The result is that inter-country adoptees will frequently be adopted by parents who suffer from health problems or who are older than would normally be considered acceptable by an adoption agency. In *Re C*,[22] for example, a woman of thirty-nine who weighed nineteen stones, who had suffered health problems requiring hospitalisation and who stood at risk of future health problems, nonetheless succeeded in adopting a six month old Guatemalan baby. When she had earlier approached two social services adoption agencies and one voluntary agency, they had all rejected her out of hand as a potential adopter. Concerns had been expressed not only about her health problems and her likely inability to care properly for an active young child, but also about "her limited understanding of adoption issues and her tendency to allow her enthusiasm [for adoption] to cloud her judgment".[23] Nonetheless, the judge in that case held that:

> There are serious concerns about the ability of the applicant to meet the entirety of [the child] J's needs but in terms of welfare those concerns are in my view outweighed by the considerable disadvantage that may accrue to J if the adoption order is not made and the immigration authorities decide to terminate or not to extend his right to remain here.[24]

Applying the same reasoning, a similar conclusion was reached, despite breaches of the statutory code, in *Re Adoption Application (Non-Patrial: Breach of Procedures)*.[25] And in *R v. Secretary of State for Health, ex parte Luff*,[26] although an adoption order was not ultimately made, the court nonetheless accepted a that a plausible argument could be made that it was in the best interests of two Romanian infants that they be adopted by a parent who was fifty-seven years old, had undergone heart bypass surgery and had a life expectancy of only ten years.[27]

In fact, in *Re C*, Johnson J's trawl of the decided cases revealed that only in one instance—where the natural parents sought to have their child returned to them—had the court declined to make an adoption order.[28] And in only one

---

[20] According to Judge Heald, "All of the cases that have come before me . . . have been by couples who would not normally be acceptable to an adoption agency": *op cit*. n. 8, at 30.

[21] *Re C, supra* n. 3, at 376 (*per* Johnson J).

[22] *Supra*, n. 3.

[23] *Ibid.*, at 372.

[24] *Ibid.*, at 381 (*per* Johnson J).

[25] *Supra*, n. 3.

[26] [1992] 1 FLR 59.

[27] *Ibid.*, at 75 (*per* Waite J).

[28] [1999] 1 FLR 370, 382.

reported case since *Re C* was decided,[29] has a court declined to make an adoption order. Yet even in that case the child was made a ward of court and care and control was ultimately awarded to the would-be adopters.[30]

There is undoubtedly much force in the argument that, once the child has resided in the UK for a considerable time, he or she cannot easily, perhaps even feasibly, be returned to his or her State of origin. But this does not necessarily mean that, in the absence of the birth parents being willing and able to have the child returned to them, the court must inevitably make an adoption order in favour of the obreptitious would-be adopters. Indeed, since inter-country adoptions frequently involve breaches of section 57 of the Adoption Act 1976[31] by those who have previously been rejected as domestic adopters, the bar to making an adoption order in their favour contained in section 24(2) of that Act ought to be seen as a crucial provision. For it is there provided that the court "shall not make an adoption order in relation to a child unless it is satisfied that the applicants have not, as respects the child, contravened section 57". Had this provision been considered in *Re C* it is difficult to see how Johnson J could have justified the adoption order that he eventually granted in favour of the woman he found to have "agreed to pay [the Guatemalan lawyers] . . . the sum stipulated and so was in breach of the section".[32]

Even where there has been no breach of section 57, it is still possible, perhaps even likely, that there has nonetheless been a breach of section 11 of the 1976 Act[33] which sets out the limited circumstances in which adoption arrangements and placements can be made by someone other than an adoption agency.[34] In my view, in those cases involving a breach of section 11, the criminal acts of the applicants[35] ought properly to figure in the court's assessment of whether it would be in the best interests of the child to be adopted by such persons. Indeed, as Douglas Brown J observed in *Re Adoption Application*:[36]

> The question for the court, bearing in mind section 6, is does public policy require that the applicants should be refused the order they seek because of their criminal conduct?

---

[29] *Re R (No. 1) (Inter-country Adoption)* [1999] 1 FLR 1014.

[30] Bracewell J was persuaded that the child in question had educational needs that were being met in the UK that would not be met in Romania. Similarly, she was concerned that the child's physical well-being would not be assured if she were returned to her natural parents who lived in impoverished circumstances and refused to acknowledge the child's special needs: see *ibid.* at 1038–40.

[31] This provision places a prohibition on payments in reward for or in consideration of an adoption, the procuration of an agreement to an adoption, custody transfers and the making of arrangements for an adoption.

[32] *Supra*, n. 3, at 381. It was precisely for this reason that Bracewell J held it to be impossible for her to make an adoption order in relation to the Romanian child in *Re R, supra* n. 29, at 1041.

[33] This is not inevitable in the present context, for where the arrangements for an adoption are made entirely outside the jurisdiction of England and Wales, the Act has no effect: see Adoption Act 1976, s. 74(3).

[34] Effectively these circumstances are limited to placements with relatives or those made under the authority of a High Court order: Adoption Act 1976, s. 11(1).

[35] Such private placements and arrangements are criminalised under s. 11(3) of the 1976 Act.

[36] *Supra*, n. 3.

The court, still bearing in mind the guidance contained in section 6, must conduct a balancing exercise.[37]

I would submit that the kinds of factors that ought to be weighed alongside the criminality of the would-be adopters include the length of time that the child has spent with them, the strength of the affective bond that the child has for them and the availability of other, more suitable adopters or foster-parents.[38] Considering that the child in question could be made a ward of court, giving the judge a free hand—as indeed happened in *Re R*[39]—it is difficult to see why the courts should feel it to be almost axiomatic that the child's long term welfare will best be served by making an adoption order in favour of those who have been rejected in the past and who have committed offences under the adoption legislation. Too much emphasis seems typically to be placed upon the advantages that accrue by virtue of remaining in the United Kingdom rather than upon those which can be attributed to the particular would-be adopters. For the advantages that accrue from being in the United Kingdom (rather than the State of origin) would be present whomever the child was placed with in this country. And it simply is not the case that the only options available to the court are either adoption by the initial applicants, or a return to the State of origin. Many alternatives exist where the child in question is a baby or infant who has been warded and who has not yet become firmly settled with the prospective adopters.

III SAFEGUARDS (?) AGAINST WRONGFUL ADOPTION

At a domestic level, it is extremely difficult for a child to be adopted by wholly unsuitable parents. At the placement stage, except where a child has been placed with relatives or in pursuance of a High Court order, it is a criminal offence for an adoption placement to be made by anyone other than an adoption agency.[40] Furthermore, the circumstances under which agencies may place children for adoption are strictly regulated,[41] and the agency that has placed the child must "submit to the court a report on the suitability of the applicants and any other

[37] *Ibid.*, at 118. See also *Re C, supra* n. 3, at 318 (*per* Johnson J).
[38] These may be found in at least two ways. First, there may be adopters known to the relevant local authority who would be prepared to adopt such a child, even though they had not yet applied to adopt a foreign child. Alternatively, there may prospective adopters who have failed in the past to adopt from abroad because, for instance, the Central Authority in the State of origin considered the child in question to be unsuitable for inter-country adoption under Art. 16 of the 1993 Convention. Such persons would necessarily be known to the Central Authority in this country by virtue of their earlier application to that authority under Art. 14.
[39] *Supra*, n. 29.
[40] Adoption Act 1976, s. 11(3).
[41] See Adoption Agencies Regulations 1983 (SI 1983, No. 1964). See also ss. 1–3 of the Adoption Act specifying the adoption services to be provided by local authorities and the requirements that must be met before voluntary agencies will be approved.

matters relevant to the operation of section 6".[42] At the hearing stage there is the further safeguard of a presumptive bar against the making of an adoption order in relation to a child where a previous application by the same persons in relation to that child was refused; and an absolute bar where the adopters have contravened section 57.[43]

While it is patently felt that the best interests of the child demand that the same safeguards should be extended to inter-country adoptees—"[t]he Government wishes to see the same principles and safeguards . . . for overseas adoption as for domestic adoption"[44]—their position remains much less well protected than that of their domestically adopted counterparts. None of the duties incumbent on adoption agencies prior to placement or hearing apply in relation to a child who comes into this country in the custody of his or her would-be adopters. All that exists to protect such a child are, first, the limited duties placed on the local authority under section 33 of the 1976 Act, secondly, the watchful eye of immigration authorities and thirdly, the possible deterrent of potential conviction for breaches of sections 11 and 57 of the 1976 Act.[45] Yet, none of these safeguards against abuse or contravention of the proper procedures is especially effective in practice.

While section 32 of the Act makes the would-be inter-country adoptee a "protected child" once the prospective adopters have given notice of their intention to apply for an adoption order, the duties placed on the local authority with respect to such a child are very limited. They amount to little more than an obligation to ensure that the child is visited from time to time and a requirement that the authority should furnish the prospective adopters with advice as to care and maintenance if it considers such advice to be needed.[46] The power to remove such children from unsuitable surroundings formerly contained in section 34 of the Adoption Act was specifically repealed by the Children Act 1989.[47]

Any effective local authority protection of these supposedly "protected children" must now depend on initiating proceedings under Parts IV or V of the Children Act 1989. But the problem with these mechanisms is their insistence of proof of extant or likely harm.[48] When, as we have already seen, the most frequent problems associated with prospective inter-country adopters are their age and health, it is difficult to see how the child in question could be shown currently or imminently to be at risk of harm during the relatively brief period that he or she remains a "protected child". Problems concerning the health and age

[42] Adoption Act 1976, s. 23(1).
[43] *Ibid.*, s. 24.
[44] *Adoption: The Future, op cit.* n. 1, para. 6.10.
[45] Clearly, ss. 11 and 57 do not apply extraterritorially so that financial arrangements and placements with would-be adopters that take place entirely abroad are not caught by the provisions of the Adoption Act: see Adoption Act 1976, s. 74(3) and *Re Adoption Application, supra* n. 3.
[46] Adoption Act 1976, s. 33(1).
[47] Children Act 1989, Sched. 15.
[48] Care proceedings will only succeed if the child "is suffering, or is likely to suffer significant harm": Children Act 1989, s. 31(2)(a). A similar condition exists with respect to the making of emergency protection orders under s. 46(1)(a) of the same Act.

of the prospective adopters usually represent only a long term, future risk rather than a present or impending one. As such, it is difficult to see what a local authority can realistically do to safeguard a foreign child residing with less-than-suitable would-be adopters.

As regards the immigration authorities, the reported cases lend adequate testimony to the ease with which a prospective inter-country adoptee can be brought into this country and kept here long enough to make his or her adoption by the applicants more or less a *fait accompli*. In *Re C*, for example, the applicant simply met the child at Schipol Airport in Amsterdam, flew with the child to Heathrow and "explained to the immigration officer her intention to apply for adoption".[49] And in *Re R*, entry clearance was gained in two very simple stages. To begin with, a Romanian passport was obtained in respect of the child in question on the basis that it would be needed to take her to the UK for medical treatment. Next, to obtain a visa, the British Embassy in Bucharest was told by the applicant that she was taking the child to the UK for "a few weeks holiday".[50] Thereafter, entry into the UK was a mere formality.

Admittedly, the judgment of Bracewell J in *Re R (Inter-Country Adoptions: Practice)*[51] should go some way to reducing the risks of deliberate evasions or abuses of the immigration system; but it can offer no guarantees. For example, her Ladyship's recommendation that "[t]he child should be permitted to enter the UK only if the accompanying adult produces to the immigration officer the written consent of the natural parents to the visit"[52] will naturally meet a stumbling block where, as in *Re C*, the parent was illiterate and unable even to write her own name. There may also be a problem for the relevant immigration officer if the documentation is presented in a language other than English in, say, the middle of the night. Furthermore, the additional recommendation that the child be afforded entry clearance for only the minimum period necessary, is not without prospective difficulties.[53] It fails, for example, to preclude the possibility of extended periods of entry being requested by the would-be adopters on the strength of a bogus claim about the child's health requiring extensive medical care that can only be supplied in this country over a lengthy period of time. Such claims would be eminently plausible to an immigration officer if made in respect of an under-nourished and emaciated orphan or abandoned child from a developing nation.

Finally, of course, immigration officers might find it difficult to refuse entry if the child were to be brought to this country following an adoption overseas, even if, ultimately, the foreign adoption would not qualify for recognition by the English courts. Unless they knew the relevant position under private inter-

[49] *Re C, supra* n. 3, at 376.
[50] *Supra*, n. 29, at 1018.
[51] [1999] 1 FLR 1042.
[52] *Re R, supra* n. 29, at 1047.
[53] *Ibid.*

national law, an official document testifying to the adoption of the child would be something in the face of which it might well be difficult to refuse entry.

In relation to the deterrent effect of breaching sections 11 and 57 of the 1976 Act, it is clear from the reported cases that any such deterrent must be minimal if any exists at all. In many instances, breaches of section 11 are effectively condoned by virtue of the courts retrospectively authorising those placements.[54] Furthermore, the simple fact of having breached section 11 probably does not impose a bar on the court making an adoption order, there being nothing in either section 11 or section 24 to this effect.[55] As regards breaches of section 57, the Act itself provides for retrospective judicial authorisation of payments made in connection with adoptions.[56] And in relation to both provisions there are three further factors that tend to undermine their efficacy as deterrents, all of which were adverted to by Johnson J in *Re C*:

> The prohibitions in the Act, and I think particularly of sections 11 and 57, are not of the kind that one would ordinarily expect to find in the criminal law. Yet the fact is that Parliament did specifically provide that breaches of these prohibitions would amount to offences under the criminal law . . . [I]t may be that Parliament recognised that breaches of these prohibitions could not in reality lead the court to a decision contrary to the welfare of the child . . . [and] there is the practical problem that the offences are to be dealt with only summarily and prosecution may be difficult because of the limitation period.[57]

Taken together, the frequency of judicial condonation, the absence of a bar to subsequent adoption, the concern not to do indirect harm to the child by prosecuting, the short limitation period and the summary nature of these offences, do little in practice to deter childless couples from illicit inter-country adoptions. And so long as the choices facing the court are seen purely in terms of *either* an adoption order in favour of the applicants, *or* a return of the child to his or her State of origin, it is difficult to see anything genuinely off-putting in the possibility of a prosecution under section 11 or section 57.[58]

IV THE RECOGNITION OF INTER-COUNTRY ADOPTIONS

Even where an inter-country adoption has been made in full accordance with the principles and provisions contained in the Hague Convention, the welfare of

---

[54] For a useful survey of the reported cases, see K. O'Donnell, "Illegal Placements in Adoption" [1994] *Journal of Child Law* 17.
[55] See *Re Adoption Application (Adoption of Non-Patrial)* [1992] 1 WLR 596; *Re Adoption Application, supra* n. 3.
[56] Adoption Act 1976, s. 57(3).
[57] *Supra*, n. 3, at 382.
[58] Of course, fines could be imposed in preference to incarceration. But these, under s. 57(2) of the 1976 Act, may not exceed level 5 on the scale which might easily be affordable to those able to pay the large sums often associated with inter-country adoptions. Alternatively, payment of a fine might represent a significant incursion into limited family resources and therefore, indirectly, have a negative effect on the welfare of the child. Either way, it is difficult to identify an effective deterrent in the threat of a fine.

the inter-country adoptee appears nonetheless to be considerably less assured and certain than that of the domestic adoptee. The reason for this stems ultimately from the fact that Convention adoptions need not necessarily take place in the Receiving State. They might just as legitimately take place in the State of origin.[59] And they frequently will do, for, as Rainer Frank has explained, many "States of origin want to protect the interests of their children, especially against the traffic in children".[60]

In such circumstances, however, there is a possibility that the receiving State may refuse to recognise the adoption obtained abroad, or that, even if the receiving State recognises the adoption, a third Convention State might refuse to recognise it where the adoption in question is perceived to be contrary to public policy.[61] And this public policy exception to the rule that Convention adoptions "shall be recognised by operation of law in the other Contracting States"[62] might well be triggered if the original (imperfect but not invalid) adoption was certified with incomplete adherence to the principles set out in the Convention by, say, a non-judicial competent authority.[63]

Foreseeable contraventions of the Convention's provisions for these purposes include a failure properly to counsel the birth parents prior to their giving consent[64] and violations of the prohibitions against inducing such consent by the making of a payment.[65] Should such violations come to the attention of the UK authorities before the child has been brought to this country (or at least before he or she has become settled here), it is conceivable that the discretionary refusal of recognition may be exercised. This would place the child in an adoptive limbo; adopted under the law of his or her State of origin, but not so under the law of the receiving State.

Further difficulties exist in this context with respect to the drafting of Article 26 of the Convention which seeks to delimit the *effects* of recognition.[66] In particular, Article 26(2) provides that:

> In the case of an adoption having the effect of terminating a pre-existing legal parent-child relationship, the child shall enjoy in the receiving State, and in any other Contracting State where the adoption is recognised, rights equivalent to those resulting from adoptions having this effect in each such State.

The intention of this provision is to enable the child's legal status as regards the degree of his or her integration into the adoptive family to be determined by the

[59] Hague Convention 1993, Art. 2(1).

[60] R. Frank, "The Recognition of Intercountry Adoptions in the Light of the 1993 Hague Convention on Intercountry Adoptions" in N. Lowe and G. Douglas (eds.), *Families Across Frontiers* (Dordrecht: Kluwer Academic Publishers, 1996) p. 591.

[61] Hague Convention 1993, Art. 24.

[62] *Ibid.*, Art. 23(1).

[63] Art. 23(1) of the Convention requires only that a Convention adoption be certified by a Competent Authority; it nowhere states that this competent authority must be a court.

[64] See Hague Convention, Art. 4(c)(i).

[65] See *ibid*, Art. 4(c)(iii), (d)(iv).

[66] As to the difference between recognition *per se*, and the *effects* of recognition, see R. Frank, *op cit.*, n. 60.

law of the receiving State *so long as* the adoption obtained in the State of origin terminates the legal relationship between the child and the birth parents.[67] But if an adoption is obtained in State X prior to the child being brought to this country, it is possible that his or her status within the adoptive family will remain uncertain because of doubts as to the effects of the adoption in State X. Rainer Frank, for example, adverts to a number of states that claim to employ a model of full adoption but which, in truth, allow the birth parents to retain a range of residual rights in respect of the child concerned. In such circumstances, it cannot be certain that Article 26(2) covers the adoption.[68] This in turn means that the precise status of the adoptee *vis-à-vis* the adoptive family cannot be ascertained. And, naturally, such confusion concerning the child's status can hardly be thought to conduce to his or her best interests.

In such a situation the only solution would be to have a repeat adoption in the receiving State. Yet Article 27 of the Convention only provides for repeat adoptions in the receiving State "[w]here an adoption granted in the State of origin *does not* have the effect of terminating a pre-existing legal parent-child relationship".[69] It is silent on the matter of whether repeat adoptions are permissible otherwise than by virtue of Article 27.[70] But it is probably against the spirit of the Convention to allow free and easy use to be made of repeat adoptions in the receiving State since this would drive a coach and four through Chapter V of the Convention which is specifically designed to provide for recognition of any adoption obtained in a Contracting State.[71] In consequence, a repeat adoption under Article 27 is probably better seen as being the *only exception* to the general rule that it is the first adoption which counts.[72] It is consequently difficult to see a way around the legal limbo in which many inter-country adoptees may find themselves.

There is a third source of confusion which, to his or her potential cost, surrounds the status of the Convention adoptee who is adopted in the State of origin. Article 26(1) of the Hague Convention does no more than stipulate that the newly established parent-child relationship (together with parental responsibility) is to be recognised among other Contracting States. It does not, however, indicate which law governs the nature of that parent–child relationship, the law of the receiving State or the law of the State of origin. The matter might be

[67] Some countries have more than one model of adoption. France, for example, has both the *adoption plénière* and the *adoption simple*. Depending upon which model is used, the adoption may or may not sever the legal tie between the child and the natural parents. Art. 26(2) quite rightly preserves the right of the State in which the adoption is obtained to determine whether the original parent-child relationship is terminated by virtue of the order.

[68] See R. Frank, *op cit*. n. 60, p601.

[69] Hague Convention, Art. 27(1) (emphasis added).

[70] *Cf.* Frank's interpretation that "Article 27 states that the repetition of an intercountry adoption domestically is excluded if the adoption leads to a termination of the natural parent-child relationship": R. Frank, *op cit*. n. 60, p. 603.

[71] There would be very little point in having a Convention to *regulate* inter-country adoptions if it failed to reduce to a minimum the need for repeat adoptions.

[72] The rationale for Art. 27 is to allow a full adoption where one was not possible in the State of origin but the birth parents are happy to consent to a full adoption.

important for at least two reasons. First, it could be important to know the extent of the adopter's parental responsibility for the purposes of decision making with respect to the child in cases where the State of origin adoption did not completely sever the initial parent–child relationship. Secondly, there would be the potential problem of the child growing up without a proper sense of belonging to the adoptive family. The acquisition of such a fractured self-image could hardly be viewed in terms of the child's best interests. Of course, the remedy in this situation would again be to repeat the adoption in this country under Article 27. But some adoptive parents, now perhaps thousands of miles from the State of origin, might not feel there to be a need to do this. Indeed, they might well consider the matter not to be an issue at all until it is too late and the birth parents have, some years down the line, already sought to re-establish contact with their child.

Finally in this context, it is noteworthy that Chapter V of the Hague Convention, dealing with the recognition and effects of inter-country adoptions, is underpinned in large part by politically motivated compromises between receiving States and States of origin. In being so drafted, its provisions give rise to interpretational confusion as well as relegating the *genuine* best interests of the child to merely a secondary status. While I am not suggesting that more work on this Chapter of the Convention would have ironed out the problems to which I have adverted in this section, it nonetheless remains the case that the status of the Convention adoptee can frequently be much less certain and assured than that of his or her domestically adopted counterpart.

V CONCLUSION

Despite a commendable effort to resolve the many problems associated with the escalating practice of inter-country adoptions, the importation of the Hague Convention into English law will provide precious few guarantees against future abuse of the proper procedures. Furthermore, the ease with which, on current judicial approaches, a non-Convention adoption can be obtained in contravention of the several legislative safeguards will do little to ensure that the inter-country adoptee is guaranteed the same quality of adoptive parents as the domestically adopted child. For this reason, it is difficult to refute the words of Johnson J in *Re C* concerning the "the reality that a two-tier system does operate".[73] There is one standard for the British adoptee; another for the foreign child.

Even within the Convention, there remains a manifest risk that the relevant rules of private international law will not guarantee the inter-country adoptee the same status as the child adopted in this country. And in time, this lesser status may prove damaging to the child's psyche. As a result, even within the

73 *Re C, supra* n. 3, at 382.

Convention, there seems clearly to be one set of rules and one status for the British adoptee, and another set of rules and another status for the inter-country adoptee. While little can realistically be done about those children adopted in accordance with the Hague Convention, I would nonetheless contend that more thought ought to be devoted to more inventive, child-centred ways of dealing with prospective adopters who have sought deliberately to evade the most hallowed principles governing private and commercial adoptions. Options via wardship—particularly while domestically the number of potential adopters outstrips the number of potential adoptees—seem an obvious port of call in this respect.[74]

---

[74] Recall that under the Adoption Act 1976, s. 11 one exception to the general rule that placements must be made by an adoption agency is an authorisation by virtue of an order of the High Court.

PART III
Miscellaneous Issues

8

Double Jeopardy: Race and Domestic Violence

ADA KEWLEY*

I INTRODUCTION

T HE REJECTION BY the Court of Appeal of Zoora Khan's appeal to have her
murder conviction reduced to manslaughter on the basis of the provocation
of her partner's physical, sexual abuse of her over a twelve year period[1] highlighted a major area of social concern that appears to have been insufficiently
recognised by academic and other commentators:[2] the significance of race in the
context of domestic violence. While the term "domestic violence" is generally
recognised to connote a situation in which a person causes, or attempts or
threatens to cause physical harm to another family or household member,[3] there
are other effects of such violence beyond simple physical injury to the victim.
These are characterised by feelings of helplessness, loss of self-respect, housing
and financial difficulties which may be especially severe where there are depen-
dant children who may be affected directly or indirectly by the violence.[4] If the
abuse takes place within a racial minority group, such problems can easily be
aggravated by cultural and social isolation which will make the abused woman
(and any children she may have) even more vulnerable to continued abuse, particularly if her residential status is that of an immigrant whose knowledge of
English and her rights is limited or non-existent.[5]

---

* Law School, University of Hull.

[1] (1998) *The Independent*, 1 May.

[2] See Madaqureshi, *Migrant and Ethnic Minority Women and Domestic Violence*, Conference
Report (London: University of London, 1997) p. 2.

[3] See, e.g., the definition offered by the Southall Black Sisters in *Domestic Violence and Asian
Women* (London: Southall Black Sisters, 1994) p. 11. Other commentators extend the definition to
include psychological and emotional abuse: see, e.g., *Crown Prosecution Series Statement of
Prosecution Policy* (London: CPS, 1993).

[4] See Farmer and Owen, *Child Protection Practice: Private Risks and Public Remedies* (London:
HMSO, 1995) and Mullender and Morley (eds.), *Children Living with Domestic Violence: Putting
Men's Abuse of Women on the Child Care Agenda* (London: Whiting and Burch, 1994).

[5] See Southall Black Sisters, *op cit*. n. 3, p. 5 and Stubbs, "Domestic Violence, Cultural Diversity
and the Legal System", Occasional Paper No. 7 (Northern Territory, Office of Women's Policy,
Northern Territory Government, 1996).

The aim of this paper is to consider at length these and other problems affecting domestic violence victims who hail from racial minority groups in order to suggest, where appropriate, reforms that can be made to ensure greater personal protection from abuse, and sensitivity in terms of institutional responses to their plight.

II WOMEN TRAPPED IN VIOLENT RELATIONSHIPS

It has been suggested that it is principally the structural difficulties that face many women that explains their being (or maybe just feeling) trapped in a violent relationship.[6] These structural difficulties include their relative poverty in comparison with men; fewer and less attractive employment prospects (particularly if they have children); frequent financial dependence on their male partners (especially where they are primary unpaid carers of children). Both individually and cumulatively, these difficulties can lead to their being trapped in violent relationships. Of course, these factors apply to white women, too. But in the case of ethnic minority women, their import is apt to be amplified by feelings of isolation and helplessness (which are themselves exacerbated where the victim is a recent immigrant who is dependent on a spouse for residential status),[7] housing problems, language and cultural differences[8] and assumptions about male dominance which "play a pivotal role in containing and policing [women's] lifestyle, behaviour and particularly their sexuality".[9] Furthermore, being a member of an ethnic minority group can lead to a feeling of entrapment because seeking help "outside the circle" may be perceived not only by her community, but by the abused woman herself, as a betrayal of her cultural values further compounding her sense of helplessness and despair. As Patel and Gaw put it:

> A woman can experience a sense of desperate entrapment and hopelessness about her future when she has to choose between continued abuse in the new situation and being an outcast in her community at a time when she most urgently needs support.[10]

---

[6] See, e.g., Pahl (ed.), *Private Violence and Public Policy* (London: Routledge & Kegan Paul, 1985) and National Inter-Agency Working Party, *Report on Domestic Violence* (London: Victim Support, 1992).

[7] The 1997 changes to the Immigration Rules regarding primary purpose rules have not diminished the Government's checks in order to root out "bogus" or "sham" marriages. As the Home Secretary has put it, "both parties must demonstrate that they can maintain and accommodate themselves and any dependants without recourse to public funds. The burden of proof in these cases will remain on the applicant. In addition, couples will continue to be subject to a 12–month probationary period, at the end of which they must show again that their marriage is genuine".: (1997) *Home Office News Release*, 5 June.

[8] The Southall Black Sisters record, for example, the control sometimes exerted by members of the victim's extended family: see Southall Black Sisters, *op cit*. n. 3, pp. 17–19.

[9] *Ibid.*, p. 22.

[10] Patel and Gaw, "Suicide Among Immigrants from the Indian Subcontinent" (1996) 47 *Psychiatric Series* 517, 520.

In such circumstances, the woman may be faced with apparently impossible options since within certain Asian communities considerable stigma is attached to unmarried or divorced women who do not choose to remain within their marriage or their community.[11] In *Banik* v. *Banik*,[12] for example, affidavit evidence supplied by the respondent to a divorce petition stated that:

> My husband knows and knew when he married me that I was a devout believer in the Hindu Religion. A Hindu woman looks to the spiritual aspect of dying as a married woman rather than for any material benefit. A Hindu woman will be destitute as a divorcée. *If I am divorced, I will by virtue of the society in which we live and the social attitudes and conventions existing in it, become a social outcast.*[13]

Failure to adhere to such powerful conventions as often exist within such patriarchal societies may lead not only to social ostracism but also, in extreme cases, to so called "honour killing" where the dishonour brought to the family name by bringing shame is judged to deserve such punishment.[14] At the very least, the mere threat of such isolation may be too much to contemplate for such abused women. For, as the Southall Black Sisters have declared, "it is precisely on the issue of honour and shame that many Asian women that we have met need the most counselling. Their fear of hostility, loneliness, lack of support and general social ostracisation [*sic*] is intense".[15]

The need for ongoing social support for abused women is a key feature of the current West Yorkshire Police domestic violence project in Killinbeck called "Cocoon Watch" which is showing considerable initial success in reducing repeat "victimisation" where it was said that, "the single most important action a woman can take to protect herself is to tell someone about the attacks on her. Cocoon Watch is designed to facilitate this process by extending the network of people who are prepared to telephone the police".[16] But the network of helpful neighbours and friends is precisely what women from close-knit ethnic minority communities may lack. This is especially so, of course, if she is a recent immigrant with little or no knowledge or understanding of her new country or the English language.[17]

III DOMESTIC VIOLENCE AND CONTACT ORDERS

Recent case law on contact disputes reveals a clear trend towards stating that, as contact with a father is the child's right, courts are "able to discount the

---

[11] See Southall Black Sisters, *op cit.* n. 3, pp. 19–23.
[12] [1973] 3 All ER 45.
[13] *Ibid.*, at 48 (emphasis added).
[14] See the graphic account of such "honour killings" supplied by the Southall Black Sisters: *ibid*, 23.
[15] *Ibid.*, 24.
[16] Hanmer and Griffiths (eds.), *Home Office Police Research Group Briefing Note* (London: Home Office, 1998).
[17] Stubbs, *op cit.* n. 5, pp. 14–17.

reasons for the mother's reluctance to allow contact on the basis that she does not appreciate her child's needs".[18] Indeed, a very strong presumption in favour of maintaining father/child contact may be gleaned that, in the absence of evidence of risk of harm to the child *by making a contact order*, the mere objection of one parent will not suffice to prevent the order being made in respect of the non-residential parent.

No matter how implacably hostile the mother may be to the making of such an order in favour of the father, the Court of Appeal has emphatically stated, more than once, that "[n]either parent should be encouraged or permitted to think that the more intransigent, the most unreasonable, the more obdurate and the more uncooperative they are, the more likely they are to get their own way".[19] Irrespective of how vitriolic the views of the objecting parent, Balcombe LJ enjoined his fellow judges to be "very reluctant to allow the implacable hostility of one parent . . . to deter them from making a contact order when they believe that the *child's* welfare requires it".[20] Though there is much to be said for the principle that implacably hostile parents should not be permitted to undermine the authority of the courts, there is a danger that the judges might misconstrue, in certain cases, the apparently "obvious" value in maintaining contact between a child and its father, for on occasion, such contact has been maintained even where the father has abused the child.[21] Indeed, in one extreme case, this was done where the father had a chronic history of severe violence for which he had once served a term of imprisonment. Yet even this background did not, in the view of the court, justify the severance of contact with his children.[22] Such judicial attitudes appear to fly in the face of the now well-established research finding of severe and long term psychological damage that is likely to result in children who have witnessed and lived with violence.[23] It also seems to overlook the research revealing the link between spousal abuse and child abuse. As Jane Fortin has pointed out: "the research indicating an extremely high correlation between spousal and child abuse suggests that the courts are naïve to think that a man who has seriously abused his partner will not abuse his children".[24]

Such worrying facets of the current law should not be taken in isolation. The strong emphasis placed upon the *child's* right to contact needs to be seen in tandem with the fact that violence within relationships often leads to a serious

---

[18] Fortin, *Children's Rights and the Developing Law* (London: Butterworths, 1998) p328. See also Madaqureshi, *op cit.* n. 2, p. 4.
[19] *Re O (Contact: Imposition of Conditions)* [1995] 2 FLR 124, 129–30 *per* Sir Thomas Bingham MR.
[20] *Re J (A Minor) (Contact)* [1994] 1 FLR 729, 736 (emphasis added).
[21] *L v. L (Child Abuse: Access)* [1989] 2 FLR 16. See also, Weyland, "Judicial Attitudes to Contact and Shared Residence since the Children Act 1989" [1995] *Journal of Social Welfare and Family Law* 445.
[22] *A v. N (Committal: Refusal of Contact)* [1997] 1 FLR 533.
[23] See *The Hidden Victims: Children and Domestic Violence* (London: NHC, 1994), Appendix 3; Kaye, "Domestic Violence, Residence and Contact" (1996) 8 *Child and Family Law Quarterly* 285 at 285–8; Mullender and Morley, *op cit.* n. 4.
[24] See Fortin, *op cit.* n. 18, p. 33.

imbalance of power in intra-spousal negotiations.[25] Equally, it ought not to be forgotten that violence between partners can often escalate following separation and divorce, further weakening the hand of the residential parent to resist further contact.[26] It should be noted, however, that some courts are prepared to take into consideration the dangers of physical harm to the child and mother in determining whether, on balance, contact with the father should continue to be maintained. This more realistic approach to the question of contact is to be welcomed, particularly in light of the fact that, as we have seen, the imbalance of power between the parties from ethnic minorities can be exacerbated by social and cultural isolation as well as economic and legal dependency where the abused woman is a recent immigrant with no access to public funds.[27]

So far as presumptive contact with a father who has abused his children is concerned, the practice has rightly been condemned on the basis that such a judicial attitude:

> [fails] to appreciate the level of fear, disgust and repulsion that mothers are likely to feel at the thought of their children having contact with fathers that have sexually abused them. Sexual abuse is such a serious betrayal of a child's trust that the notion that a child will benefit from having further contact with the abuser is likely to be totally alien to the majority of residential parents.[28]

It is hoped that the courts reassess their approach as regards the strength of the presumption to be ascribed in favour of contact in cases where the father has used violence against either or both of mother and child. Though it is right that the judicial function should not be surrendered to the obdurate parent, a more realistic attitude ought to be adopted where there remains a risk of harm to either party.[29] And where such a threat of continued violence exists, this ought to figure highly in the courts" assessment of where the best interests of the child do in fact lie.

IV RACE AND THE LEGAL SYSTEM

The legal system provides a crucial *potential* means of protecting a victim from further abuse by her partner through the criminal and civil law which can be used respectively to punish and deter such behaviour.[30] Yet the extent to which

---

[25] Smart, "Power and the Politics of Child Custody" in Stuart and Sevennhousjisen (eds.), *Child Custody and the Politics of Gender* (London: Routledge, 1989) p. 15.

[26] Kaganas and Piper, "Domestic Violence and Divorce Mediation" [1994] *Journal of Social Welfare and Family Law* 265.

[27] Hayes and Williams, *Family Law: Principles, Policy and Practice* (London: Butterworths, 1995) p. 54.

[28] *Ibid.*

[29] See, e.g., *Re D (A Minor) (Contact: Mother's Hostility)* [1993] 2 FLR 1.

[30] As regards criminal law, depending on the severity of violence, one or more offences under the Offences Against the Person Act 1861 may be committed. As regards civil law deterrence, see Part IV of the Family Law Act 1996 and more recently the Protection from Harassment Act 1997.

this potential will be realised depends ultimately on a number of fundamental principles that have been identified in Australia to be the following: (i) equality before the law and equal access to the law, (ii) non-discrimination, (iii) freedom of expression of religious and cultural values and (iv) the removal of barriers arising from language difference and/or different understandings.[31]

More generally, however, as the research of Julie Stubbs has emphasised, there is a need for what she terms "intersectionality"; that is "an understanding of the nexus between differences—culture, race, ethnicity, colour, language, class, age, religion, physical and mental abilities, immigration status and many others with that of gender".[32] In other words, it is only by understanding the complexity of the interaction between these factors that simplistic and misguided assumptions about racial issues can be avoided. In particular, such an approach emphasises the need to avoid making judgments about the nature and prevalence of domestic violence within specific ethnic groups or communities based on stereotypes rather than empirical evidence.[33] Closer to home, the work done by the Southall Black Sisters with Asian women outlines the dangers inherent in the concept of "multiculturisation" which gives priority to narrow, patriarchal interpretations of the social background in which domestic abuses take place.

> This approach stereotypes an entire community in so far as the dominant interpretations of culture and religious values, made by male religions and community genders is accepted. This seems to deny or obscure that internal divisions exist, for example, along class, caste or gender lines and thus the real power relations between men and women and between various groups within minority communities. State agencies, in an effort to appear multi-cultural and even anti-racist, are often reluctant to intervene where Asian women are concerned. Guided by the belief that the Asian community have their own internal mechanisms to resolve marital problems, they often deny Asian women the same advice and help offered to other women.[34]

Thus, ironically, it appears that the state agencies, by not appreciating or simply ignoring the complexity of the power structures within ethnic minority communities, could help to reinforce existing inequalities by the acquiesence in patriarchal values which help to foster conditions conducive to the perpetration of spousal violence and abuse.[35] Indeed, such acquiesence may itself be used by

---

[31] Australian Law Revision Commission, *Multiculturalism and the Law* (Sydney: Aitken Press, 1992) p. 14.

[32] Stubbs, *op cit*. n. 5, p. 1.

[33] *Ibid.*, p. 2. See also Southall Black Sisters, *op cit*. n. 3, pp. 15–39 and Stubbs and Tolmie, "Race, Gender and the Battered Woman Syndrome: An Australian Case Study" [1995] *Canadian Journal of Women and the Law* 122.

[34] *Op cit.*, n. 3, p. 16.

[35] See *ibid*, p. 17 where the patriarchal nature of Asian Community in the UK is outlined. See also Burley's account of the Vietnamese community in New South Wales which reveals that the Vietnamese community leaders tended to be "male, conservative and authoritarian": Burley, "Multiculturalism and the Law: Ethnicity Overlooked" (1993) 18 *Alternative Law Journal* 158. See also Humphrey, "Religion, Law and Family Disputes in a Lebanese Muslim Community in Sydney" in Bottomley and Lepervanche (eds.), *Ethnicity, Class and Gender in Australia* (Sydney: Allen and Unwin, 1994).

patriarchal figures within an ethnic community as an additional ideological weapon to reinforce their authority and control over women within that group. Accordingly, in looking at the legal system, the need for a deeper understanding of the complexity of the problems posed by race and the legal systems is essential if such well-intentioned, yet misguided, assumptions are to be avoided.

A Institutions and Procedures

One major obstacle to the provision of adequate legal services is knowledge of the legal system and what help may be available. This point is particularly apposite in respect of first generation immigrants who may deliberately be kept in ignorance of immigration and family law rights by their male partners as a strategy for wielding control.[36] It is therefore important that information is provided in the relevant languages and in places where women may obtain easy access.[37] Beyond simply being available in an accessible language, it is important that this information should explain the nature of the English legal system and its workings. For, apart from appearing remarkably alien to some immigrants, its institutions and procedures may, without such assistance, appear impenetrably complex and intimidating. The process of giving evidence is difficult for anyone who is unaccustomed to the judicial system, but it is especially so for someone from a different culture with a different set of norms and values. A clear example of this has been indicated by Julie Stubbs. In relation to Aboriginal culture, the common law approach to eliciting information—by asking difficult, sometimes personal, questions of witnesses—is seen as rude and inappropriate.[38] Equally, there are also important unexpressed cultural assumptions underlying the interpretation of silence as described by socio-linguist Diana Eades:

> Silence functions in a positive way for Aboriginal English speakers who use it for a number of reasons, including considering their response and getting comfortable in a situation. Because silence functions in a negative way amongst standard English speakers, Aboriginal English speaking witnesses typically have their silences interrupted in court. The different cultural significance of silence also creates potential for the misinterpretation of the silence of Aboriginal English witnesses in response to questions asked of them.[39]

[36] See Women's Legal Resources Centre Report, *Quarter Way to Equal: A Report on Barriers to Access to Legal Services to Migrant Women* (Sydney: Women's Legal Resources Centre, 1994). See, too, Southall Black Sisters, *op cit*. n. 3, Section Two.

[37] The recent introduction by NCH of credit-card size help numbers, available at Post Offices and doctors" surgeries is good example of providing accessible information.

[38] Stubbs, *op cit*. n. 5, p. 11.

[39] Eades, *Aboriginal English and the Law* (1992) p136. She later refers (at p. 137) to other problems encountered by Aboriginal people in the legal process such as the Aboriginal tendency to show co-operation with authority figures even if they do not agree with or understand the question and have cultural problems with providing specific information about time, location and quantity. The vagueness of their answers can be misinterpreted as evasiveness or mistrust from an Anglo-Australian perspective.

When it is remembered that such witnesses are being questioned in public about sensitive and intimate personal details[40] by authority figures who are frightening and intimidating, it would be surprising if such encounters could realistically be expected to lead to a fair means of eliciting the truth. The provision of sufficient numbers of adequately qualified interpreters would go a considerable distance towards removing such problems but the role of the interpreter is difficult to fulfil and requires a competent, independent individual who can transform messages from one culture to another.[41] Furthermore, it is usually inappropriate to ask friends or family members to interpret as many women prefer to have a female interpreter who at once can be relied upon for confidentiality as well as a degree of empathy such qualities being perceived as necessary by victims in sensitive cases. Two further problems with using friends and relatives as interpreters are that, first, second language competence often decreases in times of stress,[42] and, secondly, they may attempt to place pressure upon victims to become reconciled with their abusers.[43]

Other research studies emphasise the care that must be exercised in the interpretation of gestures and language if simplistic, unchallenged, underlying culturally based assumptions are to be avoided. Since it has been established that practically all victims of domestic violence find any involvement in the legal system stressful, such feelings of fear and confusion are legitimately expected to be compounded when problems associated with race, language and residential status are present. Consequently extra-special care, tact and sensitivity must be deployed by culturally aware staff who endeavour to elicit the information necessary to understand the social circumstances and family history of the abused woman so that the appropriate relief can be obtained.[44] Although the reforms introduced by Part IV of the Family Law Act 1996 were intended to simplify the statutory framework for civil law remedies and to extend their availability to a broader category of victims than previously, the legislation remains complex and beset by moral inconsistencies.[45] In addition, it is arguable that drafting inelegancies in the legislation make it more difficult than was intended for certain victims to obtain the remedies that the Act was designed to provide.[46] In consequence, the likelihood is that an applicant seeking to use the civil law for protection will continue to need sympathetic and well-informed advisers who

[40] It should be noted that Zoora Shah argued in her defence that the reason she did not initially disclose details of the abuse that she had suffered was "because of the shame at the sexual and physical abuse she says she suffered at his hands": (1998) *The Independent*, 1 May. See Southall Black Sisters, *op cit*. n. 3, Section Two.

[41] See Stubbs, *op cit*. n. 5, p. 9 and Dixon, Hogan and Wierzbicka, "Interpreters, Some Basic Problems" [1980] *Legal Service Bulletin* 162.

[42] The Ethnic Affairs Commission of New South Wales use interpreters in domestic violence and sexual assault cases: *Multiculturalism and the Law* (Ashfield: Ethnic Affairs Committee, 1992).

[43] See Southall Black Sisters, *op cit*. n. 3, p. 28.

[44] See National Inter-Agency Working Party Report, *op cit*. n. 6.

[45] See Murphy, "Domestic Violence: The New Law" (1996) 59 *Modern Law Review* 845.

[46] See Kewley, "Pragmatism Before Principle: the Limitations of Civil Law Remedies for Victims of Domestic Violence" [1996] *Journal of Social Welfare and Family Law* 1.

are familiar with the new legal provisions. But even here, given the recent reforms made with respect to Legal Aid,[47] the potential protection afforded by the Act may be more illusory than real.[48]

Important recommendations for improvement of the services provided by refugees and other agencies within the UK are outlined in a major report into the problem.[49] In particular, the report emphasises that support agency members should:

> assist women from these ethnic communities, by recognising the specific obstacles and barriers they confront. There is a need to understand that ethnic communities are not homogenous and important differences exist between communities. However, understanding the cultural practices of different communities should not lead agencies to assume that the needs of all women within a particular community are the same and can be met in the same way.[50]

This recommendation stresses the need for agency workers to understand the cultural pressures on the particular members of the ethnic community that seek their help, and to work in a co-ordinated way to improve the services available. On the vital issue of provision of information, the report states further that, "[a]gencies need to ensure women from different ethnic backgrounds and abilities are provided with information, counselling and other advice in a medium that they can understand" and that "[i]t is also necessary to ensure that the concerned woman is comfortable with the interpreter" who must "respect her confidentiality and have some understanding about the problem of domestic violence".[51]

B Race, Gender and Criminal Law

Central to the issues of both race and gender is the construction of "reasonableness" and its counterpart "the reasonable man" within the common law tradition and also encapsulated in section 3 of the Homicide Act 1957 whereby a successful plea operates as a partial defence reducing a murder conviction to manslaughter.[52] Such constructs, however, have developed in a manner which reflects a standard of reasonableness within the dominant (preponderantly

---

[47] For details of how the new system works and the cut-backs it brings with it in terms of funding, see Zander, "The Government's Plans on Legal Aid and Conditional Fees" (1998) 61 *Modern Law Review* 538.

[48] See Conference Report, *op cit.* n. 2, pp. 18–19.

[49] Madaqureshi, *op cit.* n. 2, pp. 18–19.

[50] *Ibid.*

[51] *Ibid.*

[52] For the import of the "reasonable man" construct in the context of the civil law see Conaghan, "Tort Law and the Feminist Critique of Reason" in Bottomley (ed.), *Feminist Perspectives on the Foundational Subjects in Law* (London: Cavendish, 1996) p. 47 and "Gendered Harm and the Law of Tort: Remedying (Sexual) Harassment" (1996) 16 *Oxford Journal of Legal Studies* 407. See also, *id*, "Tort Litigation in the Context of Intra-familial Abuse" (1998) 61 *Modern Law Review* 132.

male) group within society[53] at the expense of ignoring and thereby disadvantaging women and individuals from different ethnic and cultural backgrounds.[54] The concept of reasonableness also affects the way the notion of self-defence has developed:

> There is much similarity in the way the laws of provocation and self-defence have developed. Both use the notion of reasonableness, a concept which is apparently gender-neutral but in reality discriminates against women who are provoked and/or attempt to defend themselves against persistent male violence.[55]

Far from being a fair representation indicative of a broad cultural definition of acceptable behaviour, the narrow (gendered) way in which the "reasonableness" test is couched will be prejudicial to the interests of women or anyone else whose experiences do not fit easily within the predominantly white, male life-experience and behaviour patterns which it is urged is the principal concern of the criminal justice system. This is because "the great majority of criminal defendants have been male" and because "criminal law has been developed by male common-law judges, codified by male legislators, and interpreted by male judges".[56] This has had serious repercussions for female homicide defendants who, in particular, have "faced difficulties proving the legal excuses and justifications which either reduce a charge of murder to manslaughter or mandate acquittal" even though "they may not be exceptional women . . . [but] ordinary women pushed to extremes".[57]

Although in the UK the legal yardstick of the reasonable man was broadened by the decision in R v. *Camplin*[58] and remains ultimately an issue for the jury to decide, the guidance provided by the judge hearing the case may be highly influential. In any event, abused women and others who do not react to violence or other provocation in a stereotypically "male" manner—with sudden loss of self-control and in a way that is not premeditated[59]—will continue to have difficulty in relying on this partial defence. This is particularly so because, although the precise "characteristics" of the accused that may be taken into consideration in determining whether she behaved reasonably remain uncertain, they specifically *do not include* "exceptional excitability" associated with "ethnic origin".[60] Thus, the construction of reasonableness remains insensitive to characteristics of those women with whom this essay is concerned.

---

[53] See, e.g., Stubbs and Tolmie, *op cit*. n. 33, 122; *Multiculturalism, op cit*. n. 31, and Lacey, Wells and Meure, *Reconstructing Criminal Law* (London: Butterworths, 1996) pp. 285–303.
[54] Stubbs and Tolmie, *op cit*. n. 33, at 6.
[55] Lacey *et al.*, *op cit*. n. 53, p. 292.
[56] Taylor, "Provoked Reason in Man: Heat of Passion Manslaughter and Imperfect Self-Defence" (1986) 33 *University of California Law Review* 1679, 1684.
[57] *Ibid*.
[58] [1978] AC 705. See further Horder, "The Problem of Provocative Children" [1987] *Criminal Law Review* 658 on the effects and limitations of this decision.
[59] R v. *Thornton* [1992] 1 ALL ER 306.
[60] R v. *Camplin* [1978] AC 705, 726 *per* Lord Simon.

V PROBLEMS IN POLICING DOMESTIC VIOLENCE

A Introduction

The unexpected controversy which hailed in Part IV of the Family Law Act 1996 at least brought the subject of family violence back into the political and social spotlight. Yet the extent to which this legislation, for all the scrutiny and debate it received during its passage through Parliament, will achieve its goal of improving the protection afforded to victims of domestic violence will depend in large measure on the police service. This is principally because the Act presumptively requires the courts to attach a power of arrest to all of the variants of the civil law remedies for which it provides,[61] in the expectation that the threat of police involvement will lend valuable weight to these injunctions. Indeed, the centrality of the role of the police has been expressed thus: "the police are gatekeepers of the criminal justice system".[62] It is probably for this reason that so many academic and other studies have been concerned solely with the policing of domestic violence.[63] And the police themselves recognise their gate-keeping function.[64]

> For the victim, the police service is of particular importance. It is the most visible, accountable and available organisation and it is the key, not only to the whole criminal justice system but also to the other caring agencies.[65]

By using this gate-keeping metaphor, emphasis is placed on the key position held by the police at the entrance to the criminal justice system which embraces not only the police, but also the Crown Prosecution Service and the criminal courts. But of these agencies, it is the police who will be contacted by victims or other members of the public. As such, it is the manner in which the police respond to the report of an incident that often determines whether the victim will feel sufficiently protected to become emboldened enough to seek further protection by way of the civil law. If the matter is dealt with cursorily and trivialised as a mere "domestic", the panoply of remedies contained in the 1996 Act might never be sought. It takes merely a moment to telephone 999, which number can be called twenty-four hours a day; it takes considerably more resolve to engage professional legal assistance to pursue a prosecution and/or a protective civil law order.

[61] Family Law Act 1996, s. 47(2).
[62] Victim Support, *op cit*. n. 6, p. 11.
[63] See, e.g., Edwards, *Policing Domestic Violence* (London: Sage, 1989); *id, Sex and Gender in the Legal Process* (London: Blackstone Press, 1996); Hanmer *et al.* (eds.), *Women, Policing and Male Violence: International Perspectives* (London: Routledge & Kegan Paul, 1989); S Grace, *Policing Domestic Violence in the 1990s*, Home Office Research Study 139 (London: HMSO, 1995).
[64] Association of Chief Police Officers, *Position Statement on Domestic Violence: Memorandum to Home Affairs Committee* (London: ACPO, 1996).
[65] *Ibid.*, para. 3.2.

So, in dialling 999, much for the future will turn upon the police attitude towards the initial report of the incident. Yet the history of police attitudes towards domestic violence has generally been less than encouraging. As a Victim Support Report as recently as 1992 highlighted:

> the police tend to be a male-dominated, action-oriented organisation who like decisions to be clear-cut and problems to have a solution. Constables or investigating officers tend to see dealing with domestic violence as a low-grade activity unlikely to attract either prestige or excitement and all too likely to raise insoluble problems.[66]

In addition to these attitudinal problems, a further historical difficulty has been the fact that many police officers have been unaccustomed to, and ill-equipped to deal with the complexity[67] of cases involving domestic violence. And while some progress has been made in both these respects,[68] it is still the case that the policing of domestic violence, in general terms, remains in a far from ideal state.[69] As to policing cases in which there is the added racial element, further problems arise.

B Particular Problems of Policing and Race

Research has reflected concern about the practice of selective policing on racial grounds whereby the avowed aim of controlling of domestic violence has been used as the basis for what is, in reality, a case of simply over-policing a certain sector of society.[70] In the context of domestic violence, the first useful observation is that the police will often arrest offenders for challenging police authority rather than for the abuse of their female partner. As Elizabeth Stanko has explained:

> the role police played in domestics—as mediators or as temporary transport for drunken husbands out of the home—was and is part of police craftsmanship. People used the police to stop violence. If an arrest did occur from police intervention, it was most likely to be triggered not by the abuse rendered by the man in the house, but by his surly and disrespectful attitude to the police.[71]

While such policing may well be apparent across society generally, research suggests that the problem of such misuses of police power are intensified when the police seek to assert control over certain sub-communities and particularly when they are endeavouring to hunt out possible illegal immigrants residing

---

[66] *Op cit.*, n. 6, p. 11. See also Reiner, *The Politics of the Police* (Brighton: Harvester Wheatsheaf, 1992) p. 119 *et seq.*

[67] On the complexities of domestic violence cases, see Murphy, "Domestic Violence, Ideology and Laggardly Criminal Justice" [1999] *Northern Ireland Legal Quarterly* (forthcoming).

[68] See, e.g., Grace, *op cit.* n. 63.

[69] See further, Murphy, *op cit.* n. 67.

[70] See Stanko, "Policing Domestic Violence: Dilemmas and Contradictions" [1995] *Australian and New Zealand Journal of Criminology* 31.

[71] *Ibid.*, p. 32.

within ethnic minority enclaves.[72] Such practices obviously undermine the credibility of the police as impartial and non-discriminatory. They also illustrate the need for specialist training for police in racism awareness[73] as well as the urgent problem of under-representation in the police force of recruits from all ethnic groups.

At the other extreme, some police officers appear to be overly-cautious of intervening in cases of domestic violence within Asian communities because of their (mis)perception that the community has its own internal mechanism of policing. So, at a multi-agency forum in Southall in 1987, for example, some police officers argued that they had to be careful in their handling of domestic violence cases because of the "cultural differences" between themselves, on the one hand, and the aggressor and victim, on the other. They were either overly deferential to the views of the male members of the community or they were wholly reluctant to act for fear of fuelling a negative perception of the police among those self-same male members of the "community".[74] In either event, Asian women were denied an adequate police response.

Either in the guise of deference towards men or in the manifestation of a general "hands off" stance, this misplaced endeavour by the police to operate with a greater degree of cultural sensitivity, reveals their lack of understanding of the diversity of views within ethnic communities; especially when patriarchal attitudes are misrepresented as reflecting the views of the general community.[75]

VI DOMESTIC VIOLENCE AND IMMIGRATION

Women who do not have permanent residency or who are refugees are particularly vulnerable to abuse because they are reluctant, for understandable reasons, to seek outside help as they may fear deportation if they draw attention to themselves. Although the present Labour Government has stated that it intends to replace the existing rules on immigration and asylum, it is doubtful whether the replacement system will provide any greater sense of security for such women in this country. For the new rules will insist upon a genuine marriage (the burden of proof lying with the applicant)[76] and a probationary period of residence of a minimum of twelve months.[77]

The stringent requirements just outlined will continue to place immigrant women in a nigh-on impossible position whereby they have to choose between,

---

[72] See Mama, *The Hidden Struggle: Statutory and Voluntary Sector Responses to Violence Against Black Women in the Home* (London: Whiting and Burch, 1996) p. 144.

[73] See Association of Chief Police Officers, *Setting the Standards for Policing: Meeting Community Expectations*, Strategic Policy Document (London: ACPO, 1990).

[74] See Southall Black Sisters, *op cit.* n. 3, p. 39.

[75] See Patel, "Multi-culturalism: the Myth and the Reality" (1991) 3 *Cultural Review* 200.

[76] The difficulties associated with establishing a "genuine" marriage are dealt with the editor, elsewhere in this collection.

[77] See *Hansard*, HC, Vol 395, cols. 282 and 285.

on the one hand, continuing to suffer abuse and, on the other, a separation during the twelve month probationary period. The fact that the victim will have no access to public moneys during this period may well tip the balance in favour of the former option: she will remain not only a victim of violence but also, almost entirely under the control of an abusive husband because of her particular financial insecurity coupled with her abnormal vulnerability and isolation. A similar problem has occurred in Australia where the response has been to introduce special rules to cover the situations in which the relationship has been terminated due to domestic violence but the woman lacks the independent residential status to remain in Australia.[78] It is suggested that the British Government should consider such measures carefully with a view to their adaptation and adoption in this country. Certainly, the restrictions on access to public funds—such as housing benefits, social security benefits or the provision of housing under the homelessness provisions of the Housing Act—can mean impossible hardship for an abused woman who is socially and financially dependent on her abuser since many refuges depend upon public funds for their own financial survival. It is to be hoped, therefore, that the Government revises its current proposals in order to find a way to provide effective assistance for those comparatively few women in such desperate positions. After all, in budgetary terms, because of the limited numbers of such women, there can hardly be very serious financially rooted objections to doing so.

VII CONCLUSION

This chapter has endeavoured to review a range of problems posed by domestic violence which are peculiar to ethnic minority victims. It has attempted to demonstrate the urgent need for greater awareness and understanding, especially by state officials, of how a victim's race or ethnicity can exacerbate her difficulties. While some progress has been made in this respect, much remains to be done if the complexity of the interaction between race and violence is properly to be understood and the current simplistic and ultimately misguided assumptions and policies based on crude stereotyping are to be avoided. The simple acknowledgement that ethnicity raises additional cultural and economic barriers for women trying to escape violence is important in itself, for it is the necessary starting point for any serious attempt to address the question of how best to provide effective and realistic responses to domestic violence occurring within ethnic minority communities. It is hoped that this essay has helped to highlight the more important of these such barriers, and that it has gone some way to suggesting a number of reform measures.

---

[78] See Dignam, "The Burden and the Proof: Torture and Testimony in the Determination of Refugee Status in Australia" (1992) 4 *International Journal of Refugee Law* 343.

9

State Support for Housing Ethnic Minority Households: Spatial Segregation and Ghettoisation?

DAVID COWAN*

I INTRODUCTION

Much debate about ethnic segregation begins from the premise that even moderate levels are *by definition* a "bad thing" ... The problem is not segregation *per se* but the extent to which both the fact of segregation and the location of the segregated areas are not in keeping with the desires of the groups who reside there. In short, physical segregation is not the problem: poor housing is. Minorities may opt for concentration or segregation, but not in the poorest urban locations.[1]

STATE SUPPORT FOR housing ethnic minority households has, in the Thatcher/Major era and beyond, adopted a colour blind approach, in tune with the marketised and quasi-marketised principles more broadly engineered within the housing system.[2] Such colour blindness is at variance with the known patterns of housing settlement and discrimination against ethnic minorities, together with various research findings of their position in the housing market.[3] Patterns of segregation and tenure,[4] often resulting from settlement, reflect the

---

* University of Bristol. I am grateful to Lois Bibbings for comments on an earlier draft of this chapter. Remaining errors belong entirely to the author.

[1] Ratcliffe, "Methodological Refinement, Policy Formulation and the Future Research Agenda: some Brief Reflections" in Ratcliffe (ed.), *Ethnicity in the 1991 Census, Volume Three* (London: HMSO, 1996) pp. 301–2 (hereafter "Vol. 3").

[2] See generally, Malpass and Murie, *Housing Policy and Practice* (Basingstoke: MacMillan, 4th ed., 1994); Bramley, "Quasi-markets and Social Housing" in Le Grand and Bartlett (eds.), *Quasi-Markets and Social Policy* (Basingstoke: MacMillan, 1993). There is one exception to this—the Housing Corporation, a government quango, began a programme of promoting black and ethnic minority housing associations.

[3] This research is closely linked to the development of housing studies—see, for example, the classic texts Rex and Moore, *Race, Community and Conflict: A Study of Sparkbrook* (Oxford: OUP, 1967); Henderson and Karn, *Race, Class and State Housing: Inequality and the Allocation of Public Housing in Britain* (Aldershot: Gower, 1987).

[4] For the purposes of this chapter, "tenure" is regarded as consisting of the following categories: home ownership, private renting, local authority renting, and housing association renting/shared ownership. This is the accepted classification within housing studies. There are, however,

discrimination of local authorities, exchange professionals, and others. As Smith explains, "Even if black people prefer segregation, it is hard to understand why they should pursue this in the more run-down segments of the housing stock, rather than in areas where they could secure the symbolic and economic benefits associated with suburban life".[5] The 1991 census now provides us with a much richer, more complex statistical picture of housing disadvantage and spatial patterns of ethnic minority households. This chapter's analysis begins with a consideration of the spatial patterns of ethnic minority households, which inform the debate about ghettoisation and segregation.

These patterns suggest that "ethnic penalties" have been applied in the housing context.[6] It can be argued that broader discrimination within market processes has produced these results. The housing "product" does not exist one dimensionally but as part of a package of inputs, reflecting discrimination and widespread disadvantage (recognised in government programmes such as City Challenge or the "Housing Plus" scheme). Housing provides one piece of the jigsaw. So, for example, adults housed in poorer quality accommodation are less likely to be viewed in a favourable light by adoption agencies considering potential adopters. Indeed, family law is increasingly having to accommodate the importance of housing, whether as a consequence of support for children in need,[7] as a result of relationship breakdown,[8] or within the context of community care.[9] Housing is increasingly being regarded as the fundamental basis for the operation of policies which seek to redress disadvantage, especially in reports emanating from the Social Exclusion Unit.

The jigsaw is also multi-layered, for disadvantage operates both between and within ethnic minority groups. It is this diversity of experience which provides important insights. For example, Modood summarises this disadvantage in the employment context as (1) disadvantage confined to top jobs in large organisations: the Chinese and African Asians; (2) relative disadvantage: the Indians and Caribbeans; (3) severe disadvantage: the Pakistanis and Bangladeshis.[10] One might anticipate that this disadvantage is replicated within the housing system.

The important point to make is that market processes, on one level, provide *choice* but on another level they *constrain* the housing choices because of broader disadvantages not only in relation to racism. The second section of this chapter, therefore, seeks explanations to the tenure patterns outlined in the 1991 census

conceptual inadequacies with such categorisation: see Cowan, *Housing Law and Policy* (Basingstoke: MacMillan, 1999).

  [5] Smith, *The Politics of "Race" and Residence* (Cambridge: Polity, 1989) p. 37.
  [6] See Karn (ed.), *Ethnicity in the 1991 Census, Volume Four* (London: HMSO, 1997) (hereafter "Vol. 4").
  [7] Children Act 1989, s. 20.
  [8] See Bull, *Housing Consequences of Relationship Breakdown* (London: HMSO, 1993); Family Law Act 1996—on which, see Murphy, "Domestic Violence: The New Law" (1996) 59 *Modern Law Review* 845, 854-6.
  [9] Cowan, "Accommodating Community Care" (1995) 22 *Journal of Law and Society* 210.
  [10] Modood, "Ethnic Diversity and Racial Disadvantage in Employment" in Blackstone *et al.* (eds.), *Race Relations in Britain—A Developing Agenda* (London: Routledge, 1998) p. 65.

through an evaluation of the effect of market processes in securing disadvantage. An explanatory example may assist the reader. Pakistani households may wish to become owner occupiers because of the increased choice that gives (in terms of size, area, moving and internal household arrangements). However, that preference for ownership may in part reflect the fact that, for example, council housing is in undesirable areas, the units are too small, and is known for problems arising from racial harassment.[11] These market processes are also a reflection of broader, structural patterns of disadvantage. For example, Smith explicitly links "the problem mix labelled 'racial segregation' " to the legitimation of repatriation, and immigration legislation "which progressively stripped away the rights of entry and settlement conferred on Commonwealth citizens in 1948".[12] In the 1990s, this "stripping away" explicitly linked housing and immigration in legislation itself to the extent that one Court of Appeal judge, in the context of housing benefit regulations, suggested that "the 1996 regulations necessarily contemplate for some a life so destitute that, to my mind, no civilised nation can tolerate it".[13] Thus, broader structural factors have linked segregation to immigration to housing to welfare budgets—it is important, though, that budgetary constraints, while paraded as a principal cause for reform are not convincingly so. After all, the anticipated savings from benefit changes were £200 million against a total welfare budget of £80 billion. The rationale for these recent changes is considered in the third part of this chapter, providing a broader context. This completes the argument of this paper that housing disadvantage operates as a result of broader structural foci; it operates within the structural constraints set by government in relation, for example, to the rhetoric and practice within the welfare state.

II SPATIAL SEGREGATION AND GHETTOISATION

A The 1991 Census: General

The 1991 census provides, for the first time, a ward level picture of tenure differentiation between ten different ethnic groupings.[14] Within limits, this data has provided a useful analytical tool for it shows a wide variation among these ethnic groups, broadly consistent with earlier research findings. Table 9.1 provides this data on a general basis for Great Britain.

From this data, it is apparent that there are wide tenure differentials between various ethnic groups. Most obviously, it appears that Indian and Pakistani

[11] See, Bowes *et al.*, *"Too White, too Rough, and too many Problems": A Study of Pakistani Housing in Britain* (Stirling: Department of Applied Social Science, University of Stirling, 1998).

[12] Smith, *op cit*. n. 5, pp. 179–80 and ch. 5; see also Dummett and Nicol, *Subjects, Citizens, Aliens and Others* (London: Weidenfeld & Nicolson, 1991).

[13] *R* v. *Secretary of State for Social Security, ex p Joint Council for the Welfare of Immigrants* [1996] 4 All ER 385, 395.

[14] For a critique of the process as gendered, see Gilroy, "Women and Owner Occupation—First the Prince, then the Palace" in Gilroy and Woods (eds.), *Housing Women* (London: Routledge, 1994) pp. 31–2; on ethnicity, see Ratcliffe, "Social Geography and Ethnicity: A Theoretical, Conceptual and Substantial Overview" in Vol, 3, *op cit*. n. 1, pp. 2–12.

146   *David Cowan*

Table 3.1
Percentage of households by tenure by ethnic group of head of household, Great Britain, 1991

	All households	Owner occupiers	Local authority tenants	Housing association tenants	Private renters	Renting with a job
White	21,026,565	67	21	3	7	2
Black—						
Caribbean	216,460	48	36	10	6	1
Black—						
African	73,346	28	41	11	18	2
Black—other	38,281	37	34	11	14	4
Indian	225,582	82	8	2	6	2
Pakistani	100,938	77	10	2	10	1
Bangladeshi	30,668	44	37	6	10	3
Chinese	48,619	62	13	3	17	4
Other—Asian	58,995	54	14	4	24	4
Other—other	77,908	54	19	6	18	2
All groups	21,897,322	66	21	3	7	2

Source: 1991 Census (London: HMSO, 1993).

groupings are more likely to be owner occupiers than Whites. This disparity is particularly apparent among semi-skilled and unskilled manual workers, where the ratio is 82:85:53, respectively.[15] On the other hand, Black—Caribbean, Black—African, Black—other and Bangladeshi groupings are much less likely to be owner occupiers than Whites. For these groupings, council housing has proved extremely important. Among Black—Caribbean households, there has been a twenty-five year trend towards council housing, although between 1986 and 1991 this trend appears to have been reversed.[16] Ratcliffe suggests that owner occupation among the Indian and Pakistani groups remained reasonably constant through the 1980s, whereas over the same period White owner occupation increased from around 59 to 66 per cent. Thus, "with a few notable exceptions, we appear to be witnessing a significant narrowing of ethnic differentials in tenure patterns".[17] Be that as it may, the statistics bear out the importance of *gender*—fewer female-headed households become home owners within each ethnic grouping.[18] This reflects the difficulty women face in raising

[15] Phillips, "The Housing Position of Ethnic Minority Group Home Owners" in Vol. 4, *op cit.* n. 6, p. 173.
[16] Howes and Mullins, "Finding a Place—The Impact of Locality on the Housing Experience of Tenants from Minority Ethnic Groups" in Vol. 4, *op cit.* n. 6, p. 194.
[17] Ratcliffe, " 'Race', Ethnicity and Housing Differentials in Britain" in Vol. 4, *op cit.* n. 6, p. 135.
[18] Ratcliffe, *op cit.* n. 1; Phillips, *op cit.* n. 15.

finance.[19] This gender bias has a particular impact upon Caribbean households, in which females are more likely to head the household.[20]

B The 1991 Census: Ghettoisation

It is commonly suggested, both colloquially and by politicians, that the nature of ethnic minority settlement has caused ghettos to be created.[21] The meaning of "ghetto" is, however, contested:

> This kind of discussion is caught up with the hunt for ghettos, a labelling process which is too often infected by the kind of looseness of everyday discourse, and by a variety of pejorative connotations linking urban decay with the alleged moral/cultural identity of the residents of such areas.[22]

However, it might be defined as an area, first where "a single ethnic or racial group forms the whole population of the residential district. The second, concomitant proposition is that most members of the group are found in such areas".[23] Using this definition, it can be shown that Britain does *not* have ghettos, and is certainly different from the American phenomenon of spatial segregation. For example, in Chicago in 1930, over 92 per cent of the African–American population lived in areas where they formed over 80 per cent of the population; in London in 1991, by contrast, ethnic groupings "either individually or collectively, rarely achieve a majority of the population of urban wards and relatively low proportions of the ethnic populations are found at such high concentrations".[24] Where ethnic minorities are in a majority, this is always through a collation of *all* minorities taken together (for example, a 90 per cent non-White population in an Ealing ward).[25]

C The 1991 Census: Spatial Segregation

We have already considered the dual nature of residential segregation. The socio-political and socio-legal conceptions will be further considered in the

---

[19] See Gilroy, *op cit*. n. 14.

[20] Peach and Byron, "Council House Sales, Residualisation and Afro Caribbean Tenants" (1994) 23 *Journal of Social Policy* 363, 367.

[21] "In everyday perception and journalistic cliché, we give moral meanings to the territories of slum, downtown, safe streets, public park, suburb. This is how the word 'ghetto' is used. (It shows how language changes—nowhere in the modern world have there been ghettos of the type in which European Jews were forced to live)": Cohen, *Visions of Social Control* (Cambridge: Polity, 1985) p. 220.

[22] Peach and Rossiter, "Level and Nature of Spatial Concentration and Segregation of Minority Ethnic Populations in Great Britain, 1991" in Vol. 3, *op cit*. n. 1, p. 114. See also the important contribution of Wacquant, "Three Pernicious Premises in the Study of the American Ghetto" (1997) *International Journal of Urban and Regional Research* 341.

[23] Peach, "Does Britain have Ghettos?" [1996] *Transactions, Institute of British Geographers* 216.

[24] Peach, *loc cit.*, 232.

[25] Peach and Rossiter, *op cit*. n. 22, p. 117.

third part of this chapter. Here, however, our concentration is on the statistical underpinnings of residential segregation. The importance of this endeavour cannot be exaggerated: "Underlying the concept of segregation is a belief that unevenness of residential distributions within an urban area reflect social differences: *the greater the degree of spatial difference, the greater the social difference*".[26] While "unevenness" can be measured in a number of ways, Peach and Rossiter uncover different levels of segregation between ethnic minority groupings in certain areas. The highest level of segregation relates to Bangladeshis:

> It is not simply that Bangladeshis are highly segregated from the White population . . . they also show high rates against other minority ethnic groups. Their lowest level is with the Pakistanis (a group with which they once shared nationality.[27]

The Pakistani population has similarly high levels of segregation, although Black-African and Chinese populations have slightly lower levels. Caribbean levels of segregation depend on geographical location, and suggest an element of suburbanisation among this grouping.[28]

This spatial segregation needs to be linked to the tenure levels of each grouping. It is known that some areas, for example, have extremely limited numbers of accommodation units in the private rented sector or, by contrast, have significant levels of council housing/owner occupation. Areas of greatest concentration of ethnic minority households tend to be in urban areas, and most often inner urban areas. This, for example, accounts for the high prevalence of Black–African, Black–Caribbean, and Bangladeshi council tenants in purpose-built flats, or the higher ratio of Black–African and Black–Caribbean, households living in converted housing associations flats.[29] When account is taken of socio-economic differentials thrown up by the census, as well as geographical differences between ethnic groupings, interesting patterns become apparent. Pakistani households are 19.9 per cent more likely to become owner occupiers, and 18 per cent less likely to be found in council housing, than expected; Black-African households are 17.6 per cent less likely to be owner occupiers and 9.5 per cent more likely to be in council housing than expected. As Dorling puts it: "Most of the tenure patterns of ethnic minorities cannot be explained by the jobs they do, their household structure or by where they live. *'All else' is not equal in housing in Britain in 1991*".[30] When considering London boroughs with low levels of owner occupation, patterns of ownership between ethnic groupings roughly parallel the national picture: "the over- and under-representation of each ethnic group has been preserved within the special conditions of the local housing market".[31]

[26] Peach and Rossiter, *op cit*. n. 22, p. 113.
[27] Peach and Rossiter, *op cit*. *n*. 22, p. 123.
[28] *Ibid*., at 123–4.
[29] Howes and Mullins, *op cit*. n. 16, p. 211.
[30] Dorling, "Regional and Local Differences in the Housing Tenure of Ethnic Minorities" in Vol. 4, *op cit*. n. 6, pp. 155–6.
[31] Phillips, *op cit*. n. 15, pp. 182–3.

III STATE SUPPORT: THE EFFECTS OF COLOUR BLINDNESS

In this section, it is my intention to examine the state support for each housing tenure. It can be argued that the housing market and quasi-market differentially affects minority ethnic groups and this explains, at least in part, the disparities in tenure considered in the previous section. This also needs to be placed in the wider context of the enormous structural changes in the housing market throughout the twentieth century as well as having been significantly manipulated during the Thatcher/Major era. These wider trends shed light on the more specific circumstances of ethnic minority households, such as the changing patterns of discrimination in housing. As Ward puts it, ". . . there has been an overall trend away from overt racism and direct discrimination as a constraint on access towards a more wide ranging pattern of disadvantage built into the general working of allocative processes".[32] Thus, one can suggest that the effects of legislation such as the Race Relations Act 1976, and the duty on councils and the Housing Corporation to "eliminate unlawful racial discrimination" and promote equality together with good relations,[33] has simply been to relocate much of the discrimination. The State provides the link because its support, and lack of it, for particular tenures provides a critical backdrop to the housing position of ethnic minority households.

Ginsburg draws a contrast between three types of racism: *subjective* racism "is overt racial prejudice and discrimination by key individuals"; *institutional* racism occurs when "policies and/or processes result in adverse treatment of ethnic minorities"; *structural* racism occurs where "there are aspects of national and international processes that have an indirect but fundamental impact on black people's housing situation".[34] An analysis of housing market processes cross-cuts this schema. However, it also provides an important *critique* of those same processes, suggesting cleavages within and between housing tenures. It must be said, though, that the commodification of housing in the 1980s and the de-monopolisation of sources of finance has altered the terrain. Much of the research was conducted in the late 1970s and early 1980s.[35] However, it provides an important link between past and current housing histories of ethnic minorities, as appreciation of the agents in the housing market has potentially increased.[36] The statistical analyses presented in the previous section provide a sense of continuance, that the historical impact of different forms of racism affects the current housing choices of ethnic minority households.

[32] Ward, "Race and Access to Housing" in Smith and Mercer (eds.), *New Perspectives on Race and Housing in Britain* (Glasgow: Centre for Housing Research, University of Glasgow, 1987).

[33] Race Relations Act 1976, s. 71; Housing Act 1988, s. 58.

[34] Ginsburg, "Racism and Housing: Concepts and Reality" in Braham *et al.* (eds.), *Racism and Antiracism—Inequalities, Opportunities and Policies* (London: Sage, 1992) p. 109.

[35] See Phillips and Karn, "Race and Ethnicity in Housing" in Blackstone *et al.* (eds.), *op cit*. n. 10.

[36] See Bowes *et al.*, *op cit*. n. 11, ch. 2, where the importance of housing histories is discussed.

150   *David Cowan*

A Home Ownership

State support for housing has generally concentrated on increasing the scope of owner-occupation. While this is most often regarded as an aspect of Thatcherism, the expansion in the 1980s can be regarded as a product of broader influences of the twentieth century which has played host to a massive tenure shift away from private renting (about 90 per cent rented in 1914) to home ownership (more that 70 per cent are now home owners with more expected).[37] Home ownership has been regarded as the tenure of choice, or the "basic and natural desire", a view which has cut across the party political divide.[38]

Some ethnic minorities have also been regarded as "choosing" home ownership because their culture favours entrepreneurialism and the private market,[39] although such claims are strongly disputed.[40] The other side of the coin has emphasised the *constraints* experienced by ethnic minority households in seeking, and gaining, accommodation in other tenures (considered below). The more convincing explanation eschews such distinctions in favour of a broader, more contextual explanatory pattern which emphasises individual agency and structural pressures, needs to be considered in terms of accretion of knowledge and capability, and has a temporal and spatial dimension.[41] Institutions, such as building societies (from whom, the evidence suggests, few ethnic minorities sought finance), "have tended to rely on stereotypes of the ethnic minorities and to make decisions by relating those stereotypes to their norms. These norms are not only economic but also moralistic".[42]

Research in the 1970s suggested that polarisation of lending according to purchase price and ethnic grouping. "Redlining"—a practice of refusing to lend against security on properties in certain areas—seems to have been the practice of certain institutions in the mid-1970s, although devolved managerial discretion of such agencies makes general statements of this nature difficult.[43] Such practices have been ascribed considerable importance in stopping the suburbanisation of households: "Building society activity (and inactivity) has probably been most decisive (directly or indirectly) in sustaining the "racial"

---

[37] See DoE, *Our Future Homes*, Cm. 2901 (London: HMSO, 1995) 9.

[38] Compare, for example, DoE, *Fair Deal for Housing*, Cmnd 4728 (London: HMSO, 1971) and DoE, *Housing Policy—A Consultative Document*, Cmnd 6851 (London: HMSO, 1977).

[39] See, for example, Dahya, "The Nature of Pakistani Ethnicity in Industrial Cities in Britain" in Cohen (ed.), *Urban Ethnicity* (London: Tavistock, 1974).

[40] See for example Bowes *et al.*, *op cit*. n. 11, and below.

[41] Sarre *et al.*, *Ethnic Minority Housing: Explanations and Policies* (Aldershot: Avebury, 1989). The position of ethnic minorities in Scotland provides an excellent example of the geography of constraint: see MacEwen and Third, "Tenure Choice and Ethnic Minorities in Scotland: Recent Research and Some Legal Conundrums" in Cowan (ed.), *Housing: Participation and Exclusion* (Aldershot: Dartmouth, 1998).

[42] Sarre *et al.*, p. 318.

[43] See Sarre *et al.*, p. 281; Karn *et al.*, *Home Ownership in the Inner City—Salvation or Despair?* (Aldershot: Gower, 1985) pp. 40–50.

dimension of residential segregation at a local level in the private sector".[44] A similar point can be made about other exchange professionals. The practice of "racial steering" among estate agents—in which clients are typecast according to their supposed preferences—is well-known. Arguing that this type of "racial stereotyping is a means of handling the common-sense racism of civil society in a day-to-day context", Ginsburg suggests that this institutional racism "exposes such practices as routine and normal, without the exceptionalism associated with explicit subjective racism".[45]

The rise of home ownership among the population more generally can also be explained by the series of *incentives* given both to that tenure (and the concomitant constraints placed on alternative tenures) as well as some of those wishing to enter it. Tax relief on mortgage payments (until recently linked to income levels, so that the greater the income, the greater the relief), the belief that capital gain was always probable (and untaxable),[46] together with the disincentives to other tenures, made home ownership "natural".[47] These benefits of home ownership have, however, not been distributed equally. Concentration in inner cities has generally meant "life in run-down environments, in homes of below average quality and at a point on the housing 'ladder' where owners receive less [housing] subsidy, and accrue fewer amenities, than do their counterparts in the public sector".[48] Urban regeneration programmes have generally adopted a "colour blind" approach (the "trickle down effect") and ethnic minorities themselves have "become marginalised and attracted only limited resources" within the various programmes.[49] Improvement/repair grants have proved an important source of funding, but, after 1981–3, have not been prioritised within capital programmes and their current existence has been further marginalised within the Housing Grants, Construction and Regeneration Act 1996.[50] Thus, the general *quality* of property owned by ethnic minority households (as to which the 1991 Census has not best equipped us with the most relevant data) has proved to be an important factor in proving, at best, disadvantage in alternative tenures.[51]

Purchase of council housing was encouraged through giving sitting tenants the right to buy their accommodation at a considerable discount. These discounts increased in the 1980s.[52] However, it can also be argued that this has

[44] Smith, *op cit*. n. 5, p. 89.

[45] Ginsburg, *op cit*. n. 34, p. 120.

[46] See, for example, Saunders, *A Nation of Home Owners* (London: Allen & Unwin, 1990).

[47] Discussion on this important contextual factor can be found in Kemeny, *The Myth of Home Ownership* (London: Routledge, 1981).

[48] Smith, *op cit*. n. 5, p. 87; see also Karn, Kemeny and Williams, *Home Ownership in the Inner City: Salvation or Despair?* (Aldershot: Gower, 1987).

[49] Munt, "Race, Urban Policy and Urban Problems: A Critique on Current UK Practice" (1991) 28 *Urban Studies* 183, 185.

[50] See Hills, *Unravelling Housing Finance* (Oxford: OUP, 1991) pp. 147–50; Bowes *et al.*, *op cit*. n. 11, discuss this at pp. 69–71 and 101–3.

[51] See Bowes *et al.*, *op cit*. n. 11, pp. 30–5.

[52] On the reasons for this policy, see Cole and Furbey, *The Eclipse of Council Housing* (London: Routledge, 1994).

differentially affected ethnic minorities, both in their ability to purchase, as well as in subsequent allocations in a residualised and marginalised stock.[53]

B Council Housing

State support for local authority housing has been waning, causing the sector to become "residualised" and its occupants are now the most marginalised.[54] The better quality accommodation has generally been sold off under the right to buy, the sector itself has been subject to a massive withdrawal of state funding since about 1977, and house-building has virtually stopped. These processes have their genesis in the history of council housing. Access to the sector is governed by the housing which prioritizes certain categories, which now include homelessness (although duties to successful homelessness applicants only last for two years).[55] A market, of sorts, exists for this type of accommodation, which generates an "inequality of bargaining power". This market is based upon the ability and willingness of an individual applicant to wait for accommodation in the sector, the operation of the different rules used by councils, together with the knowledge that each applicant has of the system. So, for example, applicants approaching authorities through the homelessness legislation might be allocated a worse quality property and/or might only be made one offer.

Historically, council housing has borne the brunt of the charge of discrimination and racism. The early criticisms related to the practice of housing visitors, who were used to grade households.[56] Henderson and Karn's study of Birmingham in the 1970s found discrimination both in selection and allocation of accommodation.[57] They argued that their findings were more generally applicable outside the Birmingham arena because the pressures which caused the discrimination to appear existed elsewhere. The problem was partly located in a set of assumptions which structured the discretionary system. Crucial to the system was keeping the level of voids to a minimum and thus a process of matching applicants to properties it was believed they would accept became the norm. Such processes may well be more prevalent today as concentration on local authority void rates has become a major factor in benchmarking local authorities and assessing their effectiveness. Estate management was also a crucial

---

[53] See, for example, Peach and Byron, *op cit*. n. 20, at 363.

[54] These processes are considered in Forrest and Murie, *Selling the Welfare State* (London: Routledge, 1991) pp. 65–85. It is important that what might also be described as "polarisation" has occurred within each tenure: see Murie, "The Social Rented Sector, Housing, and the Welfare State in the UK" (1997) 12 *Housing Studies* 437.

[55] Housing Act 1996, Parts VI–VII, as amended by SI 1997/1902. For a critique, see Cowan, *Homelessness: The (In-)Appropriate Applicant* (Aldershot: Dartmouth, 1997) chs. 8 and 9.

[56] See, e.g., Lambert *et al.*, *Housing Policy and the State* (Basingstoke: MacMillan, 1978) ch. 3; and Central Housing Advisory Committee, *Council Housing: Purposes, Procedures and Priorities* (London: HMSO, 1969) para. 96.

[57] Henderson and Karn, *op cit*. n. 3, p. 271 *et seq*.

factor in the pattern of discrimination, because council officers wished to match reputable tenants to reputable areas.

It is important to appreciate that these processes are ongoing and, ironically, occur even when allocations systems are devised on the basis of an anti-racist platform. If systems of allocation are based on a bargaining process in which applicants' ability to bargain relates to the security of their current accommodation, approaching through the homelessness route will most often determine a low level of bargaining. Yet, it is clear that black people form a significant percentage of the homeless applicants in inner city stress areas,[58] and are in turn discriminated against in selection and allocation.[59]

C Housing Associations

State support for "social" housing has been transferred from councils to housing associations via the Housing Corporation. The post-1988 financial settlement has essentially required housing associations to compete with each other for a limited capital allocation which, generally, must be mixed with private sector funding at proportions set by central government. In return for this public injection, housing associations are subject to the regulatory gaze of the Corporation. Current concerns are that this sector has become marginalised by its huge reliance on housing benefit paying for the increasing market rents made possible by the tenure regime under the Housing Act 1988. Additionally, the requirement to allocate only to those in need, as well as co-operate with the local authority on allocations (for example, in allowing local authorities to nominate up to 100 per cent of their new allocations), may be causing a crisis within the sector.[60]

Housing associations have traditionally provided accommodation for those groups who have experienced difficulty in other tenures (for example, those requiring sheltered accommodation).[61] They have, thus, proved to be an important source of accommodation for ethnic minority households, although there has been the suspicion that the width of discretion in housing allocations may

[58] See, e.g., Bonnerjea and Lawton, *Homelessness in Brent* (London: PSI, 1989); see also Burrows, "The Social Distribution of the Experience of Homelessness" in Burrows *et al.* (eds.), *Homelessness and Social Policy* (London: Routledge, 1997) p. 57. Exact quantification is difficult because official statistics are not kept and ethnic monitoring has been rare in practice—see Cowan, *op cit. n.* 55, pp. 104–6.

[59] See, e.g., Jeffers and Hoggett, "Like Counting Deckchairs on the Titanic: A Study of Institutional Racism and Housing Allocations in Haringey and Lambeth" (1995) 10 *Housing Studies* 325; Commission for Racial Equality, *Race and Council Housing in Hackney* (London: CRE, 1984).

[60] See Page, *Building for Communities* (York: Joseph Rowntree Foundation, 1993); Griffiths *et al.*, *Community Lettings* (York: Joseph Rowntree Foundation, 1996); Withers and Randolph, *Access, Homelessness and Housing Associations* (London: National Federation of Housing Associations, 1994). It may well be that local authorities are using their nomination rights to "match" black applicants to inner city housing: see Howes and Mullins, *op cit.* n. 16, p. 211.

[61] For background, see Cope, *Housing Associations: Policy and Practice* (Basingstoke: MacMillan, 1990).

lead to discrimination in certain cases.[62] Ethnic monitoring has been undertaken by the Housing Corporation and, on this basis, the Corporation exercises its responsibilities. However, such statistical analyses are not apt to uncover qualitative evidence of discrimination.[63] Little empirical work exists on housing association allocations because of their diversity, although as their allocations principles have become increasingly centralised, in time this will not be the case.[64] Important work remains to be done here (especially bearing in mind the importance of the tenure in the new governance of housing). Be that as it may, the Housing Corporation instituted a five year programme in 1986 (extended for a further five years) to promote the development of black and ethnic minority housing associations.[65] This has, however, taken place against the backdrop of increasing operational difficulties for smaller associations (which black and ethnic minority associations generally are) and continuing concerns as to their viability in the post-1988 funding era.[66]

D Private Renting

Private renting has developed into a sector which provides accommodation for the mobile ("contributing to a healthy economy"), the young, those "facing a change in their personal or domestic circumstances", and others who prefer to rent.[67] The majority of tenancies—assured shortholds for a minimum six month period under the Housing Act 1988—reflect the short-termism of the market for this tenure. The deregulation of security in 1988 was backed up by de-control of rents, so that landlords are able to charge market rents. For those unable to afford the market rents, housing benefit has become essential, causing the rental market to be differentiated between those able, and those unable, to pay market rents. Attempts to restrict the Treasury's exposure to housing benefit expenditure have met with significant problems in the sector.[68] Deregulation and de-control have been avowedly the twin factors used by the government to arrest the decline in the sector (although this is controversial). This decline, from a

[62] See Niner, "Housing Associations and Ethnic Minorities" in Smith and Mercer (eds.), *op cit.* n. 32.

[63] See, e.g., Commission for Racial Equality, *Housing Associations and Racial Equality* (London: CRE, 1993).

[64] See especially, Housing Corporation, *Performance Standards and Management Guidance* (London: Housing Corporation, 1997).

[65] Discussed in Harrison, *Housing, "Race", Social Policy and Empowerment* (Aldershot: Avebury, 1995) ch. 5.

[66] See Mullins, "From Local Politics to State Regulation: the Legislation and Policy on Race Equality in Housing" (1992) 18 *New Community* 401, 408; Harrison *et al.*, *Black and Ethnic Minority Housing Associations* (London: Housing Corporation, 1996) esp. paras. 4.72–6; Cowan, *op cit.* n. 4, pp. 107, 268–70.

[67] DoE, *op cit.* n. 37, p. 20.

[68] See, for example, Bevan *et al.*, *Private Landlords and Housing Benefit* (York: Centre for Housing Policy, University of York, 1995); Kemp and McLaverty, *Private Tenants and Restrictions in Rent for Housing Benefit* (Centre for Housing Policy, University of York, 1995).

post-war market share of about 55 per cent to the current figure of about 10 per cent, has coincided with the periods of settlement of ethnic minorities, who were particularly reliant on this form of accommodation often at a premium, as well as being of the poorest quality.[69] The sector is currently characterised by having the largest proportion of any sector which is "unfit for human habitation",[70] as well as being expensive due to the lack of supply. Ethnic minority households are also known to suffer from discrimination in its allocation.[71]

IV. THE POLITICS OF SEGREGATION

We now move from discussion of the broader discriminatory tendencies within the housing market to consider the politicisation of segregation, and the creation of structural discrimination within the housing system. This politicisation provides an important backdrop to changes which have taken, and are taking place, in the housing welfare systems. Smith argues that:

> "Political imagery associated with the organization of residential space has, through its role in initiating and legitimizing policy change, contributed to the racial categorization of groups and individuals according to who they are or where they come from, where they live, and how they act or what they are presumed to think."[72]

She is able to link this association to immigration policy ("racial segregation was, in short, defined as a problem caused by immigration"), slum areas (where "public services were strained and the working class white electorate suffered"), and crime *control* ("a territorial link—grounded in the volatile 'inner city' — between the presence of black people and the escalation of urban violence").[73]

In the 1990s, the link between segregation and housing had a particular impact upon the development of asylum and immigration policies. Regularly throughout this period, politicians and the media contributed to the developing discourse that *bogus* asylum-seekers and *illegal* immigrants were accessing welfare, and particularly social housing.[74] I have elsewhere argued that this provides a significant example of the movement towards "inappropriateness" — the construction of persons who are so morally blameworthy that the issue of supply (or, in this broader context, resources) becomes irrelevant.[75] Thus, a confluence developed between the politicisation of segregation and the

---

[69] See, for example, Burney, *Housing on Trial* (Oxford: OUP, 1967).

[70] DoE, *English House Condition Survey 1991* (London: HMSO, 1993).

[71] Commission for Racial Equality, *"Sorry it's Gone": Testing For Racial Discrimination in the Private Rented Sector* (London: CRE, 1990); Ginsburg, "The Housing Act, 1988 and its Policy Context: A Critical Commentary" (1989) 25 *Critical Social Policy* 56, 74–7.

[72] S. Smith, 'Residential Segregation and the Politics of Racialization", in M. Cross & M. Keith (eds), *Racism, the City and the State*, (London: Routledge, 1993), 129.

[73] At 132, 135, 139 respectively.

[74] For further detail on this point, see D. Cowan, *op cit.* n. 55, ch. 7.

[75] D. Cowan, *Homelessness: The (In-)Appropriate Applicant*, (Aldershot: Dartmouth, 1997), 141.

contestability of welfarism.[76] As Ginsburg has noted, "The legitimation for racist immigration control is that the people most likely to want to come to Britain will be from poor countries . . . It is therefore the pressure on a welfare state in the process of retrenchment, as well as accommodation to white concern about black welfare scroungers, which expressly concerns government".[77] An important factor in the Conservative approach to the problem was the legitimation of processes of *market* discrimination (inability to pay) to justify processes of *racial* discrimination (inability to claim benefits and social housing).[78]

From 1992, both Conservative and New Labour governments have gone to quite considerable, almost absurd, lengths to withdraw all social welfare entitlements available to UK nationals from asylum-seekers and other "persons from abroad".[79] Under the current framework, put in place under the Immigration and Asylum Act 1999, support (including accommodation) is only to be provided to those asylum-seekers and their dependants "who appear to the Secretary of State to be destitute or to be likely to become destitute ..."[80] Accommodation is to be provided on a "no-choice" basis anywhere in England and Wales under a dispersal scheme (although there are recurrent concerns that insufficient levels of accommodation are being brought within the scheme)[81] operated by a newly created branch of the Home Office, the Asylum Support Directorate. The purpose of the scheme is to provide a safety net "in a way which minimises the incentive for abuse by those who do not really need the support or who would make an unfounded asylum application in order to obtain the provision".[82] The rationale for offering no choice to asylum-seekers is because those "genuinely fleeing persecution are looking for a safe and secure environment ... Such people will not be overly concerned about . . . the location in which they are supported."[83]

Nobody can doubt that the arrangements in place prior to the 1999 Act were "shambolic".[84] A mish-mash of different welfare legislation was developed through the courts which required local authority social services departments to provide accommodation and essential services.[85] Various cases show local

---

[76] "The deviant superscrounger . . . is quite often an immigrant shrewdly exploiting the guileless generosity of British welfare": P. Golding & S. Middleton, *Images of Welfare*, (Oxford: Martin Robertson, 1982).

[77] N. Ginsburg, *Divisions of Welfare*, (London: Sage, 1992), 160-1; see also P. Tuitt, *False Images*, (London: Pluto, 1996).

[78] For example, in January 1997, the Housing Corporation issued a circular warning housing associations that before they consider allocating accommodation to "applicants from abroad who do not qualify for local authority housing, they should carefully consider whether their aims and objectives allow them to do so", particularly in the light of the applicants' ability to pay.

[79] This phrase is drawn from the Housing Act 1996, s. 185(1), which created a category of persons ineligible to make a homelessness application.

[80] S. 95(1).

[81] This led to the scheme's introduction being phased in.

[82] Home Office, *Fairer, Faster and Firmer—A Modern Approach to Immigration and Asylum*, Cm 4018, (London: Home Office, 1998), para 8.19.

[83] Home Office, *Asylum Seekers Support*, (London: Home Office, 1999), para. 1.6.

[84] Home Office, *op cit*. n. 11.

[85] National Assistance Act 1948, s. 21; Children Act 1989, s. 20; for discussion of the cases, see D. Cowan, *op cit* n. 4, pp. 263–6.

authorities exploiting loopholes in the legislation to withdraw services (probably because central government funding would only cover their interpretation of what could be offered by local authorities)—for example, in *R v Newham LBC, ex parte Gorenkin*, it was held that if an asylum-seeker already had accommodation, the local authority was under no obligation to provide other goods or services such as food.[86] However, the dispersal scheme has already become bogged down by administrative and financial complexities.[87] The Audit Commission have commented that:

> "In many areas, supporting asylum seekers is not a popular policy, and if the cost of support is borne, at least in part, by local taxpayers, community tensions may increase. For some local authorities, dispersal looks like a 'no-win' option, with no incentive to participate."[88]

The dispersal system has been introduced because London and the South-East, particularly Kent, have borne the costs of providing services to asylum-seekers. Council tax rises in these areas have been said to be at least partially due to these costs.[89] Residential segregation has, once again, fuelled the exclusionary discourse.[90] In mid-August 1999, there were running attacks between asylum-seekers and locals in Dover, where asylum-seekers had been segregated in bed and breakfast accommodation in certain parts of the town.[91]

It is important that all of these policies have implications for the implementation of broader welfare strategies. Housing officers have been drawn into the enforcement of immigration laws leading to passport and identity checks on all welfare claimants. All applicants are subject to the culture of suspicion that currently exists about "persons from abroad". After the Housing Act 1996, Waddington talks of housing officers having to ask applicants unanswerable questions which effectively forces the local authority to discuss the applicants' immigration status with the Home Office unit responsible for deportation.[92] There is nothing particularly new in this relationship between welfare and immigration—it has been argued that in the early twentieth century welfare was "premised on national chauvinism".[93] The serious consequences for ethnic minorities of these changes have been described as follows:

---

[86] (1998) 30 H.L.R. 278.

[87] Audit Commission, *Another Country: Implementing Dispersal under the Immigration and Asylum Act 1999*, (London: Audit Commission, 2000), para 19. [88] *Ibid*, para 25.

[89] Kent County Council apparently brought in outside auditors to work out the costs to them of providing services to asylum-seekers: "Kent counts the £24m cost of asylum-seekers", *The Times*, 12 January 2000.

[90] See, for example, J. Goodwin, "Suburbia's little Somalia", *Daily Mail*, 12 January 1999, which cites concerns that the London Borough of Ealing would be "Somalia's seventh largest town with its 12,000 inhabitants".

[91] See, for example, "Minister steps in over refugee violence", *Daily Telegraph*, 16 August 1999; "Dover knife victims vent fury on police", *The Times*, 17 August 1999; "Port in a storm", *The Guardian*, 19 August 1999.

[92] M Waddington, 'Too Poor to Stay here: "Illegal Immigrants" and Housing Officers', in D. Cowan (ed), *Housing: Participation and Exclusion*, (Aldershot: Dartmouth, 1998).

[93] S. Cohen, "Anti-semitism, immigration controls and the welfare state", in D. Taylor (ed.), *Critical Social Policy*, (London: Sage, 1996), p. 47.

"Not only do they discourage claims from a section of the population and leave precisely those most in need with poorer provision; put in place degrading, bureaucratic and expensive machinery to save very little in the way of public money; place public sector workers in a highly dubious relationship with the state; but also they hammer home notions of illegality, undesirability and unworthiness which can be turned with similar ferocity on to single parents, gays and lesbians, criminals, the homeless, young people, old people, disabled people—indeed, anyone who does not fit the model of deserving poor."[94]

By way of contrast to these welfare cuts and exclusion from housing, until recently little was done to assist those ethnic minorities who were excluded by their housing situation. In particular, little was done to assist those suffering from the effects of harassment. Although various departments of government had called for "joint working" in relation to racial harassment for some time,[95] little was in fact done by agents on the ground. There has been a background of widespread inaction by local authorities to the extent that "initial anger [of those subjected to racial harassment] towards the perpetrators was in many cases rapidly redirected towards the police or the council once a case had been reported".[96] The "victim-centring" approach suggested by the guidance involves moving the perpetrator (and then excluding them from that housing tenure, for example through intentional homelessness) and leaving the "victim" in a situation in which they are fearful often for their lives. If the "victim" decides to surrender their tenancy, racial harassment from a person unknown to the applicant does not automatically render them homeless. The accommodation must not be reasonable for them to continue to occupy—a hard test to satisfy. Some authorities are even known to require applicants to seek legal redress before rendering themselves homeless, when it is well-known that legal redress itself is problematic and often worse than useless.[97] Despite the fact that racial harassment is now an offence (in the Crime and Disorder Act 1998), these structural problems remain (and are arguably exacerbated by the Housing Act 1996).[98]

V. CONCLUSION

In this chapter, the pattern of state support for housing ethnic minority households has been exposed as prejudicing those households within the marketplace.

[94] D. Hayes, "Outsiders within: the role of welfare in the internal control of immigration", in J. Batsleer & B. Humphries (eds.), *Welfare, Exclusion and Political Agency*, (London: Routledge, 2000), p. 75.
[95] Home Office, *The Response to Racial Attacks and Harassment: Guidance for the Statutory Agencies*, (London: Home Office, 1989); DoE, *Racial Incidents in Council Housing: the Local Authority Response*, (London: HMSO, 1994).
[96] J. Cooper & T. Qureshi, "Violence, Racial Harassment and Council Tenants", (1994) 8 *Housing Studies* 241; see also L. Bridges & D. Forbes, *Making the Law Work against Racial Harassment*, (London: Legal Action Group, 1990).
[97] D. Cowan, *Homelessness: The (In-)Appropriate Applicant*, (Aldershot: Dartmouth, 1997), ch 5; cf the *positive* changes in the Housing Act 1996 regarding violence to women.
[98] *Ibid*, ch. 9.

It has been argued that, whilst ghettoisation can, on one definition, be shown not to exist in Britain, spatial segregation is a common factor amongst and between ethnic minority groupings contained in the 1991 census. This may well reflect the choice of these households but is undoubtedly influenced by the institutional practices of housing providers and financiers. Such institutional discrimination may well have waned in certain cases as the same institutions have sought to become more competitive in the market place in order to expand their domination. However, the pattern of location suggests that old practices and prejudices may well not have dissipated. As significant a factor is the prevailing *discourse* of residential segregation which has been shown to have been a powerful driver behind changes, and linkages between, shifts towards the exclusion of those subjected to asylum and immigration control.

10

Healthcare Law for
a Multi-Faith Society

JONATHAN MONTGOMERY*

I INTRODUCTION

RUNNING THROUGH BRITISH healthcare law are a number of golden threads, offering reassurance that the law has taken the moral high ground. They purport to provide guarantees of universal objectivity promising that law is neutral, consistent and just. This essay considers the operation of some of these fundamental commitments from the perspective of their ability to recognise the diversity of cultures and faith communities that make up British society. It asks whether the conceptual currency of healthcare law can cope with the challenge of religious pluralism presented by members of ethnic minority groups.

The thesis advanced is that the application of these principles appears even handed but is in fact dominated by a secular humanist world view; a view that shows a lack of sympathy for the way in which members of faith communities might be expected to approach difficult healthcare decisions, particularly those about life and death. The claimed neutrality of our legal system therefore needs to be seen in a different light. It is not so much a question of respect for specific minority cultures as a recognition that the discourse of law and the practice of judges have underestimated the significance of religious faith in people's lives. To counter this conceptual discrimination against religion, the law needs to introduce new procedures and additional principles. Only then will it be able to accommodate the demands of our multi-faith society.

* Reader in Health Care Law, University of Southampton. I am grateful to my late friend and colleague Sebastian Poulter for stimulating my interest in the law's response to cultural and religious diversity. I wish I could have discussed this piece with him, it would have been much improved.

II THREE PRINCIPLES

A Autonomy

There can be little doubt of the rhetorical commitment of the British courts to the principle of patient autonomy. In *Re F*, Lord Goff said that it was a "fundamental principle, now long established, that every person's body is inviolate".[1] The House of Lords has persistently adopted an American formulation of this principle. As Lord Goff put it in the same case:

> in the case of medical treatment, we have to bear well in mind the libertarian principle of self-determination which, to adopt the words of Cardozo J (in *Schloendorff* v. *Society of New York Hospital* (1914) 105 NE 92, 93) recognises that:
>
> > "Every human being of adult years and sound mind has a right to determine what shall be done with his own body, and a surgeon who performs an operation without the patient's consent commits an assault."[2]

It has also been consistently held at the same highest level that the duty to respect this right to autonomy prevails over other ethical and legal obligations of doctors:

> [I]t is established that the principle of self-determination requires that respect must be given to the wishes of the patient, so that if an adult patient of sound mind refuses, however unreasonably, to consent to treatment or care by which his life would or might be prolonged, the doctors responsible for his care must give effect to his wishes, even though they do not consider it to be in his best interests to do so . . . To this extent, the principle of the sanctity of human life must yield to the principle of self-determination . . . and, for present purposes perhaps more important, the doctor's duty to act in the best interests of his patient must likewise be qualified.[3]

Again, in the words of Lord Mustill:

> Any invasion of the body of one person by another is potentially both a crime and a tort . . . How is it that, consistently with the proposition just stated, a doctor can with immunity perform on a consenting patient an act which would be a very serious crime if done by someone else? The answer must be that bodily invasions in the course of proper medical treatment stand completely outside the criminal law. The reason why the consent of the patient is so important is not that it furnishes a defence in itself, but because it is usually essential to the propriety of medical treatment. Thus, if the consent is absent, and is not dispensed within special circumstances by operation of law, the acts of the doctor lose their immunity . . . If the patient is capable of making a decision whether to permit treatment and decides not to permit it his choice must be obeyed, even if on any objective view it is contrary to his best interests. A doctor has

---

[1] *Re F* [1989] 2 FLR 376, 435.

[2] *Ibid.*, at 436. This authority was also cited in *Sidaway* v. *Bethlem RHG* [1985] 1 All ER 643 (1995) 1 BMLR 132, and *Airedale NHS Trust* v. *Bland* [1993] 1 All ER 821, [1993] 1 FLR 1026.

[3] *Airedale NHS Trust* v. *Bland* [1993] 1 FLR 1026, 1035–6 *per* Lord Goff.

no right to proceed in the face of objection, even if it is plain to all, including the patient, that adverse consequences and even death will or may ensue.[4]

Thus, patient autonomy is said to be a key concept in English healthcare law. The fundamental principles of trespass to the person ensure that no treatment can be carried out without the consent of the patient.[5] Patients who are capable of making choices are guaranteed the right to decide what happens to them even if their decisions are irrational.[6]

However, the reality of this right to accept or reject treatment is that it is fragile.[7] It depends on the patient being assessed as competent to decide. If she is assessed as incompetent, then her right to choose is destroyed and instead she is entitled to receive not the treatment she chooses but the treatment that the health professions decide is in her best interests.[8] If the processes by which competence is assessed lack consistency and objectivity then the apparent right to autonomy will be very much less valuable than it seems. We shall see below that the way in which the courts have dealt with the competence issue in cases involving religious belief throws into question their ability to make such assessments with full regard to the complexities of religious belief.

B Best Interests

For incompetent patients, then, the commitment to autonomy is supplanted by the second of the golden threads running through healthcare law, that of the best interests of the patient. Like autonomy, this principle is among the four cardinal signposts that have dominated Anglo-American medical ethics.[9] It is hard to reject such a powerful symbol of the altruistic commitment of medicine to public service. The General Medical Council's summary of the duties of doctors sees making the care of patients their first concern as the primary particular manifestation of the medical calling.[10]

The belief that doctors practise in order to look after their patients' best interests has deep roots in the common law. Indeed, at least one British judge, Lord Templeman, has come close to suggesting that the obligation to do patients good may be more fundamental than that to respect their right to choose. He said:

[4] See [1993] 1 FLR 1026, 1061–2.
[5] If they are competent: see below.
[6] *Re MB* [1997] 2 FLR 426; *St George's Healthcare NHS Trust* v. *S* [1998] 2 FCR 685.
[7] For an earlier discussion of the concept of fragility of consent rights see P. Alderson and J. Montgomery, *Health Care Choices: Making Decisions with Children* (London: Institute for Public Policy Research, 1996) pp. 34–5.
[8] *Re F* [1989] 2 FLR 376; J. Montgomery, *Health Care Law* (Oxford: Oxford University Press 1997) pp. 239–40.
[9] *Viz*: autonomy, beneficence, nonmaleficence and justice. See T.L. Beauchamp and J.F. Childress, *Principles of Biomedical Ethics* (Oxford: Oxford University Press, 1994).
[10] General Medical Council, *Duties of a Doctor* (London: General Medical Council, 1995).

The doctor, obedient to the high standards set by the medical profession, impliedly contracts to act at all times in the best interests of the patient . . . At the end of the day, the doctor bearing in mind the best interests of the patient and bearing in mind the patient's right to information which will enable the patient to make a balanced judgment, must decide what information should be given to the patient and in what terms that information should be couched.[11]

For His Lordship, patients' rights to give (or withhold) informed consent had to be balanced against their rights to be offered the care that would best promote their health. In the same leading House of Lords decision on informed consent (or rather the lack of such a doctrine in English law) Lord Diplock defined the duty of doctors thus: "to exercise his skill and judgment in the improvement of the physical or mental condition of the patient".[12] He rejected the idea that the disclosure of information was a separate duty and maintained robustly that it was part of the duty to do good for the patient and should be measured against the usual standards.

There are many ways in which the law's commitment to the best interests of patients is manifest. Sometimes it is indirect, making it difficult to identify the way in which the judges would assess the merits of cases. Thus, the duty to give incompetent patients the care that is in their best interests is usually judged not against the judicial assessment of where those interests lie but that of the doctors looking after them.[13]

Usually, the treatment of patients who are not competent to consent for themselves does not need prior sanction by the court. Consequently, the application of the best interests principle lies in the hands of health professionals rather than lawyers.

In a few areas, however, the courts have said that they should be involved prior to treatment being given and here the judges have had to address the best interest decisions themselves. In fact, the courts have typically, even here, restricted their scrutiny to satisfying themselves that the clinical judgment made by those doctors is within the margin of responsible professional decisions.[14] They have refrained from seeing it as their role to decide for themselves what is the best course of action.[15] In most cases, the courts have been reluctant to see it as their task to dictate to doctors what they should do, preferring to reassure themselves (and the public) that there has been full consideration of the options. Thus, it has been said that it would be an abuse of the court's powers to instruct a doctor to treat against her or his clinical judgment.[16] Rather, their role is to take responsibility for decisions to relieve the participants, especially parents, of

[11] *Sidaway* v. *Bethlem RHG* (1985) 1 BMLR 132, 159 *per* Lord Templeman.
[12] *Sidaway* v. *Bethlem RHG* (1985) 1 BMLR 132, 149.
[13] *Re F* [1989] 2 FLR 376.
[14] *Re F* [1989] 2 FLR 376; *Airedale NHS Trust* v. *Bland* [1993] 1 All ER 821.
[15] For cases in which they seem to have considered going further see *Frenchay NHS Trust* v. *S* [1994] 2 All ER 403, 411–13 *per* Waite LJ and *Re S* [1995] 2 WLR 38. In the latter case, the Court of Appeal confined its consideration to matters of *locus standi*, see [1995] 3 All ER 290.
[16] *Re J* [1992] 4 All ER 614.

some of their burden.[17] The supposed focus on the best interests of the patient has in reality been supplanted by a concern to scrutinise the process by which decisions are taken.[18]

The way in which the courts have addressed welfare cases has led Ian Kennedy to argue that making best interests a legal principle is actually to abdicate responsibility for regulating decisions. His argument is worth quoting at length:

> The best interests formula may be beloved of family lawyers but a moment's reflection will indicate that although it is said to be a test, indeed *the* legal test for deciding matters relating to children, it is not really a test at all . . . In fact, of course, there is no general principle other than the empty rhetoric of best interests; or rather, there is some principle (or principles) but the court is not telling. Obviously the court must be following some principles, otherwise a toss of a coin could decide the cases. But these principles, which serve as pointers to what amounts to the best interests, are not articulated by the court. Only the conclusion is set out. The opportunity for reasoned analysis is lost . . . If best interests is recited without analysis, the very purpose for involving the law is defeated . . . If any reasoning has taken place, it has occurred prior to arriving at the conclusion that a particular course of conduct is in a person's best interests. If, as is the case, this prior process of evaluation and analysis, and the factors underlying it, go unstated, accountability cannot exist. In effect, the law abdicates its responsibility. Decisions cannot readily be challenged. Discretion becomes virtually unfettered. The disequilibrium of power between patient and doctor (and others) goes uncorrected.[19]

Kennedy argues that the best interests test protects medical power rather than patients' welfare. Worse still, by hiding this fact it makes it more difficult to understand what is going on when decisions are taken. Close readings of cases where the courts take welfare decisions in medical cases seem to confirm Kennedy's argument. Thus, in the Jeanette case,[20] which he uses to illustrate his point, the court reached its conclusion (that it was in the young woman's best interests to be sterilised) by a process of defining the facts so as to highlight the arguments in favour of sterilisation and minimise the risks. The distortions involved in this process are evident from the judgments and speeches themselves in the disregard of the risks of the operation and of the possibility of the successful use of oral contraception. Perhaps most stark, however, is the ever increasing perceived risk of pregnancy. It was "possible" in the Family Division, an "immediate question" in the Court of Appeal and a "significant danger" and "unacceptable risk" before the House of Lords. The facts had not changed, but the judicial interpretations became more extreme as they felt the need to justify their decisions more strongly.[21]

[17] *Re C* [1996] 2 FLR 43, 44.
[18] J. Montgomery, *op cit.* n. 8, pp. 417–20.
[19] I. Kennedy, "Patients, doctors and human rights" in I. Kennedy, *Treat Me Right* (Oxford: Oxford University Press, 1991) pp. 395–6.
[20] *Re B* [1987] 2 All ER 206.
[21] The argument summarised in this paragraph is made more fully in J. Montgomery, "Rhetoric and Welfare" (1989) 9 *Oxford Journal of Legal Studies* 395.

There is a significant danger that best interests decision making could become little more than a mechanism for the imposition of prejudice. This essay will consider how far the cases suggest that faith communities fall foul of such a lack of sympathy for their beliefs. However, while Kennedy draws attention to the way that the vagueness of the best interests approach undermines the ability of the law to inject a balance of power into the unequal relationship between patient and health professional, this paper goes further. It suggests that the prejudicial approach of the judiciary serves to reinforce the vulnerability of patients to having their religious views overwhelmed by medical ethics.

C Sanctity of Life

The third of the principles running through English healthcare law is that of the sanctity of life. For many religious people life is a divine gift of supreme value. It should also be recognised, however, that this is not necessarily taken to mean that life is the highest value or must be preserved at all costs.[22] Most traditions recognise that martyrdom can be a heroic act, sacrificing life in order to vindicate the faith. Further, for those who believe in life after death or reincarnation, death is a natural part of the divine order that is to be welcomed rather than feared. A pluralist society would need to recognise the importance of life in such frameworks of meaning.

Like self-determination and best interests, commitment to the sanctity of life is frequently expressed by the judiciary. The principle can be seen at work most clearly in the prohibition of steps that end or shorten life, even when the patient requests active euthanasia.[23] That it is not absolute can be seen in the approach of English law to the termination of pregnancy, where social reasons are permitted to outweigh the protection of the life of the fetus.[24] It is also apparent in the judicial acceptance that it is sometimes legitimate to withdraw life-sustaining care.[25] However, for present purposes, the ability of English law to deal neutrally with people of different faiths needs to be considered in relation to the way in which individual decisions about life and death are approached.

In *Airedale NHS Trust* v. *Bland*[26] the status of the sanctity of life principle had to be faced head on. Tony Bland had been so severely injured in the Hillsborough tragedy that he survived only in a persistent vegetative state. He was apparently insensate and could experience no quality of life, good or bad. The courts had, therefore, to determine whether the law's commitment to the sanctity of life principle required that he be kept alive even though he could

[22] See J.K. Mason, *Human Life and Medical Practice* (Edinburgh: Edinburgh University Press, 1988).

[23] *R* v. *Adams* [1957] Crim. LR 365; *R* v. *Arthur* (1981) 12 BMLR 1; *R* v. *Cox* (1992) 12 BMLR 38.

[24] Abortion Act 1967, s. 1(1)(a).

[25] See, e.g., *Re J* [1990] 3 All ER 930 where this issue specifically was discussed.

[26] [1993] 1 All ER 821, [1993] 1 FLR 1026.

experience no benefit from his life and his parents now wished that his body be allowed to die. The approach taken by the court was to regard the principle of the sanctity of life as a component of the best interests test rather than a separate principle. The legality of withdrawing life-sustaining treatment was governed by whether it was in Tony's best interests to take this step. However, when assessing those interests, regard would have to be had to the principle that life was sacred.

The most extensive discussion of the principle was given by Hoffman LJ in the Court of Appeal. He said:

> we have a strong feeling that there is an intrinsic value in human life, irrespective of whether it is valuable to the person concerned or indeed to anyone else. Those who adhere to religious faiths which believe in the sanctity of all God's creation and in particular that human life was created in the image of God himself will have no difficulty with the concept of the intrinsic value of human life. But even those without any religious belief think in the same way. In a case like this we should not try to analyse the rationality of such feelings. What matters is that, in one form or another, they form part of almost everyone's intuitive values. No law which ignores them can possibly hope to be acceptable . . .
>
> But the sanctity of life is only one of a cluster of ethical principles which we apply to decisions about how we should live. Another is respect for the individual human being and in particular for his right to choose how he should live his own life. We call this individual autonomy or the right of self-determination. And another principle, closely connected, is respect for the dignity of the individual human being: our belief that quite irrespective of what the person concerned may think about it, it is wrong for someone to be humiliated or treated without respect for his value as a person. The fact that the dignity of an individual is an intrinsic value is shown by the fact that we feel embarrassed and think it wrong when someone behaves in a way which we think demeaning to himself, which does not show sufficient respect for himself as a person.

Hoffman LJ recognised the variety of approaches to interpreting the meaning of a commitment to the sanctity of life, including an explicit discussion of religious factors

> I accept that the sanctity of life is a complex notion, often linked to religion, on which differing views may be held. The Jehovah's Witness who refuses a blood transfusion even though he knows this may result in his death, would probably not consider that he was sacrificing the principle of the sanctity of life to his own right of self-determination. He would probably say that a life which involved receiving a transfusion was so defiled as no longer to be an object of sanctity at all. But someone else might think that his death was a tragic waste and did offend against the sanctity of life. I do not think it would be a satisfactory answer to such a person to say that if he could only see it from the point of view of the Jehovah's Witness, he would realise that the principle of the sanctity of life had not been sacrificed but triumphantly upheld.[27]

---

[27] These quotations from the judgment of Hoffman LJ are at [1994] 1 FCR 485, 522–3.

He expressed some reservations about using so robust a principle, worrying that "the case for the universal sanctity of life assumes a life in the abstract and allows nothing for the reality of Mr Bland's actual existence".[28]

In the House of Lords, Lord Goff referred to the sanctity of human life as a fundamental principle, recognised in the European Convention on Human Rights (Article 2) and the International Covenant on Civil and Political Rights (Article 6). However, as was shown above, the House held that the principle of sanctity of life gave way to the higher principles of self-determination and best interests. Thus, competent patients are entitled to refuse life-saving treatment and health professionals are entitled to withhold or withdraw such treatment provided they responsibly regard it to be in the patient's best interests to do so. In *Bland* itself, and a number of subsequent cases, the courts have reached the view that it is in the best interests of patients in a persistent vegetative state to be permitted to die notwithstanding the importance of the principle of sanctity of life.[29] The focus has been on how "meaningful" life is for the patient: a quality of life approach.[30] We shall see later how this approach has excluded certain religious beliefs from consideration.

In principle, the law recognises that the general value of life is not to be elevated above the rights of patients to determine its worth to them. In *Re T*, Lord Donaldson recognised:

> a conflict between two interests, that of the patient and that of the society in which he lives. The patient's interest consists of his right to self determination—his right to live his own life how he wishes, even if it will damage his health or lead to his premature death. Society's interest is in upholding the concept that all human life is sacred and that it should be preserved if at all possible. It is well established that in the ultimate the right of the individual is paramount. But this merely shifts the problem where the conflict occurs and calls for a very careful examination of whether, and if so the way in which, the individual is exercising that right. In case of doubt, that doubt falls to be resolved in favour of the preservation of life for if the individual is to override the public interest, he must do so in clear terms.[31]

III   RELIGIOUS DIMENSIONS TO ASSESSING COMPETENCE

In principle, religious views should have no particular part to play in assessing whether patients are competent to consent to, or refuse, treatment. As Lord Donaldson has put it "I personally regard religious or other beliefs which bar any medical treatment or treatment of particular kinds as irrational, but that does not make minors who hold those beliefs any less '*Gillick* competent' ".[32]

---

[28] *Ibid.*, at 516.

[29] E.g., *Re H* [1998] 3 FCR 174; *Re D* [1998] 1 FCR 498; *Re R* [1996] 3 FCR 473.

[30] *Re D* [1998] 1 FCR 498.

[31] *Re T* [1992] 2 FLR 458, 470.

[32] *Re W* [1992] 2 FCR 785, 803. "*Gillick* competence" refers to the test laid down in *Gillick* v. *West Norfolk & Wisbech AHA* [1985] 3 All ER 402 whereby a young person is competent to

Nevertheless, a close examination of the case law suggests that the judiciary has found it more difficult to act upon this neutral stance than to express it.

Questions about the courts' ability to be objective about assessing competence have come to the fore in two areas. The first concerns the refusal of pregnant women to consent to caesarean sections which their obstetricians regard as essential to saving their life and that of the baby they are carrying. The second has been where young people express their willingness to sacrifice their lives rather than compromise their faith. In the former area, a contrast can be drawn between the stance taken by the higher judiciary, where legal principle has been honoured to protect the rights of women, and the lower courts, where the desire to protect life has led judges to manipulate the concept of competence to facilitate their desired outcomes.[33] In one case where religious objections were said to be behind the woman's refusal to consent, her wishes were overridden without the issue of competence even being discussed.[34]

The first case to grapple with the problem was a blood transfusion case in which the woman concerned was not thought herself to be a Jehovah's Witness, but whose mother was a devout member of that faith. Nevertheless, the woman told nursing staff that she retained some beliefs from that religion. Ward J in the High Court examined not merely whether she understood the situation but also the "depth" of her faith:

> My conclusion of the strength of her faith is that her convictions are in fact not so deep-seated or so fundamental as to constitute an immutable decision by her as to her way of life—or her way of death. In my judgment she remains capable as she has demonstrated herself to be capable of renouncing the tenets of the faith to suit her own chosen way of life.[35]

His decision was partly based on his assessment that her lifestyle was contrary to that recommended by her faith and he inferred that she could not have taken it that seriously. Given that patients are entitled to refuse treatment for good reason or no reason,[36] this concern for the consistency of the patient's motivation seems to be an issue peculiar to cases concerning religious beliefs. In the Court of Appeal, Butler-Sloss LJ took a similar line, observing that the woman had not been baptised into the faith and holding that she was not a "practising" member.

These assessments of the degree of the woman's commitment to the beliefs of the Jehovah's Witnesses were used to suggest that her expressed views could not really have reflected her own settled opinion. Rather they were deemed to be the

consent to treatment if she or he has "sufficient understanding and intelligence to enable him or her to understand fully what is proposed" (at 423); see further, J. Montgomery, *op cit.* n. 8, pp. 283–7.

[33] See *Re MB* [1997] 2 FLR 426 (CA) and *St George's Healthcare NHS Trust* v. *S* [1998] 2 FCR 685 for discussion and review of the cases.

[34] *Re S* [1993] 1 FLR 26.

[35] Quoted in the judgment of Lord Donaldson in the Court of Appeal, *Re T* [1992] 2 FLR 458, 465–7.

[36] *Sidaway* v. *Bethlem RHG* [1985] 1 All ER 643, 666, *per* Lord Templeman.

result of undue influence exerted by her mother. In contrast to the characterisa-
tion of the woman's beliefs as superficial, the judges spoke of her "mother's fer-
vent belief in the sin of blood transfusion". On the facts of this case, the tenets
of faith were rendered insignificant; either they were not the real wishes of the
patient or they were excessively fanatical. These strategies will tend to margin-
alise doctrinal objections to care.

Lord Donaldson identified a category of people whose involvement in advis-
ing a patient should alert the court to the possibility that undue influence may
have been exercised:

> the relationship of the persuader to the patient—for example, spouse, parents or reli-
> gious adviser—will be important, because some relationships more readily lend them-
> selves to overbearing the patient's independent will than do others.[37]

He did not go so far as to assert that there is a presumption against respecting
religious beliefs, but the approach is clearly one of suspicion.

The question of undue religious influence has emerged again when the courts
have been required to assess the competence of adolescents who hold strong religious beliefs. In *Re S*, a fifteen year old girl had suffered from thalassaemia
almost since birth and required regular blood transfusions.[38] When she was ten
years of age, her mother began to attend Jehovah's Witness meetings, taking her
daughter with her. The mother's reluctance to consent to the continuation of the
transfusions was overcome by seeking the necessary consent from the father.
Subsequently, however, the girl refused to co-operate and the court was asked
to exercise its jurisdiction to determine whether she should continue to receive
blood.

Johnson J found that she had not yet been baptised into the church, but that
she held her beliefs strongly and she told him that "having someone else's blood
is having someone else's soul". He noted that she believed "that for her to submit to further transfusions would have consequences for her in the life hereafter
and it is for that reason and not because of any wish to die, so-called, that she
resists the local authority's application" for treatment to be authorised.[39] He
painted a poignant picture of her demeanour: "S seemed to me to be not only
small, frail and pale of face, but she seemed to me to be less mature than most
girls of her age in the way she spoke, responded to questions and generally conducted herself". He noted further that "holding her Bible in both her hands as
she answered questions, this young woman never wavered in her refusal to have
more blood transfusions" and that "[s]he has said on previous occasions that if
it was forced upon her it would be like rape and it would be those who had done
it who would be the sinners".[40]

[37] *Re T* [1992] 2 FLR 458, 473.
[38] [1994] 2 FLR 1065.
[39] *Ibid.*, at 1068.
[40] *Ibid.*, at 1072.

Particular difficulties were presented by her beliefs about divine intervention. There were suggestions in her account of the situation that she was hoping that God might work a miracle to save her life. In a single interview with a doctor she spoke of such a possibility no less than nine times, saying that God might decide she should live because she was faithful. This might have been an article of faith, being wholly prepared to die if that was the choice of God, or it might have been a form of denial, refusing to recognise the seriousness of the situation. The court concluded that it was a symptom of the latter, pointing to her lack of understanding of how she would die. The judge was also concerned by her inability to explain why God was opposed to transfusions. He noted that she had been found to repeat explanations of what she had heard and was unable to explain them on further scrutiny. He summed up his assessment with a biblical allusion:[41]

> "When I was a child, I spoke as a child". That seemed to me to be how S feels and speaks. There are those who are children and those who are adults and those who are in-between. I do not believe that S is in-between. She is still very much, in my view, a child. Whilst as she gave evidence I was so very strongly impressed by her integrity and her commitment, I believe they were the integrity and commitment of a child and not of somebody who was competent to make the decision that she tells me she has made. She hopes still for a miracle. My conclusion is, therefore, that she is not "*Gillick*-competent".[42]

Importantly, it should be noted that she believed in miracles was taken to be evidence of her incompetence. Yet many religious people retain a belief in miracles despite the dominant scientific scepticism about such claims.

In *Re S*, the finding of incompetence was only partly bound up with the patient's religious beliefs. There was also consideration of whether the girl's account was similar to those of other young people who were fed up with prolonged treatment but who would not explain their frustration in religious terms. The expert evidence indicated that young people in such situations tended to show similar resistance to that shown by S without any religious influence. The court felt that this reinforced its conclusion that her refusal to co-operate was not "competently" reached. Nevertheless, in other cases it is the religious nature of the patient's beliefs alone that seems to determine the assessment.

Re L[43] concerned a young Jehovah's Witness of fourteen who required a blood transfusion to save her life. She needed plastic surgery following severe scalding which would inevitably result in significant loss of blood. The girl accepted her doctors' advice that she needed a transfusion to save her life but still rejected the transfusion because of her religious beliefs. Sir Stephen Brown P found that she was not "*Gillick* competent" to give or refuse her consent to the treatment. This was partly because she was not fully aware of the way in which

41 1 Corinthians 13:11.
42 [1994] 2 FLR 1065, 1076.
43 *Re L* [1998] 2 FLR 810.

she would die, which ignorance was a direct result of the refusal of her parents and the health professionals looking after her to inform her of the facts. More important for current purposes, however, is the way in which her religious beliefs were taken into account. The judge stressed her narrow experience, saying that that she had lived a sheltered life, principally within the Jehovah's Witness community, that necessarily limited her understanding. He found that because of this she lacked the required degree of understanding for legal competence. Such an approach makes it far more difficult for those brought up in a strong faith community to establish their competence than those whose views are shaped by mainstream secular society.

This attitude can be seen even more clearly in the expert opinion on the issue of competence in the case. The psychiatrist asked to advise the court on this issue,

> [made] the point that the girl's view as to having no blood transfusion is based on a very sincerely, strongly held religious belief which does not lend itself in her mind to discussion. It is one that has been formed by her in the context of her own family experience and the Jehovah's Witnesses' meetings where they all support this view. He makes the point that there is a distinction between a view of this kind and the constructive formulation of an opinion which occurs with adult experience.[44]

This analysis effectively disregards religious beliefs on the basis that they have been formed in the context of a close family and local church where people were of similar views. The psychiatrist sought to distinguish the position from that of adults, but is doubtful whether devout adults would fare any better on such an approach. It is often the case that those with a strong faith show considerable reluctance to enter into discussion of the basis of their beliefs with outsiders. Even if adults would be assessed more sympathetically, it would seem that the psychiatrist's reluctance to respect belief risks disregarding all religious opinions expressed by young people. This is, at least arguably, a breach of their basic human rights[45] if adopted as a blanket prejudice. That it is prejudice is shown by the fact that the psychiatrist was prepared to draw so firm a conclusion without even talking to the girl. It was not, therefore, an indication of her mental capacity but of the psychiatrist's assumptions.

IV CATEGORICAL IMPERATIVES IN THE STRUCTURE
OF WELFARE DECISION MAKING

Many religious people believe that right conduct is a matter of abiding by universal principles, often (but not necessarily) of divine origin. However, this deontological approach to ethical dilemmas sits uneasily with the judicial approach to welfare decision making. The courts have maintained a more prag-

---

[44] *Re L* [1998] 2 FLR 810, at 812.
[45] See UN Convention on the Rights of the Child, Arts. 2 and 14.

matic and essentially consequentialist approach to decisions. They have preferred to consider the likely results of selecting each of the available options and to use "common sense" to determine which of these possible futures is the most attractive (or least unattractive).[46] This can be illustrated by the way in which attempts to appeal to moral principles in one of the early sterilisation decisions were firmly rejected by the House of Lords on the basis that the only principle at stake was the best interests of the patient and that appeal to other factors would detract from those interests.[47] So, too, have rules of law or thumb to guide the courts in determining whether a child's life is so awful as to make the withdrawal of life-sustaining treatment acceptable been rejected in favour of an undiluted best interests test (which has in turn proved to provide little basis for departure from medical advice).[48]

This insistence on the irrelevance of universal standards to decisions about the best interests of individual children has made it very difficult for the courts to take account of religious views that make the opposite assumption. In *Re C*, for example, the court was asked to authorise an NHS Trust to withdraw artificial ventilation from a young baby and also to refrain from resuscitating her.[49] The girl suffered from muscular atrophy and was not expected to survive for more than about a year even if ventilation were continued. Her parents were Orthodox Jews and their religion was clear on the implications of the sanctity of life in the case. The mother's affidavit stated:

> we are still of the opinion that the course of action proposed by the plaintiff would not be in the best interests of our child. Religion plays an important part in the life of myself and my family. We are all orthodox Jews and live our lives by those values. One of the principles fundamental to our religion is that life should always be preserved. Another is that someone of our faith cannot stand aside and watch a person die where their intervention could prevent that death. In such a case the person that stands by will subsequently be punished by God. Failing to resuscitate is equivalent to a situation such as this.[50]

Sir Stephen Brown P expressed great respect for the parents but held that their version of the sanctity of life was insignificant when the court came to play its role:

> The anxiety of the doctors as well as the parents can be well understood. Their objective in their profession is to save and to preserve life but, as has been said in earlier cases that whilst the sanctity of life is vitally important, it is not the paramount consideration. The paramount consideration here is the best interests of little C.[51]

[46] See, e.g., *Re C* [1998] 1 FCR 1 (discussed below).
[47] *Re B* [1987] 2 All ER 206, see especially the speech of Lord Bridge.
[48] See especially *Re J* [1990] 3 All ER 930. The cases are discussed in J. Montgomery, *op cit.* n. 8, pp. 417–20.
[49] [1998] 1 FCR 1.
[50] *Ibid.*, at 7.
[51] *Ibid.*, at 9.

The parents' claim was that the child's interests were determined by the value placed by their faith on her life, and that this value required them to take every available step to keep her alive. The court required an assessment of this child's situation, not a general consideration of principle. As there could be no compromise on the absolutist position adopted by the parents, the court's position effectively negated the parental views.

If *Re C* shows how a strong religious commitment to life was neutralised in the court's analysis, a similar resistance to faith can be seen when the religious view in question rejects life. In *Re E* Ward J adopted an approach to the construction of the welfare principle that makes it almost impossible to take a sympathetic view of religious views.[52] The patient was a boy of fifteen who was found to be suffering from leukaemia. The treatment involved drugs that would attack his bone marrow as well as the leukaemia cells, which necessitated blood transfusions to compensate for the inability of his bone marrow to produce blood cells. The boy and his parents were Jehovah's Witnesses and opposed to the blood transfusions on religious grounds. The case came to court under the wardship jurisdiction, under which Ward J found that the boy's wishes were not determinative. He had to consider what was in his best interests. He found that the best interests test was objective: what would a reasonable parent do, bearing in mind that the boy lived in his particular religious society. He also found that the boy's wishes should be taken into account. However, when he came to apply that approach he found it very difficult to give any weight to the religious considerations in the light of the importance of life:

> He is of an age and understanding at least to appreciate the consequence if not the process of his decision, and by reason of the convictions of his religion, which I find to be deeply held and genuine, he says "no" to a medical intervention which may save his life. What weight do I place upon this refusal? I approach this case telling myself that the freedom of choice in adults is a fundamental human right. He is close to the time when he may be able to take those decisions. I should therefore be very slow to interfere. I have also to ask myself to what extent is that assertion of decision, "I will not have a blood transfusion", the product of his full but his free informed thought? Without wishing to introduce into the case notions of undue influence, I find that the influence of the teachings of the Jehovah's Witnesses is strong and powerful. The very fact that this family can contemplate the death of one of its members is the most eloquent testimony of the power of that faith. He is a boy who seeks and needs the love and respect of his parents whom he would wish to honour as the Bible exhorts him to honour them. I am far from satisfied that at the age of 15 his will is fully free. He may assert it, but his volition has been conditioned by the very powerful expressions of faith to which all members of the creed adhere. When making this decision, which is a decision of life or death, I have to take account of the fact that teenagers often express views with vehemence and conviction—all the vehemence and conviction of youth! Those of us who have passed beyond callow youth can all remember the convictions we have loudly proclaimed which now we find somewhat embarrassing. I

[52] [1993] 1 FLR 386.

respect this boy's profession of faith, but I cannot discount at least the possibility that he may in later years suffer some diminution in his convictions.[53]

This assessment contains at least three prejudicial assumptions. First, the willingness to contemplate death is interpreted as evidence of the power of religious indoctrination rather than a possible assessment of where the balance of interests lies. The decision reached by the family is itself used to demonstrate its unreliability. Such a judgment is made because the judge is unsympathetic to the outcome of the patient's choice not because the process has been shown to be flawed by lack of understanding or free will. There appears to be little or no scope for the suggestion that the young man's decision could be legitimate. If this possibility is ruled out in this way it is hard to see how religious arguments can be given any weight.

A second indication of cause for concern is the way in which the alignment of the boy's views with those of other members of his faith is taken to indicate a lack of volition on his part rather than confirmation of his conviction. At least here there is some attempt to tailor the assessment to the individual circumstances, noting his desire to secure the love and respect of his parents. This is less clear in relation to the third issue, the way in which the zeal of youth is used as a reason to downplay the significance of the boy's views. Ward J used the fact that the young man might change his mind as a reason for overriding his current views. Yet this possibility is always there for all people and would not usually be regarded as a reason for ignoring their current choices. In fact, the boy did not change his mind and exercised his right as an adult to refuse treatment approximately two years later when he became eighteen.[54] If young people who hold opinions as a result of their faith are assumed to be unable to understand their own interests, then it is difficult to see how their rights to religious freedom can be respected.

It seems clear that English law finds it impossible to comprehend religious decisions that death is preferable to life. Ward J's assessment of the welfare issue indicates that, while he notes the religious question, an "objective" assessment will always result in a choice for life:

> A has by the stand he has taken thus far already been and become a martyr for his faith. One has to admire—indeed one is almost baffled by—the courage of the conviction that he expresses. He is, he says, prepared to die for his faith. That makes him a martyr by itself. But I regret that I find it essential for his well-being to protect him from himself and his parents, and so I override his and his parents' decision. In this judgment—which has been truly anxious—I have endeavoured to pay every respect and give great weight to the religious principles which underlie the family's decision and also to the fundamental human right to decide things for oneself. That notwithstanding, the welfare of A, when viewed objectively, compels me to only one conclusion, and that is that the hospital should be at liberty to treat him with the

---

[53] *Ibid.*, at 393.
[54] See *Re S* [1994] 2 FLR 1065, 1075.

administration of those further drugs and consequently with the administration of blood and blood products.[55]

Or once again:

> [I]s this choice of death one which a judge in wardship can find to be consistent with the welfare of the child? The father supplied the answer himself—life is precious. The risk of serious infection from a blood transfusion is infinitesimal and not a risk which would stand in the father's way but for his religious conviction because, as he said, life is too precious. When, therefore, I have to balance the wishes of father and son against the need for the chance to live a precious life, then I have to conclude that their decision is inimical to his well-being.[56]

The religious opinions are the incongruous stumbling block: "but for" these there could be no issue. If they are the only contrary argument then they are anomalous and illogical. It is a matter of subjective wishes against the objective value of life. Yet to the Jehovah's Witnesses, these wishes were based on an objective reality of the divine order. The analysis offered by the court is not an equal assessment of different approaches but a choice for a secular evaluation rather than seeking to see the issues from the patient's world view. Religious views are "baffling" and do not, in the court's view, fit the paradigm of welfare analysis.

The approach adopted by Ward J in *Re E* was cited with approval in *Re O*.[57] In that case, despite a sensitive explanation of the dilemma facing the parents from their faith perspective, Johnson J found that he had "no doubt" that he should authorise a blood transfusion if it became medically necessary.[58] Similarly, in *Re R*[59] the issue was found to be clear cut:

> The evidence is clear, however, that because of her medical condition the opinion of those who are responsible for her treatment supports the use of blood products. Without that treatment, the consensus is that the treatment will be unsuccessful and she will suffer harm. Only because they cannot give their consent to this treatment are her caring parents unable to meet her needs. But so overwhelming is her need for blood and so much is it in her best interests to have it in the light of current medical knowledge that, for her welfare, I am bound to override the parents' wishes and authorise the use of blood products, thus enabling the doctors to give her transfusions.[60]

The parents' religious commitment to the sanctity of life in *Re C* could not be accommodated within the best interests test. [61] Yet in *Re E, Re O* and *Re R* sanctity of life was used to show that religious views were incompatible with the best interests of the children in the line of cases just discussed. The judiciary seems

---

[55] *Re E, supra*, at 394.
[56] *Ibid.*, at 393.
[57] [1993] 2 FLR 149.
[58] See pp. 150 and 153.
[59] [1993] 2 FLR 757.
[60] *Ibid.*, at 760.
[61] [1998] 1 FCR 1.

to be happy to use the sanctity of life doctrine to override religious values but not to accept its religious foundations for people of faith.

IV CONCLUSIONS

The analysis of the above cases has shown that the courts have found it difficult to give significant weight to religious faith. They state that the perception of some judges that some religious views are irrational has no bearing on the question of whether those who hold such beliefs are legally competent to give or withhold consent to treatment. However, when cases come before them they are happy to allow their interpretation of the facts to be coloured by a reluctance to accept refusals based on faith. In *Re T* the concept of undue influence and apparent uncertainty of the patient's grasp of the facts permitted a clearly expressed view to be discounted as not having been competently made. In *Re L* the psychiatrist's assumptions about the nature of adolescent religion went unchallenged as they allowed the court to justify overriding a decision with which it was clearly uncomfortable. The overwhelming impression is that the courts are reluctant to face up to the possibility that people may choose death over life.[62] It appears, therefore, that the rights of religious people to refuse treatment are more fragile that those of humanists.

It seems clear that the usual priority between sanctity of life and respect for autonomy is reversed where faith is concerned. While the matter is complicated by the fact that most of the cases involve children, the adoption of an "objective" standard for welfare has been used by the courts to privilege the preservation of life over the countervailing theological arguments. The latter are characterised as subjective or as strongly influenced (rather than free). While there may be philosophical arguments for adopting this position, it would seem to be based on the acceptance of a secular epistemology that gives the lie to the law's claim to be neutral. As *Re C* shows, reliance on a religious version of the sanctity of life principle to support a decision can be undermined where the court so chooses.

This essay has demonstrated that, for members of faith communities, the three fundamental principles of British healthcare law do not ensure recognition of their values and interests as conceived by them. The commitment to autonomy implies that it is patients who are the ultimate arbiter of where their best interests lie. Yet because it depends on their being accepted as legally competent, this autonomy is vulnerable to ethnocentric and secularist assumptions about the nature of rationality. The judges have not succeeded in stepping above the difficulties of understanding religious perspectives to incorporate faith into the assessment of competence. Thus, autonomy is more poorly protected for those

---

[62] See also J. Montgomery, "Suicide, Euthanasia and the Psychiatrist: A Legal Footnote" (1998) 5 *Philosophy, Psychiatry and Psychology* 153.

with religious views than it is for those with more familiar (to the judiciary) belief systems.

Once declared incompetent, patients become vulnerable to medical and judicial paternalism. The purpose of judicial scrutiny of decisions taken in the "best interests" of patients is to ensure that as objective a view as possible is taken. However, as the analysis has shown, such judgments have in fact been made in ways which find it difficult to take adequate account of the perspectives of religious people. What should be an independent review of the case, recognising that each patient is an individual in a cultural and (sometimes) religious context, often collapses into the application of a generalised secularist view on what is best for people (rather than this person). The principle that decisions must be taken in the best interests of the individual patient has not guaranteed respect for the values of religious people.

Finally, the sanctity of life principle has proved to be an effective sword in the hands of those seeking to prevent religious parents sacrificing the lives of their children on the (perceived) insensitive altars of their faiths, but it has been an extremely weak shield against the pressure of a secular world view that sees it as futile to maintain that life is precious in all circumstances and at all costs. This fundamental commitment of the law to protect life seems a hollow promise to those whose faith leads them to rely on it.

This structural lack of sympathy to faith needs to be countered in a number of ways designed to enable religious arguments to become as plausible in court as secular ones. In relation to the process of assessing competence, steps need to be taken to balance the prejudice. The test itself is neutral, but the way in which it is applied to the facts is poorly controlled by the law. It is unlikely that this can be directly regulated, but guidance on how assessments should be made could draw attention to the risk that a general lack of sympathy for religious views could undermine objectivity. It could also provide a checklist to help health professionals identify whether their judgment is being coloured by the content of religious beliefs rather than the patient's understanding of the situation.[63]

The first step in reducing the dangers of welfare decision making is to increase the significance of the patient's perception of their interests. Where they are competent to express a legally valid choice, that perception will be determinative. When they are not so competent, the current law seems to disregard their views entirely. A way needs to be found to take the personal values of patients into account even when they are not legally competent. It may be difficult to draw reliable inferences from patients' previous conduct from which a court could impute decisions to them, but that process at least recognises the individuality of the lives which are being considered. In North America, this approach has been described as "substituted judgment". The principle is that the court

---

[63] The Code of Practice issued under the Mental Health Act 1983, now in its third edition, provides a model for this approach. See also the discussion in P. Alderson and J. Montgomery, *op cit.* n. 7, pp. 66–77 proposing a similar approach to confronting prejudice in the assessment of children's competence.

should try to place itself in the patient's shoes and make the decision that it believes the patient would have made had they been in a position to do so. One English decision has shown some interest in this approach,[64] but it has not yet been adopted here. An alternative would be to require the courts to presume that adherence to settled religious convictions is in the best interests of patients. Only where the implications of those convictions were unclear would that presumption be rebutted.

Without such reform, the law fails to recognise the importance of faith in some people's lives. At present, the courts have shown themselves systematically unwilling to accept strongly held religious beliefs, despite their acknowledgement that they should be able to do so. The building blocks of medical law seem to protect patients' rights. However, the truth is that, despite its concern to be neutral, English medical law has been unable to use its foundational concepts to treat humanists and members of religious faiths equally.

---

[64] *Re J* [1990] 3 All ER 930.

Index

Abduction of children. *See* Child abduction
Abuse, child,
  child abduction, 6, 7
Adoption,
  inter-country. *See* Inter-country adoptions
  transracial. *See* Transracial adoption
Affirmative action,
  transracial adoption, 34, 40, 41
Arranged marriages, 78–79
Australia,
  child abduction from, 3
  indigenous children. *See* Indigenous children
    in Australian law

Checklist, welfare,
  local authority support for ethnic minority
    children, 16, 24
Child abduction, 3–14
  abuse, child, 6, 7
  assessment of risk, 5–7
  Australia, abduction from, 3
  conclusions, 14
  Conventions,
    admission of countries to, 14
    aims, 3
    defences, 4, 5
    deterrence, 3
    UK as signatory, 3
    welfare, interpretation of, 3–4
  Council of Europe Convention, 2
  cultural relativism, 11–12
  defences, 4, 5
    assessing risk, 5–7
  deterrence, 3
  domestic violence, 6, 7
  endogenous value judgments, 11–13
  financial detriments, 5–6
  forum conveniens, 11
  generally, 3–4
  Hague Convention, 3
  male elitism, 13
  monism, 11, 13
  non-Convention cases, 9–11
  objecting child, 7–8
  pluralism, 13–14
  psychological harm, 5–7
  relativism, 11–12
  risk assessment, 5–7
  sexual abuse, 6–7
  social consensus, 12–13

  tolerance, 11
  unaccompanied returns, 5–6
  universalism, 11
  value framework, 11–14
  welfare of child, 3–4, 9–11, 14
Child protection,
  local authority support for ethnic minority
    children, 22
Children,
  abduction. *See* Child abduction
  abuse. *See* Abuse, child
  indigenous children. *See* Indigenous children
    on Australian law
  local authority support for ethnic minority .
    See Local authority support for ethnic
    minority children
  marriages between, recognition of, 80–85
Community interests,
  transracial adoption, 33, 34, 38–39
Contact orders,
  domestic violence, 131–133
Criminal law,
  domestic violence, 137–138
Criminal offences,
  inter-country adoptions, 118–121
Cultural relativism,
  child abduction, 11–12

Day care,
  local authority support for ethnic minority
    children, 16, 23
Disabled children,
  local authority support for ethnic minority
    children, 20–21
  needs, 20–21
Divorce,
  foreign. *See* Foreign divorces, recognition of
Domestic violence, 129–142
  child abduction, 6, 7
  conclusions, 142
  contact orders, 131–133
  criminal law, 137–138
  double jeopardy, 129–142
  immigration, 141–142
  institutions, 135–137
  meaning, 128
  policing problems, 139–141
  procedures, 135–137
  race and, 129–142
    contact orders, 131–133

Domestic violence (*cont*.):
  race and (*cont*.):
    criminal law, 137–138
    cultural awareness, 136
    immigration, 141–142
    institutions, 135–137
    legal system, 133–138
    policing problems, 140–141
    procedures, 135–137
    refugees, 137
    women trapped in violent relationships,
      130–131
   refugees, 137
   women trapped in violent relationships,
    130–131

Education,
  local authority support for ethnic minority
    children, 23
  transracial adoption, 35, 36–37

Family support,
  local authority support for ethnic minority
    children, 22
Foreign divorces, recognition of, 51–70
  British Isles, divorces obtained within the,
    54–55
  conclusions, 68–70
  cultural identity, 52
  current law, scheme of, 54–68
    overseas divorces. *See* overseas divorces
      below
  extra-judicial, 51
  generally, 51–52
  historical overview, 52–54
  increase, 51
  Jewish *ghet*, 51
  Muslim *talaq*, 51
  overseas divorces, 55–68
    grounds for recognition, 55
    means of proceedings, obtained by, 55–63
      country in which divorce obtained,
        61–63
      meaning, 55–56
      non-recognition, grounds for, 64–68
      proceedings, meaning of, 56–60
      situs of extra-judicial divorce, 61–63
    official documentation, 66–67
    otherwise than by way of proceedings,
      overseas divorce obtained, 64
    public policy, 67–68
    want of notice, 65–66
  religious courts, 51
Foreign marriages, recognition of, 71–86
  arranged marriages, 78–79
  child marriages, 80–85
  conclusions, 85–86
  cultural values, 77–85

    adjudicative function in context of,
      exercise of, 77–80
    arranged marriages, 78–79
    child marriages, 80–85
    failure to recognise, 77
    reasons and non-reasons, 77–80
  discretionary veto,
    public policy, 71–73
    use, 71
  generally, 71–73
  meaning, 71
  public policy, 71–73
    cultural imperialism, 74–77
Fostering,
  local authority support for ethnic minority
    children, 16

Hague Convention 3. *See also* Child abduction
Harassment,
  housing ethnic minority households, 145
Healthcare law, 161–179
  autonomy, patient, 162–163
  best interests, 163–166
  categorical imperatives in decision making,
    172–177
  competence, religious dimension to
    assessment of, 168–172
  conclusions, 177–179
  generally, 161
  multi-faith society, for,
    autonomy, patient, 162–163
    best interests, 163–166
    categorical imperatives in decision
      making, 172–177
    competence, religious dimension to
      assessment of, 168–172
    generally, 161
    religious views, 168–172
    sanctity of life, 166–168
  patient autonomy, 162–163
  religious views, 168–172
  sanctity of life, 166–168
Housing ethnic minority households, 143–159
  colour blindness, 143, 149–155
    council housing, 152–153
    effects, 149–155
    home ownership, 150–152
    housing associations, 153–154
    private renting, 154–155
    types of racism, 149
  conclusion, 159
  council housing, 152–153
  generally, 143–145
  harassment, 145
  home ownership, 150–152
  housing associations, 153–154
  politics of segregation, 155–159
  private renting, 154–155

spatial segregation, 143–159
  colour blindness, 143, 149–155
  discrimination, 143–144
  ethnic penalties, 144
  generally, 143–144
  ghettoisation, 145–148
    1991 census, 145–148
  harassment, 145
  immigration "threat", 155
  market processes, 144–145
  patterns, 143
  politics, 155–159
state support, 143–159
types of racism, 149
Human rights,
  indigenous children in Australian law, 88

Immigration,
  domestic violence, 141–142
Indigenous children in Australian law, 87–109
  Aboriginal Child Placement Principle
    (ACPP), 92–96
  child protection and placement, 92–98
    Aboriginal Child Placement Principle
      (ACPP), 92–96
    generally, 92
    self-determination, 96–98
    "stolen generation", 92
  child-rearing practice, 87
  conclusions, 108–109
  contemporary policy, 88
  family law, 98–108
    best interests principle, 105–108
    generally, 98–99
    structures, family, 99–102
    Tiwi Island case, 102–105
    values, family, 99–102
  forcible removal, 87, 92–98
  generally, 87–89
  historical issues, 88
  human rights, 88
  importance of issue, 87–88
  international treaty obligations, 88
  kinship relations, 87, 88, 99–102
  land claims, 87
  multiculturalism,
    definition, 89–91
    family law. *See* family law *above*
  percentage of population, 87
  public debate, 87
  self-determination, 87, 89–91
    child protection and placement, 96–98
  self-government, 89
  "stolen generation", 92
  territorial dispossession, 88
  United National Convention on the Rights
    of the Child, 88
Inter-country adoptions, 111–125

background, 111
conclusion, 124–125
criminal offences, 118–121
growth in popularity, 111–112
immigration, 120–121
international Conventions, 112–113
numbers, 111
protected children, 119–120
recognition, 121–124
safeguards against wrongful adoption,
  118–121
welfare of child, 113–118
  Convention adoptions, 113–115
  generally, 113
  non-Convention adoptions, 115–118
wrongful adoption, safeguards against,
  118–121
International issues,
  foreign divorces. *See* Foreign divorces,
    recognition of
  foreign marriages. *See* Foreign marriages,
    recognition of
Interpreters,
  local authority support for ethnic minority
    children, 22

Local authority support for ethnic minority
    children, 15–31
  assessment of needs, 20, 22
  care plans, 25
  checklist, welfare, 16, 24
  child protection, 22
  Children Act 1989,
    checklist, welfare, 16, 24
    duties to looked after children 16. *See also*
      looked after children *below*
    inadequacies of, 16–17
    parental responsibility, 16
    Practice Guidance and Regulations, 17
    support services, 16
    welfare of child paramount, 16
  conclusions, 30–31
  day care, 16, 23
  disabled children, 20–21
  due consideration to religious persuasion,
    racial origin and cultural and linguistic
    background, 24
  duties to looked after children, 16
  education, 23
  ethnicity, 18
  family support, 22
  fostering, 16
  generally, 15–16
  "in need", children, 19–22
  interpreters, 22
  language issues, 18
  leaving local authority accommodation, 28–30
  looked after children, 24–30

Local authority support for ethnic minority
    children (*cont.*):
  care, 24
  care plans, 25
  checklist, welfare, 24
  due consideration to religious persuasion,
    racial origin and cultural and linguistic
    background, 24
  duties owed, 24
  generally, 16
  leaving local authority accommodation,
    28–30
  length of stay, 25
  meaning, 24
  monitoring, 25
  paramount consideration, welfare not,
    24
  placement, 26–28
  planning, 25
  statistical information, 24–25
  weight to be given to child's welfare, 24
mixed parentage, children of, 17
monitoring, 21, 23, 25
nature of duties and powers vested in local
    authorities, 19
needs,
  assessment, 20
  definition, 19–20
  disabled children, 20–21
  eligibility for range of services, 21–22
  ethnicity, criteria based on, 20
  reasonable standard of health or
    development, 20
  registers, 21
  special, 18
parental responsibility, 16
partnerships with other agencies, 23
placement, 26–28
preventative work, 18, 19
priorities, determining, 21–22
proactive approach, 20
publication of information, 23
reasonable standard of health or develop-
    ment, 20
receipt of services, 21–22
recognition of ethnic identity,
  Children Act 1989, 16
  generally, 15
  Guidance, 16–17
  primary legislation, 16, 17
  regulations, 17
  secondary legislation, 17
  United National Convention on the Rights
    of the Child, 17
registers, 21
representation of ethnic minority children in
    care, 15
research, 17

resource allocation, 22
service provision, 18–23
  assessment of needs, 20, 22
  child protection, 22
  day care, 16, 23
  disabled children, 20–21
  education, 23
  eligibility of "in need" children, 21–22
  evaluation, 23
  family support, 22
  "in need", children, 19–22
  interpreters, 22
  minimal intervention, 18
  monitoring, 21, 23
  nature of duties and powers vested in local
    authorities, 19
  need, definition of, 17–18
  partnerships with other agencies, 23
  planned provision, 22–23
  Practice Guidance, 23
  preventative work, 18, 19
  priorities, determining, 21–22
  proactive approach, 20
  publication of information, 23
  reasonable standard of health or
    development, 20
  receipt of services, 21–22
  registers, 21
  resource allocation, 22
  staffing, 22
  state intervention, 18
  translators, 22–23
support services, 16, 18–23
terminology, 18
translators, 22–23
United National Convention on the Rights
    of the Child, 17

Marriage,
  child marriages, 80–85
  foreign marriages, recognition of. *See*
    Foreign marriages, recognition of
Mixed parentage, children of,
  local authority support for ethnic minority
    children, 17
Monism,
  child abduction, 11, 13
Monitoring,
  local authority support for ethnic minority
    children, 21, 23, 25

Pluralism,
  child abduction, 13–14
Public policy,
  foreign divorces, recognition of, 67–68
  foreign marriages, recognition of,
    71–73
    cultural materialism, 74–77

Race discrimination,
  race-matching policies, 40–42
  transracial adoption, 33, 40–42
Relativism,
  child abduction, 11–12

Service provision,
  local authority support for ethnic minority
    children, 18–2385
Sexual abuse,
  child abduction, 6–7

Translators,
  local authority support for ethnic minority
    children, 22–23
Transracial adoption, 33–48
  academic achievement, 35, 36–37
  affirmative action, 34, 40, 41
  attitudinal development, 37
  British Agencies for Adoption and Fostering
    Practice Notes, 36
  Children Act responsibilities, 41–42
  community interests, 33, 34, 38–39
  conclusions, 48
  costs, 39
  divisions, racial, 39
  generally, 33–35
  genetic heritage, 34
  harm, 35–38
  identity crises, 37
  integrated society, belief in, 37–38
  legal impropriety, 33–34, 40–44
    affirmative action, 40, 41

  Children Act responsibilities, 41–42
  generally, 40
  race-matching as race discrimination,
    40–42
  welfare of child, centrality of, 42–44
  opposition to, 33
  personal development, 35, 36
  race discrimination, 33, 40–42
  reforms, 44–47
    legal, 46–47
    practical, 44–46
  self-esteem, 35, 37
  survival skills, 36, 38
  urban myths,
    community interests damaged, 38–39
    generally, 35
    harmful, transracial adoptions are, 35–38
  welfare of child, 34, 42–44
  welfare concerns, 33

United National Convention on the Rights of
    the Child,
  indigenous children in Australian law, 88
  local authority support for ethnic minority
    children, 17
  recognition of ethnic identity of children, 17

Welfare of child,
  child abduction, 3–4, 9–11, 14
  inter-country adoptions, 113–118
    generally, 113
    non-Convention adoptions, 115–118
  transracial adoption, 34, 42–44